## The Knight-Errant of the Lord

*History knows no more gallant figure than Francis of Assisi, who surrendered wealth and set out—his body ill-clothed but his soul ablaze with love—to bring the good news of Christ's freedom to all who had the heart to listen.*

So magnetic was his personality that within a decade after he had founded his order of Friars Minor, some 5,000 men had flocked to follow in his footsteps.

*The Little Flowers of St. Francis,* the joyful and lyric stories woven together by his followers, is a unique gem of Western literature. It is a hymn of love to the man who called the wind and the fire his brothers, the water his sister, and who saw the image of Christ Himself in the faces of the suffering.

In his Introduction, Serge Hughes illuminates the qualities and intentions of the *Fioretti.* In his translation, he renders into English the directness and simplicity of the medieval original.

# Other MENTOR-OMEGA Books

# The Little Flowers of St. Francis

## AND OTHER FRANCISCAN WRITINGS

*Newly translated and
with an Introduction by*
SERGE HUGHES

A MENTOR-OMEGA BOOK
Published by The New American Library

> *From twenty centuries of literature and scholarship, Mentor-Omega Books present a treasury of Catholic thought for the modern reader.*

MENTOR-OMEGA BOOKS are published *in the United States* by The New American Library of World Literature, Inc., 501 Madison Avenue, New York, New York 10022, *in Canada* by The New American Library of Canada Limited, 156 Front Street West, Toronto 1, Ontario, *in the United Kingdom* by The New English Library Limited, Barnard's Inn, Holborn, London, E.C. 1, England

PRINTED IN THE UNITED STATES OF AMERICA

# The Little Flowers
## of St. Francis
### AND OTHER
### FRANCISCAN WRITINGS

For John, Superfluously

# Contents

# The Little Flowers
## of St. Francis
### AND OTHER
### FRANCISCAN WRITINGS

# TRANSLATOR'S NOTE

This translation is based on the Passerini edition of the *Fioretti*. This edition is not the most scholarly available in Italian: the editions of B. Bughetti, O.F.M., and of Mario Casella are better. But the differences for purposes of translation are very small, and the Passerini edition has several advantages. The style is less flowery and homiletic in tone, and it conveys better the cadences and happy austerity that generally grace the rhythms and images of the *Fioretti*.

The *Fioretti* is difficult to translate. The writer hopes, though, that by offering a translation that is neither excessively colloquial nor of late-nineteenth-century vintage, he has communicated something of that ideal balance between freshness and gravity that makes the *Fioretti* fascinating, perpetually elusive, and direct.

Since the *Life of Brother Juniper* and the *Life of Brother Egidio* are traditionally included in the *Fioretti*, the writer has deferred to custom and included them in this edition. In both instances, the translation is based on the texts of the *Fioretti* of B. Bughetti, O.F.M.

The writer would like to stress, however, what every reader will see for himself. The *Life of Brother Juniper* and the *Life of Brother Egidio* are not of the same stuff as the *Fioretti*. The *Life of Brother Juniper* here and there has some humorous whimsical pages, but more often than not its piety is a caricature of the spirit of Francis. In some instances, as in the story of the tyrant Niccolao, most readers will sensibly conclude that Brother Juniper's sense of sacrifice was terribly misguided, and that the tyrant, even more than good Brother Juniper, is the one who deserves to be pitied.

By and large, the *Life of Brother Juniper* is a good example of the excesses of the extreme Spiritual attitude among the Franciscans. Francis was sublimely impractical, but Brother Juniper was often ludicrously or even senselessly so. For once, as in the story of how Brother Juniper cooked for the brothers, the reader will feel some sympathy for the much-maligned Conventuals and their supposedly excessive involvement with practical matters.

The *Life of Brother Egidio,* by contrast, does not confuse the excesses of humility with lyrical Franciscan charity, but neither does it have many traces of the poetry of the *Fioretti.* It is, all in all, a valuable account of the life of a devoted and less playful member of the early followers of St. Francis.

The *Sayings of Brother Egidio* is another traditional part of many editions of the *Fioretti,* but I have omitted them for two reasons: they do not add much to the *Fioretti,* and, in the version in which we know them, they show more of a Ciceronian rotundity and sense of a balanced phrase than of Franciscan freshness.

In their place, I offer not the *Canticle of Creatures,* which to judge from the editions of the *Fioretti* of the last hundred years, bids fair to become another "traditional" part of the *Fioretti,* but two documents of Francis that are peculiarly relevant to the *Fioretti:* the Rule of 1223 and the Testament of the Saint.

The texts of the Testament and the Second Rule are taken from the mss. Riccardiano 1670 (first half of the XV century) and Palatino 141 (1485), published for the first time, to the best of my knowledge, in *Mistici del duecento e del trecento,* Arrigo Levasti, ed. (Milan, Rizzoli, 1935).

If the reader so wishes, with these documents and the *Fioretti* he can begin to sketch out for himself the dominant features of the Saint. He should know, however, that in spite of the abundance of materials on and by Francis, we have as yet only an approximate likeness, not a portrait. Francis is elusive.

*Serge Hughes*

# INTRODUCTION

*For those of us who "remember" the* Fioretti . . .[1]

In recollection, whether we ever read it or not, we "remember" the *Fioretti* as poetry, as young poetry.

We vaguely "recollect" a world of delicate stories, earnest and almost palpably fantastic at times. Tender and fragrant, the *Fioretti,* we are sure, is poetry, and that poetry is lyrical.

The people in the *Fioretti,* we also remember, move about in two spheres: the familiar world of actions understandable in terms of cause and effect, and the Other World, which directly—yet playfully and elusively—transforms everyday reality.

Above all, the people in this Franciscan world do good, and the effects of that good are fascinating and unpredictable. For example, in the story we most vividly remember, that of the wolf of Gubbio, the wolf heeds the admonitions of the Saint; we know he will go on to lead an irreproachable life. The point, we say to ourselves, is that good can come about suddenly, and it endures. Whether this incident or others like it ever took place is not the point. When we read of the discovery of a wolf's skeleton buried in the

---

[1] Throughout this introduction, I call the *Little Flowers of St. Francis* by their familiar Italian name. I do so for no grave scholarly reason. The choice was made because the word *Fioretti* rolls better from the tongue and because it sounds less effeminate and precious than the usual English translation. With equal self-indulgence I have, except for those whose names we know too well in English, let the cast of the *Fioretti* retain the Italian form of their names.

church of San Francesco della Pace in Gubbio, we are not unduly impressed. With all due deference to scholarship, we feel that the discovery is not very relevant. It offers some kind of proof for those who have no need of it, and none for those who do.

A book of young, lyrical poetry—we go on to insist on our unreliable memories—the *Fioretti* no doubt appeals as much to the old as to the young; and since most of us who come to these conclusions do not feel particularly young or particularly old, we are willing to let matters rest there. Our "memories" of the *Fioretti* are pleasant. We do not wish to tamper with them.

Yet it is precisely for those of us who are in that middle age, that prolonged adolescence that lasts from seventeen to seventy, that a rereading of the *Fioretti* is called for. There are a number of us whose simplicity is no longer that of the young nor yet that of the old who would like to find the way back to the remembered garden.

A "garden," because the *Fioretti,* usually the one source of our knowledge of Francis, does not linger in memory as a story. It is not "the account of what actually happened" that we recall, but rather the scents of the *Fioretti.* Unconcerned with the historical claims of the book, we treat them with indulgence. Whether certain personages did or did not exist, whether the version of certain historical events is reliable—this does not usually interest us. Unwilling to go so far as the learned eighteenth-century Bollandist and editor of the *Acta Sanctorum,* Constantinus Suyskins, who avowed that an ignorance of the *Fioretti* attested to the seriousness of one's interest in Francis, we are nevertheless convinced that the value of the book, which we have always meant to reread, lies in its charm.

Our "memory" is not altogether misleading. There is a great deal of charm and poetry, as well as many valuable insights, in the *Fioretti,* and none of these qualities have any obvious connection with the part of the work that offers an account of "what actually happened." There is a poetical suspension of time in the *Fioretti.*

However, for those of us who are neither truly young nor truly old, the historical aspect, the dark side of the moon, can have a unique value. If we find it distasteful to imitate the specious enthusiasm of readers pretending to be young or old, then we have an almost moral obligation to consider seriously the "historical" *Fioretti*. Considering our age and temperament, it is the one proper and fitting tribute we can offer. And who knows—it may be precisely this approach that may lead us to the remembered garden.

As a beginning, we should look at everything—including the title—with new eyes.

⌒ᕰ⌐

The title itself, *Fioretti,* is somewhat misleading. Like all Italian diminutives, it can be a term of endearment, and the diminutive of flowers invariably suggests things fresh, youthful, and humble. The use of the word is reminiscent of a passage from the introduction to a Franciscan work of the fourteenth century, the *Legenda Trium Sociorum*: "As from a pleasant meadow we pluck certain flowers which in our judgment are fairer, not following a continuous history but leaving out many things as they befell." In this sense, in its deliberate lack of concern for chronological sequence, the stories are really *fioretti*.

At the same time, however, it is certain that the compiler of the *Fioretti* did not choose the word for its poetical allusiveness. By the fourteenth century, as Professor Edmund G. Gardner has pointed out, the word *fioretto* (or its plural, *fioretti*), had already become more a common name for an anthology than a poetically evocative term. There is nothing particularly scented about such titles as *Fioretto di cronache degli imperatori, Fioretto delle morali di Santo Gregorio, Fiori e vita di filosofi e altri savi e imperatori*. As in most old metaphors, the original poetry may be reevoked once we have forgotten its acquired banality. Toward the end of the last century, we did just that and more, for example, when we imparted to the word connotations that told more of the state of our souls than of the complex world of the *Fioretti*.

It would be good, then, if on rereading the *Fioretti* we could restrain our pre-Raphaelite tendencies and our inclinations toward pastel reminiscences.

It would also be good to modify our notion of the unity of the *Fioretti*: its unity is of a complicated nature. To begin with, we should note that the *Fioretti* is a compilation.

The first part, the part that most of us have some knowledge of, consists of the first thirty-eight chapters. It is probably the oldest part and deals principally with St. Francis and his first companions. Two short chapters on St. Anthony of Padua precede the second part, Chapters 41 to 53, which contains an account of the lives and miracles of the brothers two and three generations after the death of Francis. Most of the stories take place in the province of the Marches, the section of Italy northeast of the Saint's native Umbria.

Originally, the *Fioretti* consisted of only these two principal parts. Since the fourteenth century, however, the *Considerations on the Stigmata,* an account of the receiving of the stigmata and the events leading to and from it, has become the traditional concluding part of the *Fioretti.*

As a rule, the first and last parts are those most vividly "remembered." The other parts, the two chapters on St. Anthony of Padua and a good part of the second section, are often effortlessly blotted out. We usually profess to admire the *Fioretti* without qualification, but if in fact we ever read it we quickly make our own *fioretti* of the *Fioretti.*

We do this constantly with all sorts of books, and should certainly have no misgivings about our happy faculty of forgetting much of what we read. In this case, however, there are some particularly cogent reasons for keeping in mind what was so easy to forget, for scrutinizing what appeared irrelevant or boringly naïve.

The *Fioretti* appears simple. Those of us who had the good fortune to read it in Italian, for example, found it fresh and spontaneous. We delighted in its modest cadences, its lack of sophistication. We responded to its unselfconscious gravity. At no point, in spite of a certain discontinuity of style, did we suspect that we were reading anything but an original work.

Yet not too long ago, in 1902, Paul Sabatier, the learned poet-historian who initiated both a popular and a scholarly interest in Francis that has lasted almost to our day, discovered a manuscript, the *Actus beati Francisci et sociorum eius.* Investigation showed that a good many of the stories in the *Fioretti* appeared in this manuscript in a Latin version —and the evidence indicated that this Latin version was the earlier. Whatever freshness and simplicity the *Fioretti* manifested was, therefore, not only that of a compilation but of a translation as well.

Some twelve years later, A. G. Little, the eminent English student of things Franciscan, discovered another and better version of that manuscript. It now appeared that of the entire body of work known as the *Fioretti*, at least fifty-two or fifty-three chapters had originally appeared in the *Actus*.

Scholarship ferreted out the original, and scholars will continue to work with it, and such work can be very meaningful. Italians, however, and nonscholars throughout the world, will continue to enjoy the translation. Even those of us with a smattering of Italian will usually continue to turn to the *Fioretti*, not the *Actus*, when dissatisfied with an English translation. It does not speak well of our respect for primary sources, but it does compliment our ear. Besides, if our knowledge of the *Fioretti* is to be through translation (there are, after all, Christians whose Greek is rusty) we can console ourselves: by common consent, the *Fioretti* is a masterpiece of translation.

But if the *Fioretti* is largely the result of translation and compilation, to whom do we owe so much? Who was the translator? We do not know with certainty (and how fittingly Franciscan this anonymity is!) but most scholars believe it to be one John of Marignolli, Bishop of Bisognano, who died in 1359. The bishop, to the best of our knowledge, has no other claims to literary immortality. Whoever the translator might have been, he was a superb editor; he translated, omitted, and modified with rare skill. He was also, to judge from his *Considerations on the Stigmata*, which is not a translation but his own compilation from various sources, a talented author. The *Considerations* can stand comparison with the other parts of the *Fioretti*.

And what of the author of the original *Actus*? Do we know the name of the "me" who suddenly and disconcertingly announces himself in the second part of the *Fioretti* on p. 122; ". . . and Brother Jacopo said to me. . ."? Is this "me" the "I" of p. 135: "I had a great desire to meet Brother Jacopo. . . ."? We do not know with certainty, but with respect to the proper name mentioned on p. 131: "and Brother Giovanni told me, Brother Vgolino, this story," most scholars have been in agreement that Vgolino is probably one Ugolino da Brunforte, who became a Franciscan some time before 1260 and died toward the end of the century. More recently, however, the name of another Franciscan, Ugolino da Boniscambi, active from 1270 to 1340, has been suggested; but he would have been a child when he heard the stories of some of the brothers mentioned in the second part of the *Fioretti,* and some scholars find this implausible.

We do have a more definite idea of when the original Latin version was composed. Internal evidence and references to historical personages indicate some time between 1322 and 1328.

Plausible attributions of authorship and dates of composition are no mean accomplishments of scholarship. By themselves they should be of substantial help toward a better understanding of the *Fioretti.* Similar discoveries with respect to other anonymous works have often thrown sudden light on what appeared to be murky. Yet with respect to the *Fioretti* these discoveries amount to hints, not solutions.

The *Fioretti* is not only a compilation, but a compilation based on oral traditions—and oral traditions are notoriously difficult to trace, to evaluate, and even to understand. The date on which an oral tradition was written down is, of course, important—but it is only half a discovery. A great deal still remains hidden from sight, and the problem of the origin of the oral tradition is left virtually untouched.

The beginnings of the oral traditions of the *Fioretti,* according to its own testimony, go very far back. The narrator speaks of hearing stories from Jacopo della Massa, who in turn, we know, personally knew the intimate follower and secretary of St. Francis—the timid lion, Brother Leo. And Brother Leo was among the very first followers, together with Brother Egidio, Brother Simone, and St. Clare.

The oral tradition, consequently, appears to have been written down a hundred years after the death of the Saint. A century is a long time, and particularly in the history of the Franciscan Order.

Generally, oral traditions are written down when they are challenged, threatened, or perverted. The polemical intent, though, is not always easily recognizable. Sometimes there are militant and explicit references, and then the adversary and the issues are clearly seen; sometimes, instead, the arguments are allusive, intense, and subtle—so cautious and sparse in references to the adversary that we are left perplexed, uncertain of how to distinguish the "what actually happened" from what is believed to have happened, or of how to make similar distinctions when the present is described or the future prophesied.

The initial problem raised by the *Fioretti,* therefore, is the determination of which oral tradition it embodies. In what ways is the St. Francis of the *Fioretti* different from the St. Francis of other tradition? What is stressed? What is omitted? Is its account of the ideals of the Saint and the history of the Order in agreement with other traditions, and if not, why? In a word, is the history of the Saint and of the Order—to use the most unpreRaphaelite word possible— trustworthy?

The *Fioretti,* of course, is not interested in and does not even mention the bare skeleton facts necessary for an approach to this problem. It assumes that the reader knows that Francis was born in Assisi in 1182; that in 1210 he received official approval for his Order from Pope Innocent III; that in 1217 as head of the Order he held the first great meeting of the friars, the General Chapter; and that four years later he composed a Rule that was lost, but that in 1223 he wrote another, which was approved by Pope Honorius III. In addition, the *Fioretti* assumes that the reader knows that the year before the Saint's death, in 1224, he received the stigmata.

Assuming all this knowledge on the part of the reader, the *Fioretti* shows little interest in any aspect of Francis other than that of Francis the Saint and founder of the Order. There are no references to him before his conversion. There is no mention, for example, of the great scene in which the young Francis stripped himself of his clothes and with unfathomable assurance and humility handed them back to his father as a token of irrevocable renunciation. The Francis of the *Fioretti* is a man who has already made his one great decision in life—and the story is an account of how he implemented that choice, in his personal life and through his Order.

We also encounter a large number of assumptions with regard to the Order. It is taken for granted that the reader knows that the order of Francis is unique, and without precedent in Christendom; a similar assumption is, of course, made with regard to the heart of Francis' doctrine—the ideal of evangelical poverty.

These assumptions are justified. They are also verifiable.

The order Francis envisioned *was* unique. It *was* distinct from any order that preceded it. It had some things in common with a number of lay associations that flourished at the same time, toward the end of the twelfth century, but the differences were greater. No lay confraternity, witness the Waldensians, was so docile and subject to the Pope. No lay group considered the world as its mission territory. Even in the practice of poverty, the differences were remarkable. The Cathars of the time, to cite one example, allowed for a division of functions that Francis would not have tolerated: there were the *perfecti*, or the aristocrats of the sect who practiced strict poverty, and the *credentes*, who assisted them economically. And although there were numerous lay groups of that century (the *Humiliati* and the Poor Men of Lyons among the most notable) who preached penance and poverty, their passion for poverty had little in common with the spirit of the Franciscans.

Above all, the *Fioretti* is concerned with a certain interpretation of poverty. It is the story of the form that this observance of poverty took in the Saint and in a group of his followers. The first part deals with Francis and his companions, the second with the brothers of the Marches some generations later.

Evangelical poverty is the major concern of the *Fioretti*, and if we do not recognize it as such, we are in no position to approach the world of Francis. Cultural antecedents will not help at this point. Abstractly, we know that there is nothing new under the sun; any industrious scholar knows that it is only a question of time before he will come across a precedent for any given idea. And so, with respect to the poverty of Francis, mention has been made of the idea of poverty among the Fathers, in particular the famous phrase of St. Jerome: the yearning "to be naked with the naked Christ."

The fact remains, however, that Francis' followers, his admirers, and Francis himself were right in their granite conviction that they had discovered something new. With evangelical poverty, something fresh had been restored to the world—a new wonder, a treasure lost since the death of Christ. This is the pearl of great price found in the *Fioretti*.

But the central position of the pearl is not always immediately recognizable. There are distractions that easily make us lose sight of it. For example, there is a stress on extrinsic and often contrived similarities with Christ: the twelve Apostles sent forth by Francis in pairs; the forty-day fast, with but a slight change from that of Christ; the betrayal in spirit by a traitor who, like Judas, hangs himself.

Yet if we are to be scandalized, it should not be about such relatively small matters. If we are to be scandalized, it should be about a greater claim to the imitation of Christ—the claim to have imitated Christ's spirit of poverty and to have directly experienced the freedom that is almost vertiginously Christ-like, and without precedent. In truth, no religious community before the early Franciscans had ever experienced such lighthearted, awesome trust in the providence of God, a trust that He would provide not simply spiritual bread, but daily sustenance.

Certain traits, and certain stories of this Francis, the lover of Lady Poverty, have become the knowledge of most of us who read, whether or not we have read the *Fioretti*. We all "know" of Francis singing in his deathbed—to the consternation of the friars surrounding him, who were apprehensive of scandal. We "recall" the impetuous gesture of Francis in ordering Brother Ruffino to preach naked in church, and then repenting and following him to beg his forgiveness. All of us "remember" the sermon to the birds.

More often than not, in our "recollection" we make of Francis not a plaster saint, certainly, but a lovable eccentric. Not fully grasping the depth and breadth of his notion of poverty, without an idea of its complexity, we run the constant risk of reducing him to the role of a gay troubadour of God (Francis of the stigmata!) or, worse, to being the patron saint of a medieval SPCA.

The silhouette of the lover of poverty drawn by the *Fioretti* bears no resemblance to this Francis. The lover of poverty is another person; in describing him and exalting him, the *Fioretti* embodies the oral traditions of some of his earliest followers.

Does the *Fioretti,* in its unmistakable emphasis on evangelical poverty, make implicit or explicit references to an opposing, rival tradition?

It does, but more often than not, indirectly. When it is direct, however, it is disconcerting and even shocking in its tone and mode of attack.

To begin to discern the lineaments of the opponent, it is necessary not only to have a precise idea of the *Fioretti's* notion of the Saint, but also to have a precise notion of its version of the Order's history. It is in this history, in fact, that we find the first hint of an explanation of the polemics in which the *Fioretti* was engaged—and it is from this explanation that we must decide what those polemics imply for the value of the book as a trustworthy historical account.

The account given of the Order is unilinear and unequivocal. It is no more concerned with chronological exactness in this area than it is with respect to the life of Francis, but it does have a sense of continuity. It begins with the founding of the Order and continues to some indefinite time after the generalate of St. Bonaventure.

From the very beginning, it is made clear that St. Francis will watch over the Order after his death, just as he did during his life. He will always assist those who call on him when faltering in the practice of poverty. He will help them in this world, as he does in a scene with obvious evangelical analogies when he provides for five thousand Franciscans gathered together; and he will help them in the next, for God has granted him the privilege of shortening the stay of his brothers in Purgatory. He will aid and sustain the weak, and persuade the doubtful. In the *Fioretti*, St. Dominic, his contemporary, first has doubts as to the wisdom of imposing evangelical poverty on such a growing order, which has so many unavoidable practical needs. However, he too is persuaded, and his acceptance is so total that we read that he damned all those in his order who would break away from the observance of that poverty.

During his lifetime, the *Fioretti* tells us, Francis led the Order superbly. He was successful at home, he was successful abroad. Only the counsel of Cardinal Ugolino, to whom Francis had early turned for guidance, kept him from going to France; he did go successfully to Spain, and most dramatically to Syria, where his goodness and eloquence persuaded the Sultan Malik-el Kamil to embrace Christianity in secret.

Toward the end of his life, according to the *Fioretti*, the Saint, because of an illness of the eyes—caused, we are told, by excessive weeping—delegated, but did not relinquish, his office to Pietro Catani, and withdrew, giving himself over to contemplation in preparation for death.

However, as Christ was betrayed by Judas, the order of Francis was to have its betrayals. The first great betrayal was that of Brother Elia, a proud man who so tampered with the spirit of the Order that God sent an angel to reproach him.

The sins of Elia did not surprise St. Francis. He foresaw that Elia, like Giovanni della Cappella (an early defector from the Order about whom we know very little), was proud and would betray the spirit of poverty and eventually leave the Order. He therefore avoided him. Only when Elia became aware that the Saint was avoiding him and pleaded with him to pray for him, did Francis yield. Elia died out of the Order, as Francis knew he would, but as a result of St. Francis' prayers, before dying he was allowed to wear again the Franciscan habit and was saved.

The second betrayal came some time after the death of St. Francis. Under the leadership of Giovanni da Parma, the Order had hewn closely to the precepts of St. Francis, but under John's successor, Bonaventure (the reference to "Saint" Bonaventure is in the *Considerations*, not in the second part), the practice of Franciscan poverty grew increasingly lax. When Bonaventure became head of the Order, he actually set about persecuting Giovanni da Parma for having practiced evangelical poverty. Only when stopped by Francis, who was sent from Heaven by Christ to intervene, did Bonaventure desist from further persecution.

Such, in brief, is the account of the history of the Order according to the *Fioretti*. It is, in a number of respects, unexpected and startling. It is precisely the type of historical account that invites closer scrutiny: for example, the notion of St. Francis, aware that one of the brothers was damned and for that reason avoiding him is, to say the least, disconcerting. It hardly seems in keeping with the spirit of Franciscan charity, and the suspicions and misgivings we have on this score almost inevitably make us wonder about the reliability of the silhouette traced of the Saint himself.

To resolve this doubt we must go to documents that antecede the *Fioretti*, specifically, to the earliest existing historical document concerning Francis and his order: the *Legenda of St. Francis*, composed in 1228, two years after the Saint's death. This is not to imply, of course, that contemporary sources necessarily have any intrinsic superiority over later accounts; a biased contemporary is in no way preferable to a comparatively disinterested later historian. However, disinterested observers are hard to find in any period, and there is something to be said for the freshness of bias (if it is present) as well as for the immediacy of observation.

~~✦~~

To the extent that any person personifies a class, the author of the *Legenda*, Brother Tommaso da Celano, was a good representative of a class of men increasingly drawn to the Order. Learned and articulate, in some respects similar to the law students of Bologna mentioned in the *Fioretti*, he sincerely sought to imitate Francis. He did so, however, while remaining quite different from his model.

We are not sure why he was chosen to write the *Legenda*. He had no firsthand knowledge either of the Saint or of his closest friends, but he did have literary gifts and a rather wide erudition—a good knowledge of the Bible and of classical writers. These gifts, needless to say, were a prime prerequisite for an author who had to demonstrate why a saint merited canonization. The writer of a *legenda*, after all, was not required to have a flair for psychological investigation, much less to be skilled in the problems of origins and development. A *legenda* was meant to edify, and to edify those who already believed in the sanctity of the hero. Because edification involved a time-honored style, and because Brother Tommaso was quite adept at this style, he could be relied on to do his work well. Moreover, Brother Tommaso was probably known to be conscientious. He sought out many who had known Francis personally, and to judge from the omissions in the *Legenda*, he had a rather developed sense of the differences between the plausible and the outlandish.

As in the case of the *Fioretti*, chronological sequence was not very relevant to his purposes. There was only one important chronological point, that which marked off the "old" man from the "new"—the Saint. The years that preceded conversion did not need to be dwelt on. It was sufficient to show the strong contrast, to show how totally transforming the grace of God was, and how it turned darkness into light.

Like many other hagiographers before and since, Brother Tommaso did not have an overwhelming awareness of the uniqueness of his saint. More than once his description of St. Francis seems inspired by a medieval thesaurus: "He was charming in his manners, serene by nature, affable in

conversation, most opportune in his exhortations, most faithful in what was entrusted to him, cautious in counsel, ef-
fective in business, gracious in all things." [2]

Brother Tommaso did not always write in this enumerative
style, but even when he described events and incidents that
of themselves were poetical, there was always much miss-
ing. The hagiographer may have been, as has been asserted,
the author of that great hymn, the *Dies Irae*, but whatever
poetical gifts he may have had they were not squandered
on the *Legenda*. In his version of the sermon to the birds,
for example, there is none of the freshness, the cadences,
the perfume of the *Fioretti*. By comparison, the tone is that
of a well-meaning homily.

In all justice to Brother Tommaso, he did have a sense
for the dramatic and the colorful. It is from him that we
learn how Francis, searching for guidance, determined what
he should do by opening the gospel three times and acting
on the commands he found therein. He is also the source
of the account of how Francis stripped himself before his
father, and of how, later, his mother sought to protect him
from his father, who had him virtually imprisoned in his
own house. The delightful story of the Saint before Pope
Honorius is also his: "Not being able to contain himself
for joy, when he spoke the words with his mouth, he moved
his feet as though he were dancing." He did so, Brother
Tommaso hastens to add, "not indeed lustfully but as one
burning with the fire of divine love, not provoking laughter
but provoking tears of grief." [3]

Brother Tommaso appreciated the exuberance and freedom
of the Saint, and—most reassuring—he knew very well that
the alternation of joy and austerity in Francis was not for-
tuitous, but was the natural rhythm of the growth of his
spirit of evangelical poverty.

For Brother Tommaso, the Saint is the saint of poverty,
the custodian of that treasure which drew the first followers:
Bernardo, Egidio, Filippo. On this cornerstone, Brother Tommaso believes, Francis founded an order that was pious and
orthodox and obedient. The Order of Francis, the historian
stresses, did its work with the approval of the Pope and

[2] Brother Thomas of Celano, *St. Francis of Assisi*, trans. and ed.
by Placid Herman, O.F.M. (Chicago: Franciscan Herald Press,
1963), p. 40.

[3] *Ibid.*, p. 38.

the assistance of the cardinal protector, Ugolino of Ostia, to whom Francis had turned when in need of guidance.

In the mission field (and Brother Tommaso himself had been in Germany and knew the missionary zeal of the Order) the Saint had set a remarkable example. Two years after the death of its founder, the Order had already gone far: the heroism of Francis' mission to the Sultan—and Brother Tommaso mentions the trip—apparently was bearing fruit.

However, while describing the Saint's appearance before the Sultan, Brother Tommaso makes no mention of its success. There is not a word about the secret conversion of the Sultan. In the *Legenda* the mission, in this sense, was a failure.

The contradiction between this version and that of the *Fioretti* is curious. At first glance it might seem unimportant, but with respect to another story in the *Legenda*, about Brother Elia, there can be no minimizing the seriousness of the differences between the two versions.

The Brother Elia mentioned by Brother Tommaso has little in common with the Brother Elia of the *Fioretti*. In the *Legenda*, Brother Elia is a close and solicitous friend of Francis. He loves and is loved by the Saint, the other brethren, and St. Clare. There is not a word to suggest that the Elia who went to Syria with Francis, and who became the first provincial of the Holy Land, was inordinately proud. There is nothing to indicate that Elia did anything during the lifetime of the Saint to provoke his censure, much less his enmity.

Which, then, of the two versions is the reliable one? Instinctively, we are more drawn to the version of Elia given in the *Legenda* and this response seems more in keeping with the spirit of Francis. But charitable instincts at this juncture obviously do not suffice. The only proper way out of the difficulty is to check other testimony closer to the time of Francis to see whether it corroborates the *Legenda* or the *Fioretti*.

The problem cannot be solved by simply accepting as reliable the earlier version, the *Legenda*. We are dealing with oral traditions, and we cannot say that where the *Legenda* and the *Fioretti* narrate similar stories, the *Fioretti* used materials from the *Legenda*. Possibly, if not probably, both came from a similar oral tradition. The determination of the written antecedent, therefore, does not help us much.

We can, however, make some headway by carefully scrutinizing the history of the Franciscan Order from the time preceding the *Legenda* to the period in which we date the original of the *Fioretti*, the *Actus*.

Here, too, we are immediately confronted with enormous difficulties. We know that even during the lifetime of the Saint there was a small rift in the Order over the question of what precisely constituted the proper observance of evangelical poverty. Francis himself, as we know from his own writings, had doubts and reversals, for the task of implementing evangelical poverty for a large and growing order was considerably more complex than doing so for a small band of followers. His first Rule, probably composed for his first few companions, was little more than a brief list of quotes from evangelical texts enjoining total renunciation of worldly prudence for the morrow. It was enough that he and the brothers worked, begged, prayed, met, and slept together, first in the field of Rivo Torto outside of Assisi, and later in the dilapidated church of the Portiuncola nearby. The brothers did not own anything. They had the use of these places for lodging, but it was an exclusively provisional use. When a peasant bullied his way into the Rivo Torto huts, which the brothers had built, Francis yielded and left. Similarly, when the Benedictines conceded him the use of the Portiuncola, Francis, when making some payment to them, insisted that he was renting, not purchasing.

As long as the Order remained small, such arrangements and practices were adequate, but the Order grew rapidly and prodigiously during the Saint's lifetime. The estimate of five thousand at the General Chapter mentioned in the *Fioretti* was ridiculed by an eighteenth-century Franciscan historian, but appears quite plausible today. With this expansion of the Order, the problems of housing and other practical necessities could no longer be solved by improvised expedients, and Francis was aware of this.

On some points, the Saint was determined that he would not yield. For example, while he was in Syria, he heard that the vicars he had left in charge of the Order had altered certain parts of the Rule—specifically some fasting precepts. He hurried back home, and protesting vigorously, he called on the Cardinal of Ostia to take measures against the vicars.

So concerned was Francis that even though he completely

lacked administrative talents, he took it upon himself (with
the help of Cardinal Ugolino) to compose a new rule, the
Rule of 1223,[4] three years before his death.

The changes in the rapidly expanding Order irked and
confused the Saint. He had misgivings about the construction both of larger quarters for the brothers and of richer
churches for the Order. The Order's acceptance of papal
privileges—measures that helped it in the construction of its
churches and protected it from the active noncooperation of
the secular clergy—infuriated him. Most modifications of the
letter of the Rule, he felt, sapped the strength of evangelical
poverty and accustomed the brothers to trust not to the
immediate providence of God but to all-too-human means.
The question of money, above all, tormented him. He lit-
erally abhorred money, but for a growing order it was in-
dispensable.

The last written expression of Francis' mind, the *Testament*,[5] vehemently reflected this mood. The document admonished and reproached. Let no one, Francis commanded,
accept papal privileges. Let the construction of churches and
houses reflect the spirit of evangelical poverty. Let all the
brothers live in the spirit of the poor Christ.

Some three years before his death, Francis, afflicted by
an eye disease contracted in Syria and broken in health,
stepped down from his role as spiritual leader of the community. The Order, he trusted, would go on to do its work.
The needed machinery of government was functioning. The
ministers, the equivalent of provincials, knew their scope and
responsibilities, as did the "custodians," the next in command; and in an election ordered by the Rule they could
be trusted to designate as Minister General the man among
them most capable of governing the Order. Even if they
did not choose well, Francis trusted that God would watch
over his brothers; and so the Saint, retiring with the closest
of his early friends to Mount Alverna, prepared for the receiving of the stigmata and death.

~⅃⌐⁓

In general, most of us are instinctively in sympathy with
the protestations of Francis. There is one Francis, and there

---

[4] Translation included. See p. 212.
[5] Translation included. See p. 218.

are many Franciscans. In a conflict between commonsense requirements and those of the sublimely impractical, we know very well where our sympathies lie. The conflict is reminiscent of that between poet and administrator.

As a group, scholars have also faced this conflict. Although not quite as crude in their distinctions as Sabatier, who reduces the struggle to a conflict between the prophet Francis and the professional institutional priesthood, most of them—A. G. Little, John R. H. Moorman, G. C. Coulton, Fr. Cuthbert, O.S.F.C.—have a keen appreciation of the justice of Francis' protests.

In their reconstruction of the history of the Order, these scholars understandably relied most heavily on the accounts or histories of the Spirituals, the heterogeneous group that became strong some one hundred years after the death of Francis and that claimed, in their stress on the letter of the law, to be the authentic custodians of the true spirit of St. Francis. Their opponents, the Conventuals, who favored a more latitudinarian interpretation of the Rule and stressed the spirit of the law, did not, by comparison, seem at all Franciscan.

Of late, however, we have become less confident as to the propriety of our sympathies; and with the appearance of the most remarkable work on Franciscan origins in the last fifty years, M. D. Lambert's *Franciscan Poverty,* our sympathies can now be very legitimately challenged.

Utilizing the latest conclusions of scholarship, Lambert has made a very good case for suspending judgment on Francis' ideas on the problem of implementing evangelical poverty in a large order, and for more critically examining the approach of the Spirituals.

Francis protested, yes, but often acquiesced—and not always in a passive, defeated spirit. The Saint was not always of one mind as to what measures were necessary, and his turning to Cardinal Ugolino for help in drawing up the Rule shows that he was more aware than most of us that there were things he could not do well. He could lead a small band of followers in the spirit of evangelical poverty; he found it far more difficult to do so with a growing order. He understood that the letter of the law could kill the spirit, but he was also painfully aware that a relaxed attitude to the letter of the law could pave the way to a les-

sened fervor. He never resolved this dilemma to his satisfaction.

But in loving his order, Lambert points out, Francis loved
it in loyalty and obedience, and this spirit overcame even
his gravest misgivings. In the choice between adherence to
his convictions and obedience to those who had become his
lawful superiors, he did not defend those convictions at
the price of obedience. This resolve was in character. Was
not this obedience a typically Franciscan act of faith and
trust in Divine Providence?

The *Testament,* often quoted to substantiate the protests
of the Saint, also unequivocally stresses his resolve to obey his
lawful superiors unquestioningly.

Lambert's reconstruction has some great merits. It hu-
manizes Francis. Within this framework we can consider
the differences between the Saint and the ministers and the
Order other than in terms of Christ and anti-Christ. Without indulging in an excess of sympathy for the practical
administrators, it becomes possible to grant that on occasion they were right—as in the instance of their refusal to
abide by Francis' injunction to jealously preserve all frag-
ments on which the name of God or words used by Him
appeared.

Of course, Francis' attachments were not always so un-
usual or so unyielding. For all his abhorrence of money he
did not to our knowledge object to the key decision to
have recourse to a "friend of the Order" for all the financial
needs of the rapidly expanding fraternity.

Nevertheless, in spite of these telling points—that Francis
often reversed himself, that although he could be very funda-
mentalistic on some points he was not on others, and that
he was also very much intent on observing obedience—the
interpretation that Lambert offers may still appear more in-
genious than convincing. The protests of the *Testament* are
unequivocal. Isn't to argue otherwise to do precisely what
the Saint strictly forbade—to put a gloss on his words?
The objection is well taken, but not persuasive. If Francis
reversed himself on occasion, then the only way to be sure
that he did not reverse himself after the *Testament* would
be to know that such a reversal was impossible. We do not
know that such a reversal was impossible. Moreover, we are
not even sure of the date of the *Testament.* The usual date of
attribution (1225, the year before his death) has been se-

riously questioned by a number of scholars; and even if that date were correct, it would leave some twelve months during which Francis could have made some accommodations.

If Lambert's reconstruction of Francis as a changing and even an uncertain leader of the Order, not at all unswerving and uncompromising, appears plausible, then we can deduce some additional conclusions as to the historical reliability of the first part of the *Fioretti*.

The tone of the *Fioretti*, by and large, already shows an unmistakably Spiritual tendency. The story that St. Dominic, seeing how Providence (working through the generosity of the surrounding towns) meets the practical needs of five thousand Franciscans without their having made any practical preparations themselves, was thereby moved to embrace evangelical poverty for his own order, may or may not be true. In any case, the point made is certainly in the Spiritual tradition.

We are now in a position to understand the censorious judgment passed on Elia in the *Fioretti*—the same Elia who up to 1228 had been so favorably described in the *Legenda* of Brother Tommaso. But to fully appreciate the Spiritual quality of the version given in the *Fioretti* we must check other sources (all critical of Elia, but less violently so) that deal with his life after 1228.

There is no doubt that Elia is the *bête noire* of Franciscan history. In his personal life he was among the most peculiar of all the Franciscan generals. The Minister General, who later justified himself on grounds of health, had a delicate palate. He insisted on having his personal cook; he preferred to have his meals served by properly attired servants; he prided himself on his distinguished friends, among them Frederick II, the archenemy of the Pope; he habitually rode horseback, a particularly serious infraction of the Rule; he did not hide his contempt for the ministers; and in the seven years of his generalate he did not once call a General Chapter.

In other respects, his work as Minister General was for most of the Order beyond criticism. He actively promoted missionary expansion in Syria and throughout Europe, encouraged building for the brothers in accordance with their needs, assisted those who wished to continue their studies in Paris, and following the policies of his predecessor, John Parenti, continued to accept papal privileges.

His spectacular accomplishment was the building of the lower church of the great basilica that would henceforth dominate Assisi, a basilica reminiscent of the Syrian fortresses he and Francis had seen in their travels. Designed as the resting place of Francis, the basilica was a holy place; it was also a protection against pious and energetic believers such as those who evidenced their passion for relics of saints by tearing the breasts off the corpse of St. Elizabeth of Hungary.

Elia had not hesitated to pressure the ministers and brothers to contribute to the basilica, but there is no evidence that any group was opposed to it in principle. They only resented Elia's ways. Moreover, it was a papal basilica, not one owned by the Order.

The objections that Elia met in the Order were caused by his blatantly arrogant manners, which were, in effect, a betrayal of the spirit of Francis. On other matters—the use of increased papal privileges, the growing number of Franciscan churches, the growing tendency to pursue studies in systematic theology—there were no strong or widespread objections. In fact, when Elia was finally ousted by a group of ministers led by Haymo of Faversham and Albert of Pisa, that part of his work was actually increased.

One group in the Order, however, to which the ministers who succeeded Elia did not belong, had been particularly scandalized by Elia. These brothers, the *zelanti,* shared Francis' misgivings as to the changes in the Order but did not share his trust in Providence and his willingness to obey. For the *zelanti* the Order had fallen on bad days. Compromises that another order would have approved with few misgivings appeared to them a perversion of all Franciscan principles. They were especially indignant at the bull of Gregory IX (formerly Cardinal Ugolino, the Protector of the Order), the *Quo elongati,* which declared the *Testament* of Francis not binding on the Order. That bull, for them, was nothing less than an attack on Francis himself.

Sometime after the downfall of Elia, some of the *zelanti* resorted to a mild form of active protest. In the Marches, a number of them withdrew from Franciscan communities, charging that these communities were offensively lax when they were not corrupt. They even changed their mode of dress, wearing shorter tunics to distinguish themselves from the other Franciscans. Their withdrawal incurred the anger of the minister of the area, who set about bringing them back to obedience and conformity. In spite of action taken against them, however, most continued their protest and only attenuated its mode. Their protests apparently had some effect, for when Crescentius, the minister who had once persecuted them in the Marches, was elected Minister General, he decided to settle the increasingly violent debates on evangelical poverty. To this end, he authorized a new biography of the founder of the Order, inviting all those who had known the Saint personally to write and submit what they remembered of him. As editor-author he designated, somewhat surprisingly, Brother Tommaso of Celano, who proved to be less helpful than Crescentius had expected.

In the eighteen years that had elapsed since the time of the first *Legenda*, Brother Tommaso had not remained aloof from developments in the Order. Deferential to Crescentius, he was nevertheless firmly committed to a point of view. He may not have been a *zelante* but he shared their indignation, and like most members of the Order, had been outraged at Elia's leadership. His memory of that tenure was fresh and painful.

The *Legenda Secunda* reflected this hurt and indignation. There was only one mention of Elia: how he received Francis' dying blessing, which had been intended for Brother Bernardo. Working from reminiscences of the early followers of St. Francis—Brothers Leo, Ruffino, and Angelo—Brother Tommaso found the contrast between the Franciscan spirit of that time and the spirit of the 1240's (when the second *Legenda* was being written) an indictment.

More than a life, the *Legenda Secunda* was a homily. There are sections on the poverty of houses and of furnishings, warnings against money, and praise for the practice of begging alms. There is a story that tells in detail how in Bologna an irate St. Francis drove even the sick out of a house that he believed the brothers had bought. There is a pointed catalog of all the virtues that a Minister General ought to possess. There are pages on the ideal Friar Minor. The Rule, without equivocation, is exalted. Tommaso's indignation against his own times is always recognizable—and not always subdued.

For Crescentius, who had commissioned the life, the tone was too recognizable. He made no effort to give the *Legenda Secunda* any wide circulation, and it was, in fact, to remain known to relatively few readers until the nineteenth century.

Nevertheless Tommaso's second life of Francis had a contemporary impact. It heartened men of good will who felt that some reform was called for, and it gave joy to the *zelanti*: their agitation had had some effect. They also had an explanation of why things had come to such a pass in the Order, and their feelings were considerably less restrained than those of Brother Tommaso.

Brother Tommaso expressed his resentment of Elia by virtually ignoring him, but among the fervent *zelanti* this resentment took another, most peculiar form. Their veneration of Francis gradually turned into a bellicose cult. The Saint appeared as another Moses, another Abraham, almost (and this is the point of the excessive analogies between the two) another Christ. Like God, he could neither deceive nor be deceived.

How, then, could he at any time have failed in what he set out to do, much less have been deceived? If he went to Syria to convert the Sultan, he succeeded; if it appeared that he had failed it must have been because the Sultan was converted in secret.

With respect to Elia, who did indeed become an apostate and was excommunicated after joining the court of Frederick II, it was inconceivable that Francis would not have known all along that this would happen; therefore he *knew*. The anonymous *zelante* who originated this explanation did not stop to consider the ethical implications of Francis' foreknowledge; he was concerned only with preserving Francis' infallibility. Was it likely, moreover, that in this heated atmosphere the originator of the story of the angel sent by God to reproach Brother Elia for having tampered with the regulations of the Rule of Francis should have sought first to carefully document the story? Actually, it was not Elia who made those changes in the fasting regulations but two vicars whom Francis had left in charge when he set out for Syria.

All things considered, it therefore appears that the *Fioretti*, with respect to Elia, is following the not too historically reliable oral tradition of the *zelanti*. The *Fioretti*'s account of the origins of the Order also leaves something to be desired, and it is even quite sensible to have reservations about the silhouette it draws of Francis.

This part of the *Fioretti* is not set in a perfumed landscape out of time, out of space. To some extent, it is still smoldering with the fires of polemic.

The feelings of the *zelanti,* which were to be accepted as canonical by the extreme wing of the Spirituals, explain the latter's version of the history of Elia; and that same outlook, goaded and envenomed by the events that followed the generalate of St. Bonaventure, accounts for the apocalyptic vision in which Bonaventure seeks to claw Giovanni da Parma and hurl him down from the tree.[6]

In 1247, however, sometime before the election of Bonaventure, the *zelanti,* as well as others who, without sharing their extreme views, also wanted a return to a more Franciscan spirit, were exuberant. We shall never know to what precise extent there was any serious corruption in the Order, but it is true that with the election of Giovanni da Parma to succeed Crescentius in that year the brothers spoke of a new age for the Order. Expectation and reform were in the air. The traditional story that after the election Brother Egidio greeted the new Minister General with "Well and opportunely have you come" rings true, although the concluding phrase, "but late," was possibly a later interpolation.

Giovanni da Parma was young, acceptable to moderates of all persuasions, energetic, and pious. He wanted to inculcate a renewed love for the Rule and the gospel, and he set out to do so with the vigor of the young. He systematically visited the provinces, sought to end the constant squabbling between the Order and the secular clergy, and managed to allay the resentment of the secular masters of the Sorbonne over the academic zeal and successes of the Order.

He neglected little. Stressing the need for properly conducted divine services, he promoted what had been a constant concern of Francis, the liturgy. He established better relations with the laity by granting them spiritual benefits and, for some, the important privilege of burial in the friars' cemeteries.

In every possible way, he sought vigorously to restrain the scandalous willingness of the friars to go to court over

[6] See Chapter 48 of the *Fioretti.*

land or goods or any injury done to them, and he insisted that the Order decline any additional help from the Pope for its work.

For the ten years of his generalate, most Franciscans, whether Spirituals or Conventuals, moderate or extreme, felt that the spirit of Francis had come to life again. The spirit of Elia seemed finally exorcised, and the actual death of Elia (who did, as the *Fioretti* claims, die clothed in his habit) seemed, if the word can be considered Christian, appropriate.

All promised well; but at this point there occurred a small incident that was to be the first in a series of disastrous setbacks for both the Spirituals, moderate and extreme, and the Order as a whole.

Toward the end of Giovanni's generalate there appeared in Paris a theological work, the *Introduction to the Eternal Gospel*. This was a commentary by a young Franciscan, Gerard of Borgo San Donnino, on the teachings of the Calabrian abbot and mystic, Joachim da Flora.

The Calabrian abbot was one of the most fascinating and compelling figures of the twelfth century. Dante spoke of him as a seer with the gift of prophecy—*"di spirito profetico dotato"*—and Joachim's ardent preaching of the coming of a third age in Christendom, the age of the Holy Spirit, had won a very wide following, a following which lasted well into the fourteenth century. He was especially appreciated by the Franciscans, for among the signs heralding the new age he discerned the advent of a barefoot religious order; and among the Franciscans he was particularly revered by the extreme Spirituals.

The mysticism of Joachim da Flora, however, like a number of mystical doctrines, occasionally verged on misty schism—and the enemies of the Franciscans, not entirely placated by the good will of Giovanni da Parma, took full advantage of the situation.

Gerard of Borgo San Donnino had not only dealt with a "difficult" mystic, but had made a travesty of his teachings. Soon after the Masters at Paris had denounced the treatise and brought it to the attention of the authorities in Rome, the work was officially condemned.

Giovanni da Parma fully appreciated the situation. He was quite aware that the maneuver involved something more than a defense of orthodoxy. Acting swiftly, he passed legislation requiring some central censorship on all future theological works by members of the Order. But the damage was done. The Order, which had never hidden its admiration for Joachim da Flora, was now in the difficult position of being closely identified with a heretical interpretation of a mystic-theologian who was himself not unquestionably orthodox.

Worst of all, the condemnation implicated Giovanni da Parma himself. It was openly known that although his orthodoxy was unexceptionable (he was later beatified), he did have strong Joachimite sympathies.

Alexander IV, the reigning pontiff, aware of the delicacy of the situation and of the maneuvering involved, sought to deal tactfully with the matter. Nevertheless, he had to act —and the greatest concession he could make was to respectfully invite Giovanni da Parma to resign.

At this request, the entire Order rose up in protest. It was a plot, a betrayal, they charged. Only when Giovanni pleaded with them to defer to the Pope, and designated the man of his choice as the next Minister General, did the Order grudgingly accept.

In this way, in 1257, the Bonaventure who in the *Fioretti* seeks to claw Giovanni da Parma, was made General of the Order.

A close friend of Bonaventure, Giovanni da Parma had done much to further the young man's career at the University of Paris. He had appointed Bonaventure a lector while the young man was still only a Bachelor of Arts. The move was unprecedented.

The two men had much in common. They both strove for sanctity; they both had great respect for learning; they were both interested in Joachim da Flora, although Bonaventure's interests were less conspicuous; and they both were involved in a similar political situation within the Order— an Order that tended increasingly to extreme positions in which power shifted either to the overzealous or to the over-indulgent.

During his long tenure from 1257 to 1274, Bonaventure did his utmost to continue the work of Giovanni da Parma. He made no radical changes in the Order; he persuaded the General Chapter to continue its policy of not implementing the bulls *Ordinem vestrum* and *Quanto studiosius,* which were designed to facilitate a relaxation of the rules of poverty; he sought to give greater authority to the office of the

Minister General; and he strove to extend his control over those brothers who frequently accepted ecclesiastical office without the Minister General's consent.

On all issues, therefore, including reception of money through intermediaries, the use of houses and land, the increased dedication to academic work, and the diminished emphasis on the need for manual labor, Bonaventure did not innovate; he continued the work of his predecessor.

Bonaventure was indefatigable. In addition to all this activity, he found the time to revise the constitution of the Order and to compose his *Life* of its founder.

History has not been kind to this *Life*, but the fault lies with Bonaventure himself and with the thirteenth-century ideal of hagiography. The *Life*, like the first *Legenda* of Brother Tommaso only more so, is generic; it is rhetorical; it is—and this is attributable to Bonaventure's temperament —excessively unconcerned with individualistic traits of the Saint. And there is a still more compelling reason for the harshness of history's judgment: Bonaventure ordered all previous *lives* of St. Francis destroyed.

Our instinctive "why?" is more an accusation than a question, and for those with complete trust in the extreme Spiritual position, the answer is obvious: he did so in order to destroy all the original "sacred texts." Bonaventure, according to this position, was an arrogant intellectual. Not only did he not understand Francis but he sought to snuff out the authentic teachings of the Saint.

This interpretation has the merit of being very forceful and direct. It has to ignore, however, the fact that the tone of this *Life* is in most respects that of the *Legenda Secunda* of Brother Tommaso, and that more than 85 per cent of the material in the *Life* is taken from that source. It also has to ignore the similarities and continuity in the work of Giovanni da Parma and that of Bonaventure, and, most awkwardly, it has to blind itself to Bonaventure's dominating trait, that of a peacemaker.

Dante, whose admiration for the Spirituals is well-known and who missed no opportunity to berate those Franciscans he considered lax in their duties, has Bonaventure in Paradise speak of himself as one who *"ne' grandi uffici sempre pospuosi la sinistra cura"*—one who always put the cause of temporal things last.

At worst Bonaventure stands accused of having badly miscalculated. A man of resolute ways, he perhaps thought that a drastic move—the command to destroy all previous *lives* —might ultimately pave the way for a general reconciliation. If he thought so, he proved to be very wrong indeed.

His action incensed the extreme Spirituals. When Bonaventure had taken part in the examination into Giovanni da Parma's orthodoxy after his resignation, the Spirituals had been shocked. Now, confronted with his edict to destroy all previous *lives* of Francis, they were aghast and defiant. We owe our knowledge of the two *Legendae* of Tommaso da Celano to the refusal of some Spirituals to obey this command.

Thus by 1274, the year of Bonaventure's death, dissensions had become more bitter than ever; it appeared that the centrifugal forces that had been slowly accelerating ever since the death of Francis could no longer be contained. The extremists among both the Spirituals and the Conventuals were replacing the moderates; and to make matters worse there appeared to be no strong personality in sight, no Minister General with the strength to control the situation.

The few resolute Generals who came to power after Bonaventure were with one exception Conventuals. Because the Spirituals had had the better of the argument in their books and preaching (the leaders of the Spirituals—Peter John Olivi in Provence, Angelo Clareno and Ubertino da Casale in Italy—were fiery, unyielding, and had a following), the extreme Conventuals resorted to strong measures. For fifteen years after the death of Bonaventure they actively persecuted the Spirituals, and persecution occasionally took the form of incarceration in dark cells ninety feet underground. There were few respites. During the brief generalate of Ganfredi, a group of Spirituals obtained protection to the extent of being sent to Armenia to escape their persecutors, ministers over whom Ganfredi had little control. Even there, they were not safe. The Conventuals kept after them, accused them of heresy to the authorities, and finally had them extradited.

Later, during the short pontificate of Celestine V, a group of Spirituals was allowed to break away from the Order and enter Celestine's own order of the Hermits of the Holy Spirit of Maiella. That respite, too, was short. Within six months Celestine's successor, Boniface VIII, rescinded the order and forced the Spirituals back.

At this point some of the Spirituals, including the great Franciscan poet Jacopone da Todi, broke out in open defiance of Boniface VIII and subsequently suffered imprisonment. It seemed as though the constant charge of the extreme Conventuals, that the Spirituals were schismatic if not heretical, was to be verified.

The story of Bonaventure and Giovanni da Parma included in the *Fioretti* originated in this atmosphere.

Looking back for an explanation of what had precipitated the persecution, the extreme Spirituals could find no more convincing reason than the actions of Bonaventure. Bonaventure had been an intellectual—a serious charge; he had been a systematic philosopher, at home not in a hermitage but in a university; he had turned religion into theological science; he had never begged for alms. What more vehement way to say all this than in a defiant, apocalyptic language, pointedly reminiscent of Joachim da Flora? Angelo Clareno (who as leader of the independent community of the Spirituals had, with the help of Uberto da Casale, won recognition for the cause in 1311 at the Council of Vienna) supplied the text in his *Historia septem tribulationum*—an account of the persecution of the Spirituals and a principal source for pro-Spiritual scholars. With some modifications, the story later became an integral part of the *Fioretti*.

The *Fioretti* does not allude to the final results of the conflict between the Spirituals and the Conventuals, but the story is worth telling for its ironical and paradoxical close.

The conflict came to an end in 1320 with a decision of John XXII, the Avignon Pope. This pope was notoriously not a theologian, nor was he Hamlet-like in judgment. By training he was a jurist, and when he came to deal with the long struggle among the Franciscans, of which he was weary, he approached it in the spirit of a jurist. The cause of all the polemics, he quickly decided, was the juridically untenable notion of Franciscan poverty. Regardless of its evangelical worth, as a legal notion it was not only nonsense but a dead weight on the papacy, which had to assume many of the financial responsibilities of the Order without reaping many of the benefits. The decision was a blow to the Order, but worse was to come. Applying the same sort of juridical reasoning, John XXII declared untenable the Franciscan claims that evangelical poverty was the highest form of the imitation of Christ.

The decision stunned the Order, Conventuals and Spirituals alike, and as the first consequence there was an abrupt about-face. The very Conventuals who had led the persecution against the Spirituals now outdid them in rebellion, and Michael of Cesena, William of Occam, and Bonagratia of Bergamo became the first Franciscan Conventual leaders to defy the Pope openly, as hitherto only the extreme wing of the Spirituals, the *fraticelli,* had done.

The wheel had come full circle.

Until the debacle of 1320, one group of Spirituals—a small band of brothers in the Marches—had by and large stood apart from the struggle. We find their story in the second part of the *Fioretti,* immediately after the two short chapters on St. Anthony.

To judge from this section the Order was at peace; but we know that at least one of its leaders, Corrado da Offida, was involved in the struggle and narrowly avoided imprisonment. There is no mention of this in these chapters, just as there is no allusion to the conflict between the Spirituals and the Conventuals. These brothers prayed and talked to God. They were not the authentic Franciscans they believed themselves to be—they were much too anti-intellectual and (partly out of necessity, considering the jealous zeal of the Conventuals) almost pure contemplatives—but they did capture some of the fragrance of the Franciscan soul at a time when the fanaticism of both contending parties had almost stifled it. They were edifying. Without rancor or bitterness they led the life they were persuaded Francis wanted them to lead.

Comparing them to Francis, though, we are bound to feel a sense of disappointment. There is in these accounts an excessive stress on the miraculous, and the miracles are heavy-handed. The story of the friar who flew like an eagle has little of the poetry of the story of the wolf of Gubbio, and among the many feats of levitation accomplished by the brothers there is nothing to remind the reader of the delicacy of St. Clare's miracle of the loaves. (There are, incidentally, no women saints in the very monastic second part of the *Fioretti*.) At times, as when Brother Simone reproaches the birds for making too much noise and banishes them, the tone inadvertently becomes comically non-Franciscan.

Heavy-handed in its concept of the miracle, this part of the *Fioretti* also leaves something to be desired in its main theme, the exaltation of theological simplicity. We read often in these pages of the deep understanding of theological doctrines—even of the doctrine of the Holy Trinity—on the part of unlettered brothers who knew only prayer and penance; but there is no intimation, at any point, of the truism that prayer and penance of themselves cannot yield an authentic theological knowledge without a sustained meditation of some breadth and experience.

There was an even more disturbing consequence of this excessive stress on theological simplicity, a consequence for which, ironically, the brothers of the Marches, like most Spirituals, incur partial responsibility: the very nature of Franciscan sanctity was misunderstood. The widespread notion that Francis abhorred all theology and mistrusted Bible reading, for example, is rooted precisely in this kind of theological simplicity, which lapses at this point into theological simplism.

The brothers of the Marches and their many followers did not understand that Francis did not condemn all systematic theology but only the desiccated forms that were of no spiritual help to the teacher or the taught. Francis was not opposed to the first recognized theologian of the Order, St. Anthony of Padua. We have a letter of his, which most recent scholarship now accepts as authentic, that expresses praise and admiration for St. Anthony's work. As for his asserted lack of enthusiasm for Bible reading, who better than Francis, as evidenced in the story of perfect joy in the *Fioretti*, understood the Pauline doctrine of suffering found in the Epistle to the Galatians: that in offering God our sufferings we offer Him that which is most truly ours? As for the doctrine of evangelical poverty, the core-conviction of Francis, would it have occurred to Francis without an unprecedented reading of the Bible, of the heroic texts of the New Testament?

Although he was obviously not averse to all forms of systematic theology, much less to a meditation of the Bible, the Saint has been misrepresented in these areas by the Spirituals and, more indirectly, the *Fioretti*. The wrong is reminiscent of that done to Bonaventure by the Spirituals. To the last, they did not realize that it was the doctor of the University of Paris who had provided the Order with the one systematic theological defense of the doctrine of evangelical poverty.

In a number of cases, therefore, the cult of theological simplicity espoused so fervently by the authors of the *Fioretti* led to sins of omission and, as often happens, turned humility itself into a subtle arrogance. On some occasions, as in the story of the brother who can think of no more appropriate expression of his love for a deceased friar than to eat and drink out of his skull, the "simplicity" itself becomes disconcerting. It shows a spiritual tonality that we do not associate with Francis.

The dark side of the moon of the second section of the *Fioretti* is dark indeed. Is there no light at all, however? Is this second section anything more than a heavily partisan account of the history of the Order and of the spirit of the Saint?

It is. A markedly partisan account in the one apocalyptic reference to Bonaventure, it is also, considering the intensity of the polemic in which it moves about, a remarkably serene document—a Franciscan oasis. At a time when Spirituals were being buffeted about in a persecution involving exile and incarceration, the second part of the *Fioretti*—with its stories of the mystical experience of Giovanni of Alverna seeking his God, the brother learning how to wait wisely for death, the brother who joyfully comes to see the inadequacy of all words in the presence of God—makes us touch the hem of the Timeless. For all the reservations we may have concerning the views of the Spirituals and their interpretation of Francis, in these splendid testimonials of poverty they have captured for all time some of the fragrance of that joyous mystical ideal.

That ideal is perhaps most exquisitely and humanly conveyed in the *Considerations on the Stigmata*. Like all the other parts, it too has a polemical motif—the defense of the stigmata at a time when they were being increasingly questioned; also like the preceding parts it shows little concern for the niceties of chronological sequence. Historical time for the *Considerations* is poetical time, the time which best expresses the mystery and humanity of the event. There is a place in that time for the trembling ecstasy of Francis —and also for the vulgar doubts of Brother Leo as to whether Francis had really always been chaste, for the itchy curiosity of the brothers to touch the stigmata, for the peasant's admonition to Francis to be truly saintly so that the people would not be appalled by the deception. In no other work of Franciscan literature is the mixture of the grandiose and the intimate so fresh and felicitous. Whoever else Francis might have been, he was also without a doubt the mystic of the *Considerations*. It was with reason that this part of the *Fioretti* was especially meditated on by St. Bernard of Siena and that it became a classic text for reform movements among the Franciscans.

*The garden.* At the end of this brief probing and testing, are we tempted to conclude that for all our verifying, comparing, and rejecting, the only thing of value in the *Fioretti* is the fragrance, to feel that the *Fioretti* should remain as we "remember" it—fragrance and not history?

For some of us this will be an inevitable conclusion. Having briefly experienced what the problem of historical reliability involves, we have become disenchanted—and most of us do not want to be disenchanted.

Others among us will not feel so discomforted. Having come to some conclusions, we feel that we may have taken a step towards becoming genuinely old—that we have grown a bit out of our state of prolonged adolescence.

It is good to be completely convinced that the *Fioretti* is in no way a pre-Raphaelite text. It is a gain to see that it is even more difficult to know the mind of a saint than it is to know ourselves. In catching but a glimpse of the travail of Francis and his Order, in trying to determine what evangelical poverty ought to be, we have had an inkling of the enormous problem, not confined to Francis and the Franciscans alone, of trying to preserve, in one religious experience, respect for both the letter and the spirit of the law. It is neither outrageous nor amusing if in working out a problem of such dimensions the Christian virtues were not always in command; those of us whose experience of evangelical poverty is vicarious will certainly not be tempted at the end of this story to feel *au-dessus de la melée*.

However we respond to the attempt to assess the historical value of the *Fioretti,* one conclusion forces itself upon us: nostalgia will not lead us back to the remembered garden. The garden is not for those who seek it for itself. Should we, though, search for something more, it is quite probable that at some one point, some unexpected turn, we may suddenly discover it. At that moment we may feel that a "middle-aged" reading of the *Fioretti* pointed in the right direction.

*Serge Hughes*

# IN THE NAME OF CHRIST, ON THE 31ST OF MAY, 1396, THE VIGIL OF THE PASSOVER OF HIS BODY, BEGIN THE LITTLE FLOWERS OF ST. FRANCIS

## CHAPTER I

*How Messer St. Francis, at the founding of his Order, chose twelve companions, just as Christ chose twelve Apostles; and how one of the twelve companions of St. Francis, and that was Brother Giovanni della Cappella, hanged himself by the neck, just as one of the twelve Apostles, and that was Judas, hanged himself.*

We must first consider that the glorious St. Francis, in all the acts of his life, modeled himself on Christ. Thus, as Christ at the beginning of His mission chose twelve Apostles who were to abandon all things worldly and follow Him in poverty and in the other virtues, so St. Francis at the founding of his Order chose twelve companions, who espoused the most high poverty. As one of the twelve Apostles of Christ, cast off by God, finally hanged himself by the neck, so one of the twelve companions of St. Francis, by name Brother Giovanni della Cappella, apostate, finally hanged himself by the neck. And all this is for the elect a great example and cause of humility and fear, considering that no one is certain to persevere in the grace of God until the end. And as the twelve Apostles were to all men marvels of sanctity, and filled with the Holy Spirit, so those most holy companions of St. Francis were men of such marvelous sanctity as the world had not seen from the time of the Apostles: so much so that one of them was swept up to the third heaven, like St. Paul, and this was Brother Egidio; the lips of another, that is,

47

tall Brother Filippo, were touched by the angel with a burning coal, like Isaiah the prophet; one of them, Brother Silvestro, used to speak with God as one friend to another, as did Moses; another, the most humble Brother Bernardo, soared by flight of intellect to the very light of divine wisdom, like the Eagle, John the Evangelist, and expounded Holy Scripture most profoundly; still another was sanctified by God and canonized in Heaven while still living in the world, and this was Brother Ruffino, nobleman of Assisi. And thus all were privileged with unique signs of sanctity, as will become clear in the course of these tales.

## CHAPTER II

> *Of Brother Bernardo da Quintavalle, first companion of St. Francis.*

The first companion of St. Francis was Brother Bernardo of Assisi, who was converted in this way. St. Francis was still in secular garb, although he had already renounced the world and in order to do penance went about scorned and mortified. Many thought him out of his wits, and he was derided as mad and chased away with stones and mud by his family and by strangers; and he endured every injury and derision patiently, as if he were deaf and dumb.

Messer Bernardo of Assisi, who was one of the noblest and richest and wisest men of the city, began to ponder on St. Francis' intense contempt for the world, his great patience when others did him injury, and on the fact that although he had been detested and scorned by all for two years, he seemed ever more constant and patient. He began to think and to say to himself: "This Francis must have grace with God." And so he invited him to dine and lodge with him that evening; and St. Francis accepted and dined with him and slept in his home. Then Messer Bernardo resolved in his heart to observe carefully the holiness of St. Francis; he set up a bed for him in his own room, in which a lamp was always burning. And St. Francis, to conceal his sanctity, as soon as he had entered the room, threw himself on the bed and pretended to sleep; and similarly Messer Bernardo after a short time lay down and began to snore loudly, as if he were sleeping very deeply. At this, St. Francis, believing that Messer Bernardo was really asleep, in that first deep sleep, got up from the bed and knelt down to pray; raising his eyes and his hands, and with great devotion and fervor, he said: "My God, my God." And so saying, and weeping copiously, he remained until morning, repeating: "My God . . ." and nothing more. St. Francis said this as he contemplated and admired the excellence of the Divine Majesty who had deigned to reach down to the perishing world and through His Francis, the dear poor one, graciously grant a remedy for the health of his soul and those of others. Illumined by the spirit of prophecy, foreseeing the great things that God was to do through him and through his Order, and considering his own insufficiency and limited virtue, he was calling on God and pleading that with His pity and omnipotence, without which human frailty can do nothing, He might make up for his deficiencies and help and complete that which he, Francis, could not do by himself.

Messer Bernardo, seeing by the light of the lamp the very devout acts of St. Francis, and diligently considering the words that he spoke, was touched and inspired by the Holy Spirit to change his life. When morning came, he called St. Francis and said to him: "I have resolved in my heart to abandon the world and to follow you in that which you command."

When he heard this, St. Francis rejoiced and said: "Messer Bernardo, what you have said is so great and marvelous that we must ask counsel regarding it of our Lord Jesus Christ and pray that He be pleased to show us His will on the matter, and to teach us how we can carry it out. Therefore let us go together to the bishop's church, where there is a good priest, and we will have him say Mass. We will then remain in prayer until tierce, praying God that when we open the missal three times He will show us the way He wishes us to choose." Messer Bernardo replied that this plan pleased him greatly.

So they set out and went to the bishop's church, and after they had heard Mass and remained in prayer until tierce, the priest, at the request of St. Francis, took the missal and, having made the sign of the cross, opened it in the name of our Lord Jesus Christ three times; and the first time they found the words in the gospel that Christ spoke to the young man who asked how he might be perfect: "If you wish to be perfect, go and sell all you have and give to the poor and come follow Me." The second time they opened the missal they found the words that Christ spoke to the Apostles when He sent them to preach: "Take nothing for the journey, neither stick nor purse nor shoes nor money," wishing by this to teach them that they should place all their hope in God and direct all their energies to the preaching of the gospel. In the third opening of the missal they found the words of Christ: "He who would come after Me, let him abandon himself and take up his cross and follow Me."

Then St. Francis said to Messer Bernardo: "This is the counsel that Christ gives us. Go therefore and do thoroughly that which you have heard; and may our Lord Jesus Christ be blessed, who has deigned to show us His evangelical way."

When Messer Bernardo heard this, he left and sold all that he owned, for he was very rich. With great joy he distributed it all to the poor, to widows, to orphans, to pilgrims, to monasteries, and to hospitals; and in all this St. Francis faithfully and providently aided him.

There was a man, by name Messer Silvestro, who, when he saw that St. Francis gave and had others give so much money to the poor, was gripped by avarice; and he said to St. Francis: "You did not pay me all you owed me for those stones that you bought from me to repair the churches. Now that you have money, pay me." St. Francis, marveling at his avarice and not wanting to argue with him, as a true observer of the gospel placed all the money he had in his hands in Messer Silvestro's lap, saying that if he wanted more he would give him more. Messer Silvestro, happy with this, went off and returned home. In the evening, thinking over what he had done, he reproached himself for his avarice and meditated the fervor of Messer Bernardo and the holiness of St. Francis. On the following night and two other nights he had from God a vision in which he saw coming from the mouth of St. Francis a cross of gold, whose highest point touched the sky and whose arms stretched out from the east to the west. Because of this vision he gave all that he had for God and became a Friar Minor; and in the Order he was full of holiness and grace, and he spoke with God as to a friend, and St. Francis experienced this more than once, as will be told later.

Messer Bernardo similarly had much grace from God and was often rapt in contemplation of God; and St. Francis used to say of him that he was worthy of all reverence, and that it was he who had founded the Order, since he was the first to renounce the world, keeping nothing for himself but giving all to Christ's poor. Once he had embraced evangelical poverty, he offered himself naked to the arms of the Crucified One, may He be blessed forever and ever. Amen.

## CHAPTER III

*How St. Francis became troubled when he called to Brother Bernardo and received no answer.*

Because of the harshness of his penance and his constant weeping, St. Francis, the devoted servant of the crucified Lord, had become nearly blind and could barely see light. On one occasion he went to visit Brother Bernardo to speak with him of things divine, and having come to where Brother Bernardo was, he found him in prayer, lifted up and joined with God. As he approached the wood where Brother Bernardo was praying, St. Francis cried out: "Come and speak to this blind man." But Brother Bernardo did not answer, for as a great contemplative, his soul was lifted up and rapt in God.

St. Francis had many times experienced Brother Bernardo's singular grace in speaking of God and had come to him for that reason. After a short while he called him a second and then a third time in the same way, but Brother Bernardo did not hear him and neither answered nor moved toward him. Disconsolate and perplexed, St. Francis left, wondering to himself why Brother Bernardo, after being called three times, had not come to meet him.

Walking a bit further on and still feeling the disappointment, St. Francis said to his companion: "Stay here and wait for me." He made his way to a solitary place and knelt in prayer, asking God to reveal to him why Brother Bernardo had not answered him. While in prayer, he heard the voice of God saying: "O poor little man, what troubles you? Ought man leave God for a creature? When you were calling Brother Bernardo he was one with Me and therefore could not answer you or come to you. Be not surprised, then, if he did not answer you, since in that state he could not hear you."

Having received this answer from God, St. Francis immediately and with great haste returned to Brother Bernardo to confess humbly the thoughts he had had about him. Brother Bernardo, seeing St. Francis approaching, went toward him and threw himself at his feet. St. Francis bade him arise and with great humility informed him of the thoughts and misgivings he had had, and how God had reproached him for them, and he concluded: "I command you, in the name of holy obedience, that you do as I tell you."

Brother Bernardo, who feared that St. Francis might order him to some excessive action, as he was wont to do, wanted to evade this injunction as best he could, and he answered: "I am disposed to obey you, if you will in turn promise to obey me."

And when St. Francis promised, Brother Bernardo asked what it was that Francis willed, and St. Francis said: "I order you, in the name of holy obedience, as a punishment for my presumption and the rashness of my heart, to put one foot on my throat and the other on my mouth as I lie down flat on the ground; and I order you to walk across me three times in this manner, reproaching me harshly for my temerity. I order you in particular to say, 'Lie down, peasant, son of Pietro Bernardone. How do you come by such pride, you abject creature?' "

Brother Bernardo, although he found it hard to do so, in the name of obedience carried out St. Francis' instructions as gently as possible. Whereupon St. Francis said: "Now order me to do what you will, for I have promised you obedience."

And Brother Bernardo said: "I order you, in the name of holy obedience, each time that we are together to correct and reproach me harshly for my shortcomings."

St. Francis marveled greatly at this, for Brother Bernardo was of such sanctity that St. Francis held him in great reverence and did not find anything wanting in him. From that point on, therefore, because of that injunction, St. Francis took care to spend little time with him, whose sanctity he knew, for he did not want to reproach and correct him. When he desired to see him or to hear him speak of God, he left him as soon as he could; and it was greatly edifying to see with what charity and reverence and humility the holy father Francis spoke with Brother Bernardo, his firstborn son. To the praise and glory of Christ. Amen.

## CHAPTER IV

*How St. Francis went to the shrine of St. James and left Brother Bernardo to care for a sick man and to go to the shrine later; and how the angel came to speak to Brother Elia, who did not want to listen to him, but who later repented.*

In the beginning, when the Order was first founded and the friars were few and had no fixed places, St. Francis out of devotion went to the shrine of St. James in Galicia, taking with him a number of friars, among whom was Brother Bernardo. And as they were walking along together on the way, they came across a poor sick man; and St. Francis, feeling pity for him, said to Brother Bernardo: "Son, I want you to stay here to take care of this sick man." And Brother Bernardo, kneeling humbly and bowing his head, complied with the order of the holy father and remained behind while St. Francis, together with his other companions, went on to the shrine.

Having passed the night in prayer in the church of St. James, St. Francis received a revelation from God that he was to establish many houses throughout the world, because his Order was to spread and to grow into a great multitude of friars. Because of this revelation, St. Francis began to establish places in various regions.

As he returned along the same route he had followed to the shrine, St. Francis once again met Brother Bernardo and the sick man with whom he had left him, now completely well. The following year St. Francis allowed Brother Bernardo to go to St. James, and he himself returned to the Valley of Spoleto.

There in that deserted place he stayed together with Brother Masseo and Brother Elia and others; and they all took great pains not to molest St. Francis or distract him from prayer because of the great reverence they had for him and because they knew that God revealed great things to him in prayer.

It happened one day that as St. Francis was deep in prayer in the forest, a fair young man in the garb of a traveler

came to the door of the friars' hut and knocked so loudly
and in such great haste and so insistently that the brothers
were quite astonished. Brother Masseo went to the door and
opened it and said to the young man: "Where do you come
from, son, for from your manner of knocking it seems as
if you have never knocked at a friar's door before."

The young man answered: "And how should one knock?"

"Knock three times," answered Brother Masseo, "one after
the other, with pauses in between; then wait for as long as
is required to say an Our Father, for a brother to come to
you; and if he does not come in this interval, knock once
again."

"I am in a great hurry," replied the young man, "and
I knocked loudly because I must go on a long journey and
I have come to Brother Francis. But he is in the woods
praying and I do not want to disturb him. Call Brother Elia,
for I want to ask him a question, since I have heard that
he is very wise."

Brother Masseo then went and asked Brother Elia to see
the young man. Brother Elia, annoyed, did not wish to go,
and Brother Masseo did not know what to do or how to
answer the young man. If he were to say, "Brother Elia
cannot come," he would be lying, and if he were to say that
Elia was angry and refused to come, he was afraid of giving
scandal.

While Brother Masseo hesitated, the young man knocked
once more as he had before, and soon after, Brother Masseo
went to the door and said to the young man: "You did not
knock as I told you to."

The young man answered: "Brother Elia does not wish to
come to me; go then and tell Brother Francis that I came to
speak with him, but since I don't want to take him away
from prayer ask him to send Brother Elia to me."

Then Brother Masseo went to St. Francis, who was praying
in the woods with his face raised to Heaven, and informed
him of the young man's request (the young man was the
angel of God in human shape) and of Brother Elia's answer.

St. Francis, without moving or lowering his face, said to
Brother Masseo: "Go and, in the name of obedience, tell
Brother Elia to go immediately to that young man."

Brother Elia, having heard the order of St. Francis, became
angry and brusquely went to the door, opened it, and said to
the young man: "What do you want?"

"Brother, take care," the young man answered, "that you be not as angry as you seem to be, since wrath is a stumbling block to the soul and does not allow it to discern the truth."

And Brother Elia answered: "Tell me what you wish from me."

"I ask you," said the young man, "if those who observe the holy gospel are allowed to eat what is placed before them, as Christ told His Disciples; and I ask you further if it is licit for any man to impose any rule that is contrary to evangelical liberty."

Brother Elia answered haughtily: "I can answer this, but I do not wish to. Go about your business."

"I," replied the young man, "could answer this question better than you."

Then with great anger, Brother Elia, upset, slammed the door and left. Later he began to think of that question and to have doubts about it, for he did not know the answer. Since, when he was Vicar of the Order he had added to the constitution, contrary to the gospel and to the rule of St. Francis, that no brother in the Order should eat meat, the question was obviously directed against him. Not knowing how to resolve the difficulty himself, and remembering the modesty of the young man, who had nevertheless said that he could answer that question better than Brother Elia could, he went back to the door and opened it to ask the young man the answer. But the young man had left because the haughtiness of Brother Elia made him unworthy of speaking with an angel.

St. Francis, to whom the whole encounter had been revealed by God, came back from the forest and strongly and loudly reproached Brother Elia, saying: "You do ill, haughty Brother Elia, to drive away from us the holy angels who come to teach us. I tell you that I greatly fear that your pride might make you end your days outside the Order." And it came to pass as St. Francis had predicted, for Brother Elia did die out of the Order.

On the same day, in that hour in which the angel left, he appeared in the same form to Brother Bernardo, who was returning from the shrine of St. James and was on the shores of a great river. Speaking in Bernardo's tongue, he said: "God grant you peace, good brother."

And Brother Bernardo marveled at the beauty of the young man and at hearing his mother tongue, and at his peaceful greeting and joyous face. He asked him: "Where do you come from, my good young man?"

And the angel answered: "I come from that place where St. Francis is. I went to speak to him and was not able to do so, for he was in the woods contemplating things divine, and I did not wish to disturb him. And Brother Masseo and Brother Egidio and Brother Elia are staying with him. Brother Masseo taught me how to knock at the door as the brothers do, but Brother Elia, since he did not wish to answer the question I put to him, later repented and wished to see me and he was not able to do so." After having said these words, the angel asked Brother Bernardo: "Why don't you cross over to the other side?"

And Brother Bernardo replied: "Because I am afraid of the depth of the water."

"Let us cross together," said the angel. "Do not fear." And taking him by the hand, in the twinkling of an eye he set him down on the other side of the river.

Then Brother Bernardo knew that he was an angel of God, and with great reverence and joy cried aloud: "O blessed angel of God, tell me your name."

And the angel answered: "Why do you ask my name, which is itself a wondrous thing?"

And having said this, the angel disappeared, leaving a much heartened Brother Bernardo to finish his journey in great joy. And thinking about the hour and the day that the angel appeared to him, when he came to the place where St. Francis and his companions were staying, he told them in great detail what had happened to him. And knowing with certainty that it was the same angel who had appeared to them and to him in the same hour of the same day, they gave thanks to God. Amen.

## CHAPTER V

*How Brother Bernardo went to find a place in Bologna*

Because St. Francis and his companions were called and chosen by God to bear in their hearts, in their works, and with their words the cross of Christ, they seemed to be and were crucified, in their actions and in their austerity; and they therefore desired more to endure shame and insults out of love of Christ than to obtain worldly honor or fame or human respect. In fact, they rejoiced in abuse and were saddened by honors, and thus they went through the world as pilgrims and strangers, taking with them only Christ crucified. They were the true branches of the true vine that is Christ, and they brought forth good fruit from the souls that they won over to God.

In the early days of the Order it came about that St. Francis sent Brother Bernardo to Bologna so that he could, according to the grace that God gave him, bring forth good fruits for the Lord. And Brother Bernardo, crossing himself, in the name of holy obedience left and came to Bologna. The children there, seeing him in his uncommon and coarse garb, mocked him, insulted him, and buffeted him, as children are wont to do with idiots. Brother Bernardo patiently and joyously endured all, out of love of Christ; in fact, so that he would be all the more mocked, he deliberately went to the square of the city, and there, when he sat down, many children and men gathered around him; and some pulled on his cowl, others threw dust at him, others stones, and still others pushed him now to one side, now to the other. Remaining firm and patient, and with joyous countenance, Brother Bernardo did not complain and did not move; and moreover, for many days thereafter he returned to that very same place to endure such tribulations.

And since patience is a work of spiritual perfection and a mark of virtue, a learned doctor of the laws, seeing and considering such constancy and virtue in Brother Bernardo, who remained impervious to all abuse, said to himself: "This man must be a saint." And he approached him and said: "Who are you and why have you come here?"

And Brother Bernardo, in answer, put his hand in his tunic and took out the Rule of St. Francis and gave it to him to read.

When the learned judge had read it, considering the lofty tone of its perfect counsel, with great amazement and admiration he turned and said to those around him: "In truth, I have never heard of a loftier religious rule, and this man and his companions are among the holiest men of this world. To abuse him is to commit a great sin, for he ought to be honored as a great friend of God." And he said to Brother

Bernardo: If you would wish a place in which you could fittingly serve God, I would gladly give it to you for the good of my soul."

"Sir," replied Brother Bernardo, "I believe that our Lord Jesus Christ has inspired your offer, and I gladly accept it for the honor of Christ."

Then the judge, with great joy and charity, took Brother Bernardo to his home, and later gave him the place he had promised him, and out of his own pocket paid for repairs and furnishings. And from that time on, he became the father and protector of Brother Bernardo and his companions.

And Brother Bernardo, because of the holiness of his conversation, began to be honored by the people, and whoever could see him or touch him considered himself blessed. But he, like a true disciple of Christ and of the humble St. Francis, fearing that the honors of this world might endanger the peace and salvation of his soul, left that place and returned to St. Francis and said: "Father, the place is ready in the city of Bologna. Send friars to reside there and keep it in order, for I could no longer profit from my stay there. On the contrary, because of the excessive honor that they paid me, I was afraid that I would lose more than I would gain."

St. Francis, hearing how God had used Brother Bernardo, thanked the Lord, who was thus beginning to multiply and send forth the poor disciples of the cross. He subsequently sent other companions to Bologna and to Lombardy, where they found many places for the Order. In praise and reverence of the good Jesus. Amen.

## CHAPTER VI

*How, after the death of St. Francis, Brother Bernardo became Vicar or Minister General.*

Brother Bernardo was of such sanctity that St. Francis held him in highest reverence and frequently praised him. One day when St. Francis was kneeling devoutly in prayer it was revealed to him by God that Brother Bernardo, with divine permission, was to endure many harsh battles with demons; and St. Francis, having great compassion for Brother

Bernardo, whom he loved as his son, for many days with prayers and tears pleaded to God for him, beseeching Jesus Christ that He might give Brother Bernardo victory over the devil. And as he was devoutly in prayer, St. Francis one day heard God's answer: "Francis, do not fear; for all the temptations by which Brother Bernardo is to be buffeted are allowed by Me as a test of his virtue and as a crown of merit. In the end he will triumph over all his enemies, for he is to enjoy the banquet of the kingdom of God." St. Francis rejoiced exceedingly at this answer and thanked God, and from that time on, he showed even more love and reverence for Brother Bernardo.

He manifested that love not only during his life but in death as well, for as St. Francis lay dying, as had the patriarch Jacob, with all his devoted sons grief-struck and weeping over the loss of their beloved father, he asked: "Where is my firstborn son? Come to me, son, so that I may bless your soul before I die."

Then Brother Bernardo whispered to Brother Elia, who was Vicar of the Order: "Father, go to the right hand of the Saint so that he may bless you."

And when Brother Elia went to the right side, St. Francis, who had lost his sight because of his too frequent tears, placed his right hand on the head of Brother Elia and said: "This is not the head of my firstborn, Brother Bernardo."

Then Brother Bernardo went on his left side and St. Francis then crossed one arm over the other and placed his right hand on the head of Brother Bernardo, his left on that of Brother Elia, and said to Brother Bernardo: "May the Father of our Lord Jesus Christ bless you with every spiritual and celestial benediction in Christ, for you are the first chosen one in this holy Order to give evangelical example in following Christ in evangelical poverty. You not only gave all of your goods freely to the poor, out of love of Christ, but offered yourself to God in this Order in gentle sacrifice. May you be blessed, then, by our Lord Jesus Christ and by me, His poor little servant, with eternal benedictions, in going, coming, awake or sleeping, living and dying. May he who blesses you receive abundant blessings, and he who curses you not go unpunished. Be the leader of all your brothers. May all the friars obey your orders. Exercise the right of receiving into this Order and expelling from it all whom you wish, and may no brother have authority over you; and may you go and stay as you wish."

After the death of St. Francis the brothers loved and revered Brother Bernardo as their venerable father. And when he came to die, many brothers from many parts of the world came to see him, among whom was the divine and angelic Brother Egidio, who said with great joy: *"Sursum corda,* Brother Bernardo, *sursum corda."* And the holy Brother Bernardo told a brother secretly to prepare for Brother Egidio a place fit for contemplation. And so it was done.

When Brother Bernardo had come to the last hour of his life, he had himself propped up and said to the friars around him: "My dearest brothers, I do not wish to say much, but you must consider that I have been in the state you are in now, and that you will be in the state I am in now; and I find in my soul that I would have given up a thousand such worlds to serve our Lord Jesus Christ, and I accuse myself before our Saviour Jesus Christ of every fault I have committed. I beg of you, my dearest brothers, that you love one another." After these and other words of good counsel, he lay back on the bed, his face so radiant and joyful that his brothers greatly marveled at it. In that joy his most holy soul, crowned with glory, passed from this present life to the blessed life of the angels. In praise and glory of Christ. Amen.

## CHAPTER VII

> *How St. Francis fasted an entire Lent and ate nothing but half a loaf of bread.*

Since in certain things the true servant of Christ, Messer St. Francis, was almost another Christ, given to the world for the salvation of peoples, God the Father wished to make him in many acts one with His Son Jesus Christ, as can be seen in the venerable confraternity of the twelve companions, in the admirable mystery of the holy stigmata, and in the continual fasting during holy Lent, which he practiced in the following way.

One day St. Francis, who had gone on carnival day to the home of one of his devoted friends near the Lake of Perugia and was spending the night there, was inspired by God to pass Lent on an island of that lake. And so St. Francis begged his devoted friend, out of the love of Christ, to take him in his boat to an island on the lake where no one lived, and to do so on the night of Ash Wednesday, so that no one would see them. St. Francis' friend, who had great devotion for him, carried out the request in all haste, and St. Francis took with him nothing but two small loaves of bread. When they came to the island, St. Francis strongly besought his friend, who was about to return, not to reveal to anyone that he was there, and not to come for him till Holy Thursday. And so the friend left and St. Francis remained alone.

Since there was no shelter of any kind in which he could stay, he entered into a thick wood in which many young saplings and plum trees had formed something similar to a small hut or an animal's lair, and in this place he began to pray and to contemplate heavenly things. He remained there for the entire period of Lent without eating and without drinking, except for a half of one of those two loaves of bread—as his devoted friend discovered when he came back for him on Holy Thursday and found the two loaves of bread, one untouched and the other only half consumed. And it is believed that St. Francis ate the other half out of reverence, to distinguish his fast from that of the blessed Christ, who fasted forty days and forty nights without taking any food. And so with that half loaf he cast from himself the poison of vainglory and still fasted forty days and forty nights in imitation of Christ.

Later on, in that place where St. Francis had abstained so marvelously, God, because of the Saint's merits, performed many miracles. Men began to build there and live there, and in a short while a mighty and beautiful castle was built, and there stands the place of the friars that is known as the Place of the Island. And even today the men and women of that castle have great reverence and devotion for that place where St. Francis passed Lent. To the glory of Christ. Amen.

## CHAPTER VIII

*How St. Francis taught Brother Leo the meaning of perfect joy.*

One winter day as St. Francis, together with Brother Leo, was coming from Perugia to St. Mary of the Angels, the intense cold made them shiver, and St. Francis called Brother Leo, who was walking slightly ahead, and said: "O Brother Leo, may God grant that the Friars Minor give good example in sanctity and edification in every corner of the earth; and yet write down, and mark it carefully, that in that work there is not perfect joy." And walking a bit further, St. Francis said to him: "O Brother Leo, although a Friar Minor might give sight to the blind, cure paralytics, cast out devils, make the deaf hear, have the lame walk, make the mute speak, and even greater, have the dead of four days come alive again, write down that in that there is no perfect joy." And going on further, St. Francis cried out loudly: "O Brother Leo, if the Friar Minor were to know all languages and all learning and all Scripture, so that he could prophesy and reveal not only the events of the future but the secrets of minds and souls as well, write down that in that there is no perfect joy." And going a bit further on, St. Francis again said loudly: "O Brother Leo, little lamb of God, although the Friar Minor might speak with the tongue of an angel and know the course of the heavens and the virtues of herbs, and if all the treasures of the earth were revealed to him and he were to know all the properties of birds and of fishes and of all men and animals and of trees and stones and roots and waters, write down that in that there is no perfect joy." And going on a bit further, St. Francis cried out: "O Brother Leo, even though the Friar Minor were to know how to preach so well that he could convert all the infidels to the faith of Christ, write down that in that there is no perfect joy."

And when St. Francis had spoken in this fashion for about two miles, Brother Leo asked him in great wonder: "Father, I beg of you in the name of God, tell me where perfect joy is to be found."

And St. Francis answered: "When we shall come to St. Mary of the Angels, drenched with rain, and frozen and spattered with mud, and sick with hunger, and we shall knock at the door and the doorkeeper will come out angrily and say, 'Who are you?' and we shall reply 'We are two of your friars,' and he will retort, 'That is not true. You are in fact two evildoers who go about deceiving the world and stealing money from the poor. Go away!' and he will not open up to us and we will have to stay outside in the snow and rain, where with cold and hunger we shall spend the night; then if we shall be able to endure so many abuses and so much cruelty and so many rebuffs patiently, without upset, without murmuring against the doorkeeper, and humbly and charitably believe that he truly knows us and that God has him speak against us, O Brother Leo, write down that that is perfect joy. And if we were to continue knocking and he were to come out exceedingly upset, and he would throw us out as importunate idlers, with strong words and with blows, saying, 'Leave, wretched thieves, go to the alms-house, for here you will neither eat nor sleep'; if we can endure all of this patiently and with bliss, O Brother Leo, write down that therein is perfect joy. And if we, forced by hunger and cold and the night, continued to knock, and with great tears beseeched him for the love of God to open up and let us in, and if he, increasingly irate, were to say, 'These are wretched, insistent idlers and I will deal with them as they should be dealt with!' and he would come out with a gnarled club and grab us by the cowl and hurl us to the ground, turning us over in the snow and beating us with that club; if we could endure patiently and cheerfully all these things, which we must endure for the love of Christ, dwelling on the sufferings of the blessed Christ, O Brother Leo, write down that in that there is perfect joy. And therefore mark down the conclusion, Brother Leo: the highest gift and grace of the Holy Spirit that Christ concedes to His friends is to conquer oneself and, out of love of Christ, to endure willingly sufferings, injuries, insults, and discomfort. We cannot glory in all the other gifts of God because they are not ours but they are of God, because of which the Apostle says, 'What do you have that does not come from God? If you have had it from God, why do you glory in it as if it were your own?' But we can glory in the cross of tribulation and affliction, for this is ours, and the Apostle therefore says, 'I will glory only in the cross of our Lord Jesus Christ.'" To whom be honor and glory, world without end. Amen.

## CHAPTER IX

*How St. Francis taught Brother Leo how to answer matins, and how Brother Leo always said the opposite of what St. Francis taught him.*

In the early days of the Order, finding himself in a place where there were no books with which to recite the Divine Office, St. Francis, at the hour of matins, said to Brother Leo: "My dear one, we have no breviary with which to recite matins; but so that we may spend the time in the praise of God I will speak and you will answer me as I instruct you. I will say as follows, 'O Brother Francis, you committed so many sins in the world that you are worthy of Hell.' And you, Brother Leo, will answer, 'You speak the truth, and you deserve the deepest Hell.'"

And Brother Leo, with the simplicity of the dove, answered: "Gladly, Father. In the name of God, begin."

Then St. Francis began to say: "O Brother Francis, you committed so many sins in the world that you are worthy of Hell."

And Brother Leo answered: "Through you God will do so much good that you will go to Heaven."

St. Francis said: "Do not say that, Brother Leo; but when I say, 'O Brother Francis, you have done so many sinful things against God that you are worthy of being damned by Him,' do you answer in this fashion: 'You speak the truth and you are worthy of being placed among the damned.'"

And Brother Leo replied: "Gladly, Father."

Then St. Francis, with many sighs and tears, beating his breast, cried aloud; "O my Lord God of Heaven and earth, I have committed so many sins against You and have done so much evil that I am completely worthy of being damned by You."

And Brother Leo answered: "God will make of you

such a one that among the blessed you will be singularly blessed."

St. Francis, marveling that Brother Leo answered only the opposite of what he had ordered him to, began to reproach him, saying: "Why don't you answer as I have instructed you? I order you, in the name of holy obedience, to answer as I have taught you. I will say as follows, 'O little wretched Brother Francis, do you think that God will have mercy on you, even though you have committed so many sins against the Father of Mercy and the God of all consolations that you are not worthy of finding forgiveness?' And you, Brother Leo, my little lamb, will answer, 'In no way are you worthy of finding mercy.'"

But then when St. Francis said: "O wretched little Brother Francis," etc., Brother Leo answered: "God the Father, whose forgiveness is infinitely greater than your sin, will be very merciful towards you, and to that mercy will add many other graces."

Considering this answer, St. Francis, sweetly angered and patiently upset, said to Brother Leo: "Why have you had such presumption to deny obedience and to answer so many times the direct opposite of what I ordered you to answer?"

Brother Leo replied with humility and reverence: "God knows, my father, that each time I resolved in my heart to answer as you directed me, but God makes me speak as it pleases Him."

Whereupon St. Francis marveled and said to Brother Leo: "I beseech you in all affection to answer me this time as I directed you."

Brother Leo answered: "Speak, in the name of God, for certainly this time I shall answer as you wish."

And St. Francis, weeping, said: "O little, wretched Brother Francis, do you think that God has mercy on you?"

Brother Leo answered: "Glorious graces will you receive from God, and you will be glorified and exalted in eternity, for he who humbles himself will be exalted; and I can say no other thing, since God speaks through me."

And so in that humble argument, with many tears and with great spiritual consolation, they passed the night in prayer until the dawn. In praise of Christ. Amen.

## CHAPTER X

*How Brother Masseo asked St. Francis why everyone followed him and wished to see him.*

Once St. Francis was living in the place near Portiuncola with Brother Masseo da Marignano, whom he loved because of his great sanctity and discretion and grace in speaking of God. One day as St. Francis was about to come out of the woods where he had been in prayer, Brother Masseo wished to test his humility and went towards him, reproaching him almost insultingly, and said: "Why you? Why you? Why you?" and St. Francis answered: "What do you mean?"

Brother Masseo said: "I mean, why does everyone follow you and everyone want to see you, to hear you, to obey you? You are not a handsome man, you do not have great wisdom, and you are not noble. Why is it, then, that everyone wishes to follow you?"

On hearing this, St. Francis, overjoyed, raised his face to Heaven and for a long time stayed with his soul rapt in God. Coming back to himself, he knelt, and gave praise and thanks to God, and then with great fervor of spirit turned to Brother Masseo and said: "Do you want to know why it happens to me? Why to me? Do you want to know why everyone follows me? The answer I have from the eyes of the Most High God, which look into the good and into the evil. Those most holy eyes have found among sinners no one more wretched, more inadequate, nor a greater sinner than I. To perform that marvelous work which He intends to do He has found no viler creature on the whole earth, and therefore He has chosen me to confute the nobility and the pride and the strength and the beauty and the wisdom of the world, so that it may be known that every virtue and every good comes from Him and not from the creature, so that no creature may glory in his own sight; but he who glorifies, let him glory in the Lord, to whom is all honor and glory in eternity."

Then Brother Masseo, considering this humble answer, spoken with such fervor, was frightened, and he knew with certainty that St. Francis was rooted in true humility. In praise of Christ. Amen.

## CHAPTER XI

> *How St. Francis had Brother Masseo turn around and around when they came to a cross-roads; and how they then went to Siena, where St. Francis did holy works.*

One day St. Francis was walking with Brother Masseo, and Brother Masseo walked a bit ahead. When they came to a convergence of three roads, one of which led to Siena, another to Florence, and a third to Arezzo, Brother Masseo said: "Father, which way should we go?"

And St. Francis answered: "We shall take that road which God wishes us to follow."

Brother Masseo said: "And how can we know the will of God?"

St. Francis replied: "By the sign that I shall show you; for I command you, in the name of holy obedience, that where these roads meet, in the place where you are standing, you turn around and around as children do, and do not stop until I tell you to do so."

Then Brother Masseo began to turn around and around until, because of dizziness, he fell repeatedly to the ground. But since St. Francis did not tell him to stop and since he wanted to obey faithfully, he would each time start to spin again.

Toward the end, when he was turning around very rapidly, St. Francis said: "Stop, and do not move."

And he stopped and St. Francis asked him: "Toward which city are you looking?"

Brother Masseo answered: "Toward Siena."

St. Francis said: "That is the road which God wishes us to take."

On the way, Brother Masseo marveled greatly at what St. Francis had made him do, having him act like a child in sight of the people passing by; but out of reverence he did not dare speak of it to the holy father. As they approached Siena, the people within, who had heard of the coming of St. Francis, went toward him and out of devotion carried him and his companion to the bishop's house, so that they did not touch the ground with their feet.

At that very same hour, certain citizens of Siena were fighting among themselves, and two of them had already died in the fray. When St. Francis arrived at that spot, he preached to them with such devotion and with such holiness that he pacified them in a holy way and made them one in friendship and unity. The Bishop of Siena, hearing of this holy work of St. Francis, invited him to his home and received him with great honor that day and that night. And the following morning the truly humble St. Francis, who in his work sought only the glory of God, arose early with his companion and left without notifying the bishop.

On the way, Brother Masseo kept murmuring to himself, saying: "What has this good man done, who made me turn around and around like a child, and who did not even say a good word or thank the bishop who paid him such great honor?" And it seemed to Brother Masseo that St. Francis had acted thoughtlessly.

But then, coming back to himself through divine inspiration, he reproached himself, saying in his heart: "Brother Masseo, you are too proud in judging divine works, and you are worthy of Hell for your rash pride; for yesterday Brother Francis performed such holy deeds that had an angel of God performed them they would not have been more marvelous. And because of this, if he were to order you to throw stones you ought to obey him, for what he has done in this way was ordained by Divine Providence, as is evident by the good end that came from it; if he had not pacified those who were fighting, not only would many more bodies have been stabbed to death, but even more important the devil would have drawn many souls down to Hell. You are extremely foolish and proud, therefore, in murmuring against that which manifestly proceeds from the will of God."

And all of these things that Brother Masseo uttered in his heart as he was walking were revealed by God to St. Francis. Wherefore St. Francis, approaching him, said: "Hold firmly to those thoughts, for they are good and useful and inspired by God; but your first murmuring was blind and vain and proud, and it was a devil who put it into your soul."

Then Brother Masseo clearly recognized that St. Francis knew the secrets of the heart, and he fully understood that all the acts of the holy father were directed by divine wisdom. In praise of Christ. Amen.


## CHAPTER XII

*How St. Francis put Brother Masseo in charge of the kitchen and of the door and of the distribution of alms.*


St. Francis wished to make Brother Masseo humble, so that he would not come to vainglory because of the many gifts and graces that God gave him but would, through humility, ascend from virtue to virtue. St. Francis was then living in a solitary place with his first companions, truly saintly men, and one day he said to Brother Masseo before all the companions: "O Brother Masseo, all of your companions have the grace of contemplation and of prayer, but you have the grace of preaching the word of God to help the people. And therefore, so that your friends can devote themselves to contemplation, I want you to take charge of the door, and of the distribution of alms, and of the kitchen. When the other friars are eating, you will eat outside the door, so that those who come to visit us may be met before they knock by some good holy words from you, and so that no one but you will have to go to meet them; and do this in the name of holy obedience."

Then Brother Masseo pulled down his cowl and lowered his head and humbly received and carried out this order, performing the assigned tasks for many days.

But his friends, as men enlightened by God, began to feel great remorse in their hearts, considering that Brother Masseo was a man of great perfection, more so than they, and yet the whole burden of the work was placed on his shoulders and not on theirs. Because of this, moved by one will, they went to the holy father to pray him to distribute those tasks among them, for their consciences could in no way allow them to have Brother Masseo endure such hardships.

On hearing their requests, St. Francis accepted their counsel and bowed to their will. He called Brother Masseo and said: "Brother Masseo, your companions want a part of the tasks that I have given to you, and therefore I want those tasks to be divided among them."

Brother Masseo said with great humility and patience: "Father, whatever you impose on me, all or part, I consider imposed by God."

Then St. Francis, seeing the charity of the companions and the humility of Brother Masseo, gave a marvelous sermon on most holy humility, teaching them that the greater the gifts and graces given to us by God the more humble we ought to be, for without humility no virtue is acceptable to God. And after he had finished the sermon he distributed those tasks with great charity. In praise of Christ. Amen.

## CHAPTER XIII

*How St. Francis sent his companions to preach in many places, and how he and Brother Masseo went in another direction, where they begged for bread and placed it on a stone table next to a fountain.*

The marvelous servant and follower of Christ, Messer St. Francis, wished to conform himself perfectly to Christ, who according to the gospel sent His disciples in pairs to all the cities He was to visit. And so, in imitation of Christ, when he had gathered twelve companions he sent them in pairs throughout the world to preach. And to give them an example of true obedience, he began first, following the practice of Christ, who first practiced what He taught. Having assigned other parts of the world to his companions, he himself took Brother Masseo as his companion and set out for the province of France.

Coming to a town and being quite hungry, they went, according to the Rule, to beg for bread in the name of God. St. Francis took one street and Brother Masseo another.

But since St. Francis was very small and insignificant looking and was therefore considered a common little man by those who did not know him, he succeeded in obtaining only a few pieces of dry bread. But Brother Masseo was a big and handsome man and he managed to get many big pieces of bread and even an entire loaf. After they had begged, they met outside the town in a place where they could eat, near a lovely fountain that had beside it a long beautiful stone on which each one put what he had been given. And St. Francis, seeing that Brother Masseo's pieces of bread were more numerous and more beautiful and bigger than his, was extremely happy and said: "O Brother Masseo, we are not worthy of such great treasure!"

He repeated these words many times and Brother Masseo answered: "My beloved father, how can we call such poverty and the lack of those things we need, a treasure? Here there is neither tablecloth nor knife nor cutting board nor bowl nor house nor table nor servant nor maid."

St. Francis answered: "And that is what I consider a great treasure, where there is nothing prepared by human industry, but all that there is, is prepared for us by Divine Providence, as is made manifest in the bread we begged for, in the very beautiful stone table, and in the clear fountain. Therefore let us pray to God that the treasure of holy poverty, this noble treasure that has God as provider, may make us love Him with all our hearts." And having said these words and having prayed and eaten those pieces of bread and drunk of that water, they rose and set out for France.

They came to a church, and St. Francis said to his companion: "Let us enter this church and worship." And St. Francis went behind the altar and began to pray. In that prayer he received a divine visitation that inflamed his soul with such love of holy poverty that from the color of his face and the frequent opening of his mouth it seemed as if flames of fire came from him.

Coming towards his companion as if aflame, he cried out: "Ah, ah, ah! Brother Masseo, come to me!" He repeated this three times, and the third time lifted Brother Masseo into the air with his very breath, and propelled him the distance one could hurl a spear.

Brother Masseo was greatly astonished and later told his companions that when he had been raised by the Saint's breath and so softly thrown, he had felt such sweetness of soul and consolation of the Holy Spirit as he had never felt before or since.

Afterward, St. Francis said: "My beloved friend, let us go to St. Peter and St. Paul and pray them to teach us and to help us to possess that measureless treasure of most holy poverty. That treasure is so valuable and so divine that we wretched vessels can never be worthy of containing it, for it is a celestial virtue by which all earthly and transitory things are trodden underfoot and all impediments removed from the soul, so that it can freely unite itself with the eternal God. This is that virtue which allows the soul, still bound to earth, to converse in Heaven with the angels. This is that virtue which accompanied Christ on the cross, was buried with Him and rose again, and with Christ ascended into Heaven; and which furthermore allows the souls who love it the ease of rising to Heaven, and which protects the arms of true humility and charity. Therefore let us pray to the most holy Apostles of Christ, who were perfect lovers of this evangelical pearl, that they beg this grace from our Lord Jesus Christ, who in His most holy mercy will concede to us the grace to be worthy of being true lovers, observers, and humble disciples of the most precious and most beloved evangelical poverty."

And talking this way they came to Rome and into the church of St. Peter, where St. Francis began to pray in one small corner of the church and Brother Masseo in another. There they remained for a long time in prayer with many tears and much devotion, and then the holy Apostles Peter and Paul appeared to them in great splendor and said: "Since you ask and wish to serve that which Christ and the holy Apostles served, our Lord Jesus Christ sends us to you to announce that your prayer is granted and that the treasure of most holy poverty is conceded by God to you and to your followers in the most perfect form. And still speaking for Him, we tell you that whoever, imitating your example, will follow this desire perfectly, will be sure of the blessedness of eternal life. And you and your followers will be blessed by God." And having said these words they disappeared, leaving St. Francis much consoled.

St. Francis rose from prayer and went to his companion and asked him if God had revealed anything to him, and the answer was no. Then he told Brother Masseo of the apparition of the holy Apostles and what they had revealed to him. And so, filled with great joy, they decided to return to the Valley of Spoleto, abandoning the idea of going to France. In praise of Christ. Amen.


## CHAPTER XIV

*How while St. Francis and his friars were speaking of God, Christ appeared among them.*


In the early days of the Order, when St. Francis was gathered with his friends to speak of Christ, with great fervor of spirit he ordered one of them to speak of God, following the inspiration of the Holy Spirit. The friar complied with the order. After he had spoken wondrously of God, St. Francis imposed silence on him and ordered another to talk. And the other friar obeyed and spoke of God in a most subtle, perceptive way. Then St. Francis imposed silence on him and ordered a third friar to speak of God. He too began to speak profoundly of the secret things of God, as had the other two, inspired by the Holy Spirit. And that they were inspired by the Holy Spirit was made manifest by a clear sign, for as they spoke, the Blessed Christ appeared in their midst in the guise of a most beautiful youth and, blessing them all, filled them with such sweetness that they were all lifted out of themselves and were as dead, feeling and hearing nothing of this world.

When they came back to themselves, St. Francis said to them: "My beloved brothers, thank God, who has wished to reveal the treasures of divine wisdom through the mouths of simple people; for it is God who gives speech to the mute and makes the tongue of the simple speak wisdom." In His praise. Amen.

## CHAPTER XV

> *How St. Clare went to eat with St. Francis at St. Mary of the Angels, and how it seemed that that place was on fire.*

When St. Francis was in Assisi he often visited St. Clare, giving her holy counsel. And although she had the greatest desire to eat with him, and asked him many times, he would never grant her request. His friends, who knew the wishes of St. Clare, said to St. Francis: "Father, it seems to us that this inflexibility is not in keeping with divine charity; considering that St. Clare, a most holy virgin beloved by God, abandoned the riches and the pomp of this world because of your preaching, you ought to grant her modest wish. And in truth, if she were to ask you a greater favor than this, you ought to grant it to her, the flower of your spirit."

St. Francis answered: "Do you think I should grant her wish?"

And the brothers said: "Yes, Father. She is worthy of it."

St. Francis then said: "Since it seems so to you, so it seems to me. But so that she may be even more comforted, I would want the meal to be taken at St. Mary of the Angels, for she has been cloistered at St. Damian's for many years and it will do her good to see St. Mary's, where she was shorn and became a bride of Christ. There we shall eat together in the name of God."

The day arrived and St. Clare, accompanied by the brothers of St. Francis, left the cloister with a companion and came to St. Mary of the Angels; and she devoutly greeted the Virgin Mary before the altar where she had taken the veil. And so they showed her the place until the time came to eat. In the meantime St. Francis had the meal spread out on the ground, as was his custom. And when mealtime came, St. Francis and St. Clare sat down together, and first one of the companions of St. Francis with the companion of St. Clare, then all of the other brothers, humbly gathered around the table. As they began to eat, St. Francis began to speak of God so gently and profoundly and marvelously that divine grace descended upon them in such abundance that they were all lifted up to God. And they remained enraptured, with their eyes and hands raised up to God.

At that same time the men of Assisi and Bettona and the surrounding towns saw St. Mary of the Angels, the surrounding land, and the forest all aflame, and they ran down with great haste to extinguish the flames. But when they came to the place, they found nothing on fire. They entered and found St. Francis with St. Clare and all the brothers seated around that humble table, rapt in the contemplation of God. They understood then that the fire was a divine and miraculous fire, a sign of the divine love burning within the souls of those holy brothers and sisters. And they returned to their towns comforted in their hearts and edified.

Later, a long while after, St. Francis and St. Clare and all the others came to themselves, so well comforted with spiritual nourishment that they had little concern for bodily food. And when that blessed meal was over, St. Clare, well accompanied, returned to St. Damian's.

The sisters, seeing her, were extremely glad, for they had feared that St. Francis might have sent her to govern another convent, as he had already sent holy Sister Agnes, Clare's sister, as an abbess to rule the convent of the Monticelli in Florence. St. Francis had once said to St. Clare: "Be prepared, should I ever send you elsewhere," and she, as a daughter of holy obedience, had answered: "Father, I am always ready to go where you send me." And that is why the sisters greatly rejoiced when they had her with them again. And St. Clare remained from that time on much comforted. In praise of Christ. Amen.

## CHAPTER XVI

*How St. Francis asked St. Clare and Brother Sil-
vestro whether he should devote himself exclusively to prayer or whether he should preach from
time to time.*

The humble servant of Christ, St. Francis, a short time
after his conversion, having gathered many companions into
the Order, was greatly perplexed as to which he should do:
devote himself completely to prayer, or preach from time
to time; and he wished to know the will of God concerning
this problem. Since his humility allowed him to trust completely neither himself nor his prayers, he thought of seeking to discover what God willed through the prayers of
others. And he called Brother Masseo and said to him:
"Go to Sister Clare and ask that she, together with some of
her more spiritual sisters, devoutly pray that God show me
which would be better: to devote myself to preaching or exclusively to prayer. And then go to Brother Silvestro and do
likewise."

Brother Silvestro, before he entered the Order, had been
that Messer Silvestro who had seen a cross of gold, as high
as the sky and as wide as the ends of the earth, coming
from the mouth of St. Francis. This Brother Silvestro, who
frequently spoke with God, was of such devotion and such
sanctity that God granted what he asked; and therefore St.
Francis had a great devotion to him.

Brother Masseo left and made the wishes of St. Francis
known first to St. Clare and then to Brother Silvestro. No
sooner had Brother Silvestro heard the request than he began
to pray, and immediately received a divine answer. Turning to Brother Masseo, he said: "God tells me that you
should say as follows to Brother Francis, 'God has not called
him to this state exclusively for himself but so that he may
reap the fruits of souls, and that many may be saved by
him.'"

With that answer Brother Masseo returned to St. Clare to
find what she had learned from God. She answered that she

and her companions had received the same answer as Brother Silvestro.

When Brother Masseo returned to St. Francis, the Saint received him with great charity, washing his feet and preparing food for him. And after the meal, St. Francis called Brother Masseo into the wood and knelt before him and, baring his head and crossing his arms, asked: "What does my Lord Jesus Christ ask that I do?"

Brother Masseo answered: "Christ has answered Brother Silvestro and Sister Clare and her sisters, and wills that you go through the world preaching, for he has not chosen you for yourself alone but more for the salvation of others."

Then St. Francis, when he had heard this answer and knew the will of Christ, stood up and said with great fervor: "Let us go, in the name of God."

And he took Brother Masseo and Brother Angelo, both holy men, as companions, and setting out with great impetus of spirit, without taking into account roads or paths, they came to the castle of Cannara.

St. Francis began to preach there, first ordering the swallows that were singing to be quiet until he had finished preaching; and the swallows obeyed. And he preached with such fervor that the men and women of that castle, out of devotion to him, wanted to abandon the castle and follow him. But St. Francis did not let them, saying: "Do not hurry, and do not leave. I will ordain what you must do for the salvation of your souls." And he thought then of establishing the Third Order, for the salvation of all.

Leaving them greatly comforted and inclined to penance, he left there and came to a place between Cannara and Bevagna. And as he went by, still fervent, he looked up and saw at the side of the road a number of trees, in whose branches were an infinite multitude of birds. Marveling at this, St. Francis said to his companions: "Wait for me here on the road and I will go to preach to my sisters the birds." And he entered the field and began to preach to the birds on the ground. Immediately those in the trees came to him and they all remained still as long as St. Francis continued to preach; and then they would not leave until he had given them his benediction. And according to what Brother Masseo later told Brother Jacopo da Massa, not one of them moved, even though St. Francis moved among them and touched them with his robe.

This was the substance of the sermon of St. Francis: "My sister birds, you owe much to God and you must always and in every place give praise to Him; for He has given you freedom to wing through the sky and He has clothed you two- and three-fold; and more, because He kept your seed in Noah's ark, so that your kind would never be wanting in the world; and also you should be grateful for the nourishment of the air, which He has assigned to you. In addition to this, you neither sow nor reap, and God feeds you and gives you rivers and fountains for your thirst, and mountains and valleys for shelter, and tall trees for your nests. And although you neither know how to spin nor weave, God dresses you and your children, for the Creator loves you greatly and He blesses you abundantly. Therefore, my sisters, guard yourselves against the sin of ingratitude, and always seek to praise God."

When St. Francis had uttered these words, all the birds began to open their beaks, to stretch their necks, to spread out their wings, to reverently bow their heads to earth, and to show in gesture and in song that the words of the holy father gave them great joy. And St. Francis rejoiced with them, marveling greatly at the multitude of birds, at their most beautiful diversity, and at their attention and affection, and he devoutly praised the Creator for them.

When he had finished the sermon, St. Francis made the sign of the cross over them and gave them leave to go. Then all the birds as one soared to heaven with sweet songs and, according to the sign of the cross that St. Francis had made, flew in four different directions—toward the east, the west, the south and the north—and each group continued to sing marvelously. Their flight signified that as St. Francis, standard-bearer of the cross of Christ, had preached to them and had made the sign of the cross over them, they were now to set off singing throughout the four parts of the world. So the preaching of the cross of Christ, renewed by St. Francis, was to spread throughout the world through him and through his friars, who, like the birds, owned nothing of their own in this world and entrusted their lives only to the providence of God. In praise of Christ. Amen.

## CHAPTER XVII

*How a boy friar, wishing to know what St. Francis did at night in the woods, followed him unseen, and saw him speak with Christ.*

While St. Francis was still living, a very pure, innocent boy was received into the Order. The place where the brothers stayed was very small, so that they had to sleep on the ground. St. Francis came once to this place, and in the evening, after they recited compline, he went to sleep, so that he might get up at night to pray while the other friars were wont to sleep. The boy decided to spy on St. Francis in order to observe his sanctity, and especially to find out what he did during the night after he arose from bed. And so that he would not sleep through the night, the boy slept beside St. Francis and tied his cord to that of St. Francis, so as to be awakened when he got up; and St. Francis did not notice. But in the first deep sleep, when all the brothers were sleeping, St. Francis arose, and finding his rope knotted to the other, undid it so quietly that the boy was not awakened. St. Francis then went alone into a wood near the place where they were sleeping, entered into a small hut, and began to pray.

A short time after, the boy awoke, and finding the rope untied and St. Francis gone, he got up and left in search of him. When he found the door open, he thought that St. Francis must have gone into the wood and he too made his way there, and came to the place where St. Francis was praying, and heard voices. Drawing closer in order to understand what was being said, he saw a wonderful light surrounding St. Francis, and in that light he saw Christ and the Virgin Mary and St. John the Baptist and St. John the Evangelist, and a vast multitude of angels, all speaking with St. Francis. Seeing and hearing this, the boy fainted.

When that miraculous apparition had vanished and St. Francis returned toward the place where they were staying, he stumbled on the boy, lying across the path as if he were dead. With great compassion he took him in his arms and laid him in bed, as the good shepherd does with his sheep.

Later, when he found out from him that he had witnessed the miraculous vision, he ordered him not to speak of it to anyone as long as he, St. Francis, was living. And the boy grew up in the grace of God and in devotion to St. Francis, and was a valiant man in the Order; and only after the death of St. Francis did he reveal that vision to the brothers. In praise of Christ. Amen.

## CHAPTER XVIII

*How St. Francis held a General Chapter attended by more than five thousand friars, and preached to them.*

The most faithful servant of Christ, Messer St. Francis, once held a General Chapter at St. Mary of the Angels, and there were more than five thousand friars attending. To it came St. Dominic, the head and founder of the Order of Preachers, who was then on his way from Bologna to Rome. Hearing of the chapter that St. Francis was convening on the plain around St. Mary of the Angels, he went there with seven friars of his Order. Also attending the chapter was a cardinal, very devoted to St. Francis, to whom the Saint had prophesied that he would become pope; and so it came to pass. The cardinal had come from the papal court at Perugia to attend the chapter, and every day he came to see St. Francis and his brothers. One time he would sing Mass, another time he would preach to the friars; and he felt constant delight and devotion when he came to visit that holy gathering. Seeing on that plain around St. Mary's friars seated in groups—here sixty, there a hundred, another place two hundred, elsewhere three hundred—and all concerned only with speaking of God and with prayer, with weeping tears of repentance and performing acts of charity, in such silence and modesty that not a sound or a rustle could be heard, he greatly marveled at it and with tears and great devotion said: "This is the field, this is the army of the knights of Christ."

No one in the multitude was telling stories or jokes, but wherever there was a group of friars they either prayed or recited their offices, or wept for their sins or for those of their benefactors, and spoke together of the salvation of souls.

In that field there were huts whose walls were covered with rushes and mats, and they were separated into groups from various provinces, and that is why that chapter was called the Chapter of Rushes or Mats. For beds they used the bare earth or a little straw, and their pillows were wood or stone. Because of these things, whoever heard or saw the friars felt great devotion. And so great was the fame of their sanctity that from the court of the Pope, which was then in Perugia, and from many other regions around the Valley of Spoleto, there came many counts and barons and knights and other gentlemen, and common people, and cardinals and bishops and abbots and other clerics, all to see that humble and saintly congregation, more numerous than any the world had ever seen. They came principally to see the leader and holy father of that saintly people, who had stolen from the world such beautiful prey and gathered together such a beautiful and devout flock to follow in the footsteps of the venerable Shepherd, Jesus Christ.

The General Chapter having been convened, the holy father and Minister General of all, St. Francis, with great fervor of spirit proposed the word of God to them. In a loud voice he said to them what the Holy Spirit made him say and, as the theme of the sermon, suggested the following words: "My sons, we have promised great things, but even greater things have been promised by God; let us observe those promises we have made and await with certainty those that have been promised to us. The joy of this world is short-lived, but the suffering that follows is perpetual. Brief is the suffering of this life, but the glory of the life to come is infinite." Preaching on this theme with great devotion, he comforted the brothers, and induced them to obedience and reverence for holy mother Church, and to brotherly charity. He besought all people to adore God, to be patient in the adversities of this world, to show temperance in prosperity, and to preserve purity and angelic chastity; to have peace and concord with men and God and one's own conscience, and to love and practice most holy poverty. And he added: "I charge you in the name of holy obedience, all of you gathered here, that no one concern himself with what he has to eat or drink or with those things that the body needs, but let him attend only to prayer and the praise of God, and leave all the concerns of your body to Him, for He has special care of you." And each one received this command with a happy heart and countenance. After his sermon all those present began to pray.

St. Dominic, who was present when all this occurred, marveled greatly at the commandment of St. Francis and judged it indiscreet, for he could not conceive how such a multitude could be ruled without any care or solicitude for the things of the body. But the Blessed Shepherd, Christ, wishing to show how He cares for His fold, and His singular love for the poor, inspired the people of Perugia, Spoleto, Foligno, Spello, Assisi, and other surrounding towns to bring food and drink to that holy gathering. And men came with donkeys and horses and carts laden with bread and wine, beans and cheese, and such other good things to eat as the poor of Christ needed. In addition to this they brought with them tablecloths, pitchers, glasses, and other drinking vessels that the multitude needed. And he who could bring more, or more solicitously help, considered himself most blessed; for barons and knights and other gentlemen who had come to observe, now served the friars with great humility and devotion.

St. Dominic, who saw all this, recognized that Divine Providence was working through them, and humbly acknowledged that he had erred in judging St. Francis' commandment indiscreet. Kneeling down in all humility, he acknowledged his fault and added: "God has in truth a special care for these poor little holy ones, and I did not know it. From now on I promise to observe holy evangelical poverty and in the name of God I damn all the friars of my Order who in the Order will presume to hold goods." St. Dominic was much edified by the faith of St. Francis, and by the obedience and poverty of such a great and orderly gathering, and by Divine Providence and the abundance it bestowed upon them.

At that same chapter, St. Francis was told that many friars wore iron vests and iron bands beneath their habits, because of which many fell sick and died and others were hindered in praying. As a perceptive and loving father, St. Francis ordered all those who had these vests or iron bands to remove them and bring them to him. And they did so, and some five hundred iron vests and a great number of armbands and chest bands formed a small hill, and St. Francis left them all there. When the chapter was over, St. Francis comforted the friars, and teaching them the ways of the good and how to escape without sin from this evil world, he sent them back to their provinces with God's benediction and his own, filling them with spiritual joy. In praise of Christ. Amen.

## CHAPTER XIX

*How St. Francis went to Rieti to have his eyes treated, and how while he was staying in the house of a priest, those who came to see St. Francis took all the grapes from the vineyard of the priest, and the vineyard produced more wine than ever before.*

Since the condition of St. Francis' eyes had seriously worsened, Messer Ugolino, Cardinal Protector of the Order, because of the great love he bore him, wrote to him, urging him to go to Rieti and consult the excellent eye doctors there.

When he received the letter from the cardinal, St. Francis went first to St. Damian's to comfort St. Clare, the most devoted bride of Christ, intending to go on from there to the cardinal. But during that night St. Francis' eyes worsened, so that he could no longer see light. Unable to leave, he stayed at St. Damian's, where St. Clare made a small hut of reeds for him so that he might rest better. But St. Francis, between the pain of the affliction and the great number of rats that molested him constantly, could find no rest, either during the day or the night.

As he endured this long pain and tribulation, he began to reflect and to recognize that it was a scourge of God for his sins. And he began to thank God with all his heart, crying out in a loud voice: "My God, I deserve this and much more. My Lord Jesus Christ, my Good Shepherd, who for us unworthy sinners, through many sufferings and much bodily pain have shown us Your mercy, concede to me, Your little lamb, such grace and strength that no sickness, no suffering or pain may separate me from You."

And after praying thus, he heard a voice from the heavens,

saying: "Francis, answer Me. If all the earth were gold and all the seas and rivers and fountains were of balsam, and all the mountains, hills and rocks were precious stones, and you were to find another treasure much greater than any of these, as gold is greater than earth, balsam than water, precious stones than mountains and rocks; and if this greater treasure were given to you for this infirmity, should you not find great joy and happiness in it?"

St. Francis answered: "Lord, I am not worthy of such a precious treasure."

And the voice of God said to him: "Rejoice, Francis, for the treasure is that of eternal life, which I have kept for you and now grant you. This affliction and sickness is a sign of that promise of future blessed treasure."

Then St. Francis called out to his companion with great joy, because of this glorious promise, and said: "Let us go to the cardinal." And first comforting St. Clare with holy words and humbly taking his leave, he set out toward Rieti. As he approached, such a great multitude came toward him that he wished to avoid entering the town, and went to a church approximately two miles away. When the crowd found out that he was in that church, they flocked in droves to see him. They gathered all the grapes there and were making spoil of the vineyard. The priest of that church began to grieve over this in his heart, and he repented of having had St. Francis in the church.

Since St. Francis knew from a revelation what the priest was thinking, he called him and asked him: "My beloved father, how many donkeyloads of wine does this vineyard give you each year at its best?"

The priest answered: "Twelve."

St. Francis said: "I beg of you, Father, that you patiently endure my stay here for several days, for I find it restful here. Let everyone take grapes from your vineyard, out of love of Christ and of me, poor little one; and I promise you in the name of my Lord Jesus Christ that He will repay you a full twenty donkeyloads." And St. Francis did this so that he could remain there for the good of the souls of the people that came there, many of whom left drunk with divine love and forgetting the world.

The priest, trusting in the promise of St. Francis, freely left the vineyard to those who came. And marvel of marvels, although the vines had been completely stripped except for a few clusters, when harvest time came and the priest gathered those few bunches and put them in the press, in keeping with the promise of St. Francis, he found he had twenty donkeyloads of excellent wine.

This miracle clearly shows that as, through the merits of St. Francis, the stripped vineyard gave abundant wine, so the Christian people, stripped of virtue by sin, through the merits and doctrine of St. Francis, frequently abound in the good fruits of penance. In praise of Christ. Amen.

## CHAPTER XX

*How a young friar who so despised and abhorred his habit thought of leaving the Order.*

A young man of noble family joined the Order of St. Francis and, after a few days, as a result of the promptings of the devil, began to loathe the habit he wore, looking upon it as a vile sack. He despised the sleeves and the cowl, and the length and the coarseness of the habit seemed to him unbearable. The Order itself had become increasingly unattractive to him, and so he thought of returning to the world.

It came about that the night he was to leave the Order, he had to pass in front of the altar of the monastery. The young man had been taught to kneel with great reverence, bare his head, and cross his arms each time he passed in front of the altar, where the body of Christ was kept. He did so this time too, and as he knelt there, he was suddenly lifted in spirit and shown a marvelous vision. He saw an almost infinite multitude of saints in procession, walking in pairs, all clothed in the most beautiful and rich cloth, their faces and hands shining like the sun. They walked before him, singing with the voices of angels. Two of them were more richly arrayed than the others, and so radiant with charity that they filled him with amazement. Toward the very end of the procession he saw one adorned with such glory that he seemed a newly dubbed knight, more honored than the others.

The young nobleman, contemplating this vision, was greatly amazed, and did not know what it meant. He did not dare ask its meaning, and so remained there in sweet amazement. But when nearly all of the procession had passed by, he took courage and, running toward the last, with great fear and reverence he asked: "O my dear ones, I beg of you to tell me who are these marvelous men whom I see in this venerable procession?"

And they answered: "Know, son, that we are Friars Minor coming to the glory of Paradise."

And the young man asked: "Who are those two more radiant than the rest?"

And they answered: "They are Saint Francis and Saint Anthony. The last one you see is a holy friar who died recently, and since he valiantly fought against temptations and persevered until the end, he is being led by us in triumph to the glory of Paradise. These beautiful vestments that we are wearing are given to us by God in exchange for the coarse habits that we patiently bore in the Order. And the glorious charity that you see in us is given by God as a reward for humble penance and holy poverty, obedience, and chastity, which we served until the very end. And therefore, son, do not find it hard to wear the sack of Saint Francis, which bears such fruit. For if, with the sack of Saint Francis, for the love of Christ, you will have contempt for the world and will mortify the flesh and fight valorously against the devil, you, together with us, will have such vestments and charity and glory."

And after hearing these words, the young man came to himself and, comforted by that vision, cast off every temptation and acknowledged his fault to his guardian and to the brothers. From that point on, he desired harsh penance and coarse garments, and he died in the Order in the odor of great sanctity. In praise of Christ. Amen.

## CHAPTER XXI

> How St. Francis converted the very fierce wolf of Gubbio.

At the time that St. Francis lived in the town of Gubbio, there appeared a great wolf, terrifying and ferocious, who devoured men as well as animals. All the inhabitants lived in great fear, and whenever he would approach the city they would go out armed to fight him, as if they were going out to do battle. Yet in spite of this, they were helpless against him, especially if one man alone came face to face with him. And the fear of this wolf had so grown that no one dared to leave the confines of the town.

St. Francis, hearing of this and having compassion on the inhabitants of that city, determined to seek out the wolf, although everyone advised him against it. And making the sign of the cross, he left the city, together with some companions, placing all of his trust in God. When his companions feared to go any further, St. Francis by himself took the path that led to the place where the wolf was usually found. Many people had come to see this miracle, and when the wolf saw them he went toward St. Francis with his mouth open. St. Francis made the sign of the cross above him, called him to himself, and said: "Come here, brother wolf; I command you, in the name of Christ, to hurt no one, neither me nor anyone else."

And miraculously, as soon as St. Francis had made the sign of the cross, the terrible wolf closed his mouth and stood still; and hearing the order, he came with the docility of a lamb to lie down at the feet of St. Francis.

Then St. Francis said: "Brother wolf, you do much harm in these parts and have done great evil, preying upon and killing creatures of God without His permission. You have not only killed and devoured animals but you have had the daring to kill men, who are made in the image of God; and because of that you deserve to be hanged, as an evil thief and a murderer. All the people accuse you and curse you, and they are all your enemies. But, brother wolf, I would like to make peace between you and the people, so that you will no longer offend them, and they in turn will forgive all past injuries, and neither men nor dogs will persecute you."

When he had said these words, St. Francis saw that the wolf, with his body and his tail and his ears and his bowed head, accepted what he proposed and wished to observe it. Then St. Francis said: "Brother wolf, since you are willing to make and keep this peace, I promise you that I will have these people give you sustenance as long as you live, so that you will not go hungry, for I know that you have done evil out of hunger. But since I will beg this grace for you, I want you, brother wolf, not to hurt any man or any animal henceforth. Will you promise me?"

And the wolf, bowing his head, showed that he did.

And St. Francis said: "Brother wolf, I want you to give me your word on this, so that I can trust you completely." And when St. Francis extended his hand to him, the wolf lifted his paw and put it tamely into St. Francis' hand, thereby giving him what reassurance he could.

St. Francis then said: "Brother wolf, I order you in the name of Jesus Christ to come with me without fear, and we shall sign this treaty of peace in the name of God."

The wolf went with him obediently, like a gentle lamb, and the citizens, who looked on from a distance, marveled greatly. The news spread quickly throughout the entire town and everyone, young and old, men and women, children and grown men, came to the square to see the wolf together with St. Francis.

Before this large crowd St. Francis stood up and began to preach, saying among other things how God allows certain calamities because of sins, and how the flames of Hell, since they are to last for all time, are much more dangerous than the fury of the wolf, who can kill only the body. How much more, then, is the mouth of Hell to be feared, considering that the mouth of a small animal can provoke such fear and trembling? "Turn once more, dearest brethren, to God, and do fitting penance for your sins, and God will free you in the present from the wolf and in the future from the fires of Hell."

And when he had delivered the sermon St. Francis said: "Hear me, my brothers: brother wolf, who stands before us, has promised me and given me his word to make peace with you. He will not offend you in any way, if you promise to give him his daily needs. And I will pledge for him that he will strictly observe the treaty of peace."

The people then with one voice promised to give the wolf his daily needs. And before them all, St. Francis said to the wolf: "And do you, brother wolf, promise to maintain the peace and the treaty of peace and to offend no one, neither men nor animals nor any living creature?"

And the wolf knelt and bowed his head, and with meek ways, moving his ears and his tail, showed to the best of his ability that he wanted to observe the pact.

St. Francis said: "Brother wolf, as you did give me evidence of your promise outside the city gates, I want you now before all of these people to give me a sign of your promise that you will not betray the pledge I have made for you."

Then the wolf, lifting up a paw, placed it in the hand of St. Francis. At this gesture the people rejoiced greatly, out of devotion for the Saint and the novelty of the miracle, as well as because of the pact with the wolf, praising and blessing God who had sent them St. Francis, whose merits had freed them from the attacks of that cruel animal.

The wolf lived for two years in Gubbio and tamely went from house to house and door to door. He did not hurt anyone, and no one hurt him. He was courteously fed by the people, and as he went about from house to farm, no dog barked at him. After two years brother wolf finally died of old age, and the people grieved, because when they had seen him go so tamely about the town, they were constantly reminded of the virtue and sanctity of St. Francis. In praise of Christ. Amen.

## CHAPTER XXII

*How St. Francis tamed doves that were given to him.*

A young man who had caught many doves was going one day to market to sell them. On his way he came across St. Francis, who always had great pity for meek animals. Looking at the doves with eyes full of compassion, the Saint said to him: "My good young man, I beg you to give me these innocent birds, compared in Holy Scripture to chaste, humble, and faithful souls. Do not let them come into the hands of cruel men who would kill them."

The young man then and there gave them all to St. Francis and he, holding them in his lap, began to speak to them sweetly: "O my sisters, sweet, innocent, and chaste doves, why do you let yourselves be caught? I want to rescue you from death, and I want you to make nests so that you will have young and will multiply, according to the wishes of your Creator."

And so St. Francis went and made nests for them. And the

doves used them and began to lay eggs in them and to have their young in front of the brothers; and they were as tame and gentle around St. Francis and the other brothers as if they had been hens raised by them. They did not leave until St. Francis, with his benediction, gave them leave to go.

St. Francis had also said to the young man who had given them to him: "Son, you will one day be a friar in this Order and you will graciously serve Jesus Christ." And so it came to pass, for the young man became a brother and lived a saintly life in the Order. In praise of Christ. Amen.

## CHAPTER XXIII

*How St. Francis saw the devil enter into one of his friars, and how he had the friar brought to him and gave him penance for the sin and healed him.*

One day as St. Francis was praying in the shelter at Portiuncola, he saw through divine revelation the shelter surrounded and besieged by demons as numerous as a great army. But not one of them could enter into the shelter, for those friars were of such sanctity that the demons found no place in which to enter. But yet they persevered, and it came to pass that one of those friars within was angry with another and was thinking in his heart how he could accuse him and avenge himself. While he was prey to this evil thought, a devil, finding an opening, entered into the shelter and alighted on and clung to the neck of this brother.

The pious and solicitous shepherd, who always watched over his sheep, seeing that the wolf had entered to devour his lamb, had that brother brought to him. He immediately ordered him to reveal the poison of the hatred he had for his neighbor, which hatred had made him fall into the enemy's hands.

The frightened brother, seeing that the holy father had seen into him, confessed his poison and hatred, acknowledged his fault, and humbly asked for a merciful penance. When he had been absolved from the sin and had received his penance, the devil left him. The brother, freed from that cruel beast by the good shepherd, gave thanks to God. He returned, reproved and perfected, into the fold of the holy shepherd, and lived thereafter in great sanctity. In praise of Christ. Amen.

## CHAPTER XXIV

*How St. Francis went abroad to preach the Christian faith to the Sultan and to the Saracens.*

St. Francis, inspired by the zeal of the faith of Christ and the desire for martyrdom, once crossed the seas with twelve of his most holy companions and went straight to the Sultan of Babylon. And when he came to the land of the Saracens, where the passes were guarded by such cruel men that to pass those points was in effect to die, it happened that, as it pleased God, they were not killed but taken, beaten and tied, and brought before the Sultan. When St. Francis stood before him, inspired by the Holy Spirit, he preached with holy eloquence on faith in Christ, and would willingly have gone into the fire for it. The Sultan began to feel a great devotion for him, for the constancy of his faith, and for his contempt of the world; for St. Francis wanted no gifts from him, though he was most poor, and was only concerned with fervently suffering for the faith. And from that point on, the Sultan willingly listened to him and begged him to come to him frequently, freely allowing him and his companions to preach wheresoever they wished. He gave them a safe-conduct that they might not be hurt by any of his men. With this permission, St. Francis sent his chosen companions in pairs to several lands of the Saracens to preach faith in Christ. Toward the end, however, when he saw by divine revelation that no more fruits could be gathered in those parts, St. Francis prepared himself to return with his companions to the faithful. Gathering all his brothers together, he went to the Sultan to take his leave.

The Sultan then said to him: "Brother Francis, I would gladly be converted to the faith of Christ, but I am afraid to do so now. If my subjects were to learn of it, they would kill me and you and all your companions. Since you can still do much good and I have to resolve a number of grave problems, I do not wish to bring about your death and mine. Teach me, though, how I can be saved, and I will do what you tell me."

St. Francis then said: "Lord, I leave you now, but when I will have come among my own again and will have gone to Heaven, thanks to the grace of God, as it will please God I will send you two of my friars. You will receive the baptism of Christ from them and be saved, as is revealed by my Lord Jesus Christ. And do you in the meantime loosen yourself from every entanglement, so that when the grace of God comes to you it will find you ready for faith and devotion."

This the Sultan promised and this he did.

After this, St. Francis returned home with the venerable group of his holy companions, and after a number of years St. Francis through corporal death gave his soul to God.

The Sultan, ill at this time, was waiting for the fulfillment of the promise of St. Francis and had stationed soldiers at various points, ordering them that if two friars dressed in the garb of St. Francis were to appear they should immediately be brought before him.

At the same time St. Francis appeared to the two friars and ordered them to go without delay to the Sultan for his salvation, in keeping with his promise. The friars left immediately and, having crossed the sea, were taken to the Sultan by the soldiers. The Sultan rejoiced when he saw them and said: "Now I truly know that God has sent me His servants for my salvation, according to the promise that St. Francis made to me through a divine revelation."

Having thus been instructed in the faith of Christ and having received holy baptism from the friars, he died in his illness, reborn in Christ, his soul saved by the merits and works of St. Francis. In praise of the Blessed Christ. Amen.

## CHAPTER XXV

*How St. Francis healed a leper in body and soul.*

The true disciple of Christ, Messer St. Francis, sought to imitate Christ, the perfect teacher, with all his strength; whence it often came about, through divine intercession, that as he was healing the body of someone, God was healing that person's soul, as it is written of Christ. That is why he not only gladly served lepers, but commanded the friars in his Order, whether stationed in one place or traveling throughout the world, to serve lepers out of the love of Christ, who Himself wished to be considered as a leper.

It happened one day that in a shelter near the one in which St. Francis was staying, the friars serving in a hospital for the sick and the leprous were treating such an impatient, unbearable, and arrogant leper that everyone was convinced, and it was so, that he was possessed by a devil; for he so abused with words and actions whoever served him, and worse, he so viciously cursed the Blessed Christ and His Mother, the most holy Blessed Virgin Mary, that no one could be found who could or would take care of him. For although the friars were prepared to patiently endure curses and insults directed at them, they could not in conscience endure the abuses towards Christ and His Mother, and hence decided to abandon the care of this leper altogether. The brothers, however, did not want to do so until they had properly informed St. Francis of their decision.

After they had done so, St. Francis went to this vicious leper, came up to him, and greeted him, saying: "May God give you peace, my most dear brother."

And the leper, grumbling, answered: "And what peace can I receive from God, who has taken away my peace and all my goods, and has turned me into something foul-smelling and putrid?"

To which St. Francis answered: "Have patience, for the sickness of the body is given to us by God for the salvation of our soul; for sickness is of great merit when it is endured in peace."

The sick man answered: "And how can I endure in peace the pain that afflicts me day and night? Not only am I afflicted by my sickness, but I am made worse by your friars, whom you directed to care for me, and who do not care for me as they should."

Then St. Francis, who knew through revelation that the leper was possessed by an evil spirit, began to pray God devoutly for him. And when he had prayed he came back to the leper and said: "Son, I want to care for you, since you are not satisfied with the others."

"I accept," answered the sick man, "but what could you do more than the others did?"

St. Francis answered: "That which you wish, I shall do."

And the leper said: "I want you to wash me completely, for the stench is such that I cannot bear it."

And then St. Francis had water heated and put scented herbs into it. He then began to undress the man and, while another friar was preparing more water, began to wash him with his own hands. And miraculously, wherever St. Francis touched him with his holy hands, there the leprosy disappeared and healthy flesh took its place. As the flesh was being healed, so was the soul; and the leper, once healed, began to have great sorrow and remorse for his sins and to weep bitterly, so that as the body was being washed on the outside with water, the soul within was being cleansed from sin by contrition and tears. When he had been completely healed in body and soul, the sick man accused himself and, weeping, cried out: "Woe unto me, for I am worthy of Hell for all the abuses and insults I have given to the friars, and for my impatience and the curses I have hurled against God!"

So for fifteen days he remained in bitter lament for his sins, asking pity from God and making a full confession to the priest. And when St. Francis saw this manifest miracle that God had worked through him, he thanked God and left there, going off to distant lands. Out of humility he wished to flee from all worldly glory, for in all his works he sought only the honor and glory of God and not his own. Then, as it pleased God, the leper, healed in body and soul, after fifteen days of penance, fell sick once again, and armed with the sacraments of the Church, died in holy death.

As his soul was going to Heaven he appeared in the air to St. Francis, who was praying in a wood, and said to him: "Do you recognize me?"

"Who are you?" asked St. Francis.

And he answered: "I am the leper whom the Blessed Christ, through your merits, healed, and today I go to eternal life. I thank God and I thank you. May your body and soul be blessed, and your words and your works, for because of you many souls will be saved in this world. Know that there is no day that passes in which holy angels and other saints do not thank God for the holy fruit that you and your Order have gathered in the different parts of the world. Take comfort, therefore, and thank God, and rest in His benediction."

And having said these words, he went to Heaven, and St. Francis remained much comforted. In praise of the Blessed Christ. Amen.

## CHAPTER XXVI

*How three thieves were converted and became friars of St. Francis, and how one of them saw a marvelous vision.*

One day as St. Francis was going through the district of San Sepolcro and was passing by the castle of Mount Casale, a young and very delicate nobleman came to him and said: "Father, I would very much like to become one of your friars."

St. Francis answered, "Son, you are young and delicate and of noble birth; perhaps you might not be able to endure poverty and our harsh lives."

And the young man answered: "Father, are you not men just as I am? If you can endure that life so can I, with the grace of Christ."

St. Francis was very pleased with that answer, and blessing him, he received him into the Order then and there, giving him the name of Brother Angelo. This young man bore himself so graciously that in a short time St. Francis made him the guardian of the shelter of Mount Casale.

At that time there were in that region three notorious thieves who did a great deal of evil there; and one day they came to the shelter of the friars and begged Brother Angelo to give them something to eat. The guardian answered them in harsh reproach: "Thieves and cruel murderers, are you not ashamed to steal the fruits of others' labor; and worse, presumptuous and brazen, you now would want the alms that are given to the servants of God. You are not worthy of the earth that sustains you, for you have reverence neither for men nor for God, who created you. Go about your business, then, and do not come here again." The thieves, troubled, left in great bitterness.

At this time St. Francis returned with some bread and a small flask of wine for which he and his companion had begged; and when he was told by the guardian how he had driven away the thieves, St. Francis strongly reproached him, saying: "You have acted very cruelly, for sinners are brought back to God more by sweetness than by reproaches. Our teacher, Christ, whose gospel we have promised to observe, says that it is not the healthy who need a doctor but the sick, and that He came not for the just but to call the sinner to repentance. And that is why He often ate with them. Since, therefore, you have acted against charity and against Christ's holy gospel, I order you in the name of holy obedience to take this bread and this flask of wine that I have begged for and to go after them immediately, past mountains and through valleys, until you have found them, and to offer them all this bread and wine in my name. Then kneel before them and humbly acknowledge your cruelty; and beg them in my name to no longer commit wrongdoing, but to fear God and no longer offend their neighbors. And if they do this, I promise to assist them in their needs and provide them constantly with food and drink. When you have told them this, return here in all humility."

While the guardian went to obey the orders of St. Francis, the Saint began to pray, asking God to soften the hearts of those thieves and turn them to penance.

The obedient guardian caught up with the thieves and presented them with the bread and wine, and he did and spoke as St. Francis had directed. And as it pleased God, while these thieves were eating the food that had been brought to them, they began to say among themselves: "Woe to us unfortunates, whom the harsh sufferings of Hell await, and who go about not only stealing from our neighbor and beating and wounding him, but killing as well; and yet from all these evils and criminal deeds we have no remorse nor fear of God. And now this holy friar has come to us, and because of some just words that he said to us because of our malice, he now humbly accuses himself. He has brought us, moreover, bread and wine and a liberal promise from the holy father. These friars are in truth saints of God and merit Paradise; and we are the children of eternal damnation and deserve the sufferings of Hell. Every day we heap up perdition to ourselves, not knowing if, for all of the sins we have committed up to this hour, we shall find mercy from God."

These and similar words were said by one of them, and

the other two said: "You speak the truth, but now what are we to do?"

"Let us go," the first one answered, "to St. Francis, and if he gives us hope that we can find mercy from God for our sins, let us do what he orders us to, and we can thereby freely escape the sufferings of Hell."

This counsel pleased the other two, and so all three together came in all haste to St. Francis and said: "Father, because of our many and wicked sins, we do not think that we can find any mercy from God; but if you have any hope that God will show His mercy to us, we are disposed to do what you want us to, and to do penance with you."

Then St. Francis, receiving them kindly and with great charity, comforted them with many examples of conversion and assured them of the infinite mercy of God; for if our sins were infinite, the mercy of God would be still greater, according to the gospel; and the holy Apostle Paul said: "The Blessed Christ came into this world for the redemption of sinners."

Because of these words and teachings, the three thieves renounced Satan and all his works, and St. Francis received them into the Order, where they began to do great works of penance. Two of them lived but a short time after their conversion and then went to Paradise; but the third, surviving and meditating on his sins, gave himself to such penitential works that for fifteen years, with the exception of Lent (which he kept in the old way), he always fasted three days of the week on bread and water, always went about barefoot and with but one tunic, and never slept after matins.

In the meanwhile, St. Francis had passed away from this wretched life.

The third friar, after many years of penance, one night after matins was so tempted by sleep that he could in no way resist it and could not remain awake as was his custom. Unable to resist sleep or to pray, he finally lay down on the bed to sleep. No sooner had he put down his head than he was swept away and led in spirit to a very high mountain with a sheer cliff, and on one side and on the other there were jagged stones, splinters, and rocks of varying heights coming out of boulders. It was a terrifying sight to look down from this cliff. And the angel who was leading this brother pushed him and threw him down from the cliff; dashed from one stone to the other, he finally came to the bottom of the cliff, all shattered and broken, or so it seemed to him.

As he was lying there on the ground in that battered condition, the angel leading him said: "Come, arise, for you still have far to travel."

The friar answered: "You are a heartless and cruel man; you see me, all broken, about to die from that fall, and you tell me to get up."

And the angel came near to him and, touching him, healed and perfectly restored all his members. Then he showed him a great plain covered with sharp and cutting stones and thorns and told him to cross with bare feet until he came to the other side, where he could see a burning furnace, which he should enter. When the friar had crossed that plain with great suffering and anguish, the angel said to him: "You must enter this furnace."

The friar answered: "Oh, how cruel a guide you are! I am almost dead because of that painful plain. Now, for a rest, you ask me to enter into this burning furnace."

And as the friar looked at the furnace he saw many demons with iron forks in their hands, and as he hesitated they quickly pushed him in. Inside the furnace he looked about and saw one who had been his godfather, all aflame, and he asked him: "O unfortunate Godfather, how did you come here?"

And he answered: "Go on a bit further and you will find my wife, your godmother, who will tell you the reason for our damnation."

The friar, going on a bit further, saw his godmother all aflame, enclosed in a measure of corn, and it too was burning. He asked her: "O unhappy and wretched Godmother, why have you come to this cruel torment?"

And she answered: "Because at the time of the great famine that St. Francis had predicted, my husband and I gave short measure in the grain and hay we sold. That is why I am burning confined in this measure."

And when she had said these words, the angel pushed the friar out of the furnace and said to him: "You must prepare yourself for a horrible voyage."

The friar, complaining, answered: "O harsh guide, you are without compassion. You see that I am all aflame in this furnace, and now you wish to lead me on a dangerous voyage."

But the angel touched him and made him all well again, and then led him to a bridge that could not be crossed without great danger. It was very thin and very slippery, without railings on the side, and beneath it was a terrible river filled with serpents and dragons and scorpions, from which arose a dreadful stench. The angel said to him: "You must cross this bridge."

The friar answered: "And how can I cross it, without falling into that terrifying river?"

The angel said: "Come, follow me, and place your foot where I place mine, and this way you will cross it safely."

The brother followed the angel as he was told to until he was halfway across the bridge. At that point the angel flew away, up to an extremely high mountain, quite distant from the bridge. And the friar continued to look up to the place where the angel had flown, but finding himself without the guide, he also looked down and saw those terrible beasts with their heads out of the water and their mouths open, ready to devour him if he should fall. He was trembling so that he had no idea of what to do or what to say, for he could go neither backward nor forward. Considering himself in this affliction, and that he had no other refuge but God, he knelt down and held on to the bridge as tightly as he could, with many tears beseeching God in His most holy mercy to succor him.

When he had offered this prayer it seemed to him that he was beginning to sprout wings and with great joy he waited for them to grow, so that he could fly away beyond the bridge, there where the angel had flown. After some time, because of the great desire that he had to cross this bridge, he started to fly, but because the wings had not grown sufficiently, he fell down to the bridge and the feathers dropped from his wings. Again he hugged the bridge as he had done the first time, trusting to God and praying. Once more it seemed to him that he was sprouting wings, but as before he did not wait for them to grow sufficiently. Starting to fly before the proper time, he again fell back on the bridge and the feathers dropped from his wings. Realizing that he was falling because of his haste in wanting to fly before the proper time, he said to himself: "If I put on wings a third time, I will wait as long as is needed, so that I will fly without again falling back." While he was meditating thus, he felt the wings coming back a third time. He waited a long time, so that they

would be large enough and strong enough; and it seemed to
him that from the first to the third sprouting of wings he
had waited for something close to 150 years. Finally he got
up for the third time with a mighty effort, and flew as high
as the place where the angel had flown, and knocked at the
door of the palace into which the angel had disappeared.

A doorman came and asked: "Who are you who have
come here?"

The friar answered: "I am a Friar Minor."

The doorkeeper said: "Wait here; I want to bring St. Francis and see whether he knows you."

While the doorman went to get St. Francis, the friar began
to look at the marvelous walls of the palace. These walls
were so translucently clear that he could plainly see the
chorus of saints and what they were doing in there. And as
he remained there, stupefied by what he saw, there came St.
Francis and Brother Bernardo and Brother Egidio, and after
St. Francis such a multitude of saints who had followed
his way that they seemed countless.

When St. Francis arrived, he said to the doorkeeper: "Let
him enter, for he is one of my friars."

No sooner was he within than he felt such consolation
and sweetness as to make him forget all past tribulations as
if they had never been. And St. Francis led him within and
showed him many marvelous things, and then said to him:
"Son, you must return to the world and remain there seven
days; during that time you will diligently and with great devotion prepare yourself, for after seven days I will come for
you and then you will return with me to this blessed place."

St. Francis was adorned with a marvelous mantle, resplendent with most beautiful stars, and his five stigmata
were as five beautiful stars and so radiant that they lit the
entire palace with their rays. Brother Bernardo had on his
head a most beautiful crown of stars, and Brother Egidio
was adorned with a marvelous light; and the friar recognized
among them many other friars whom he had not seen in the
world.

Given leave by St. Francis, he returned, although reluc-
tantly, to the world. When he woke up and came to himself,
he noticed that the friars were sounding prime; the vision
had lasted only from matins to prime, although it had
seemed many years to him. And he told his guardian all
about the vision, and within seven days he began to grow

feverish. On the eighth day St. Francis came to him as he had promised, with an exceedingly great multitude of glorious saints, and led his soul to the realm of the blessed in eternal life. In praise of Christ. Amen.

## CHAPTER XXVII

*How, when St. Francis preached in Bologna, many, among whom were two scholars of saintly life, were converted and practiced penance.*

When St. Francis once came to the city of Bologna the entire population came out to see him, and the crowd was so great that St. Francis could barely get to the square, which was filled with men, women, and scholars. St. Francis made his way to the center of the square and, slightly raised above the crowd, began to preach as the Holy Spirit inspired him; and he preached so marvelously that he seemed more angel than man. His heavenly words were like shafts of lightning that pierced the hearts of those who heard him, for among those who heard him a great multitude of men and women were turned to penance.

Among these were two noble students from the March of Ancona, one na ned Pellegrino and the other Riccieri. Both were touched in their hearts by the sermon and came to St. Francis, saying that they were completely willing to renounce the world and become friars. Then St. Francis, knowing through revelation that these men were sent by God and were to lead a holy life in the Order, considering their great fervor, received them with great joy, saying: "You, Pellegrino, hew closely to humility in the Order; and you, Brother Riccieri, wait on the brothers."

And so it was, for Brother Pellegrino never sought to present himself as a cleric but remained a layman, although he was learned in letters and a great student of canon law; and because of this humility he came to such perfection of virtue that Brother Bernardo, the firstborn of St. Francis, said of him that he was one of the most perfect friars in this world. And in the end Brother Pellegrino, filled with virtue, passed from this life to the life of the blessed, with many miracles before and after death.

And Brother Riccieri, living in great sanctity and humility, faithfully and devotedly served the friars and became very intimate with St. Francis, who revealed many secrets to him. Having been made Minister in the province of the March of Ancona, he ruled it for a long time in great peace and moderation.

After some time, God allowed him to be subjected to a very great temptation, and troubled and anguished, he greatly afflicted himself with fasting, discipline, tears, and prayers day and night. But he could not cast off that temptation and was frequently in great desperation, for he considered himself abandoned by God. Lost in this despair, as a last remedy he thought of going to see St. Francis, and reasoned this way: "If St. Francis will be gracious to me and show me friendship, as he usually does, I will believe that God will have mercy on me. If he does not, it will be a sign that I am abandoned by God."

And so he left and went to St. Francis, who was at that time gravely ill in the palace of the Bishop of Assisi; and God revealed to St. Francis the story of the temptation and despair of the friar and the reason for his visit. St. Francis immediately called Brother Leo and Brother Masseo and said to them: "Go quickly to my most beloved son, Brother Riccieri, and embrace him in my name and greet him. Tell him that of all the brothers in this world I love him in a singular way."

They left and found Brother Riccieri on the way and told him what St. Francis had ordered them to say. And he received such consolation and sweetness that he was almost beside himself. Thanking God with all his heart, he went on to the place where St. Francis was lying sick. Although St. Francis was gravely ill, when he heard Brother Riccieri come, he got up and went toward him and embraced him tenderly, saying: "My most beloved son, Brother Riccieri, among all the brothers in the world I love you in a singular way."

And as he said this, he made the sign of the cross on Brother Riccieri's forehead, kissed it, and said: "My beloved son, God has permitted this temptation for an increase in merit, but if you do not want it anymore, you may be released from it." And in a marvelous fashion, no sooner had St. Francis spoken these words than all temptation left him, as if he never experienced it, and he remained quite comforted. In praise of Christ. Amen.


## CHAPTER XXVIII

*How Brother Bernardo da Quintavalle remained rapt in ecstasy from matin until none.*


How much grace God often shows to the evangelical poor who out of love of Christ abandon the world was shown in Brother Bernardo da Quintavalle. After taking the habit of St. Francis, Brother Bernardo was frequently lifted up to God in contemplation of celestial things.

Among other things, it happened once that in church, as he was hearing Mass, with all his mind suspended in God, he became so absorbed and lifted up in contemplation that he gave no sign of being aware of the elevation of the Host and did not kneel nor pull down his cowl as others did, but without blinking he stood looking fixedly ahead from matin until none.

Coming back to himself, he went about the shelter, shouting out in admiring tones: "Brothers, O brothers, brothers! There is no one in these parts so great or so noble that, were he promised the most beautiful palace filled with gold, would not, in order to gain that treasure, willingly carry to it a sack of dung."

This heavenly treasure, promised to those who love God, was so abundantly given to Brother Bernardo that for fifteen consecutive years he always went about with his mind and countenance raised to the heavens. In that time he never satisfied his hunger at the table, although he always ate a bit of what was placed before him. He used to say that abstaining from that which one does not enjoy is not perfect abstinence, but true abstinence is partaking modestly of things that taste good to the palate.

In keeping with this belief he acquired such clarity and intellectual light that even great clerics came to him to solve difficult questions and difficult passages in scripture, and he solved their every difficulty. Since his mind was completely freed from and cut off from terrestrial things, he, like a swallow, soared high in contemplation, so that sometimes for twenty and other times for thirty days he would stay alone on the summits of high mountains, contemplating heavenly things. Brother Egidio used to say of him that the gift which had been given to Brother Bernardo da Quintavalle, who, soaring, nourished himself like a swallow, was not given to other men.

And because of this high grace he had from God, St. Francis gladly and frequently spoke with him day and night; and they were often found together in the wood throughout the night, lifted up in God, both of them intent on speaking of God, who is blessed for all eternity. Amen.

## CHAPTER XXIX

*How the devil appeared in the form of Christ to Brother Ruffino and told him that he was damned.*

Brother Ruffino, one of the most noble men of Assisi, a companion of St. Francis and a man of great sanctity, was once sorely tempted in his soul by the demon of predestination. He became deeply melancholy and depressed, for the demon had put it into his heart that he was damned and not one of those predestined to eternal life, and that all he did in the Order was thus for nought. This temptation lasted for many days, and out of shame he did not reveal it to St. Francis; but he did not cease praying and performing his customary acts of abstinence.

In answer, the enemy increased his anguish, subjecting him to false apparitions. For the devil once appeared to him in the form of a crucified man and said to him: "O Brother Ruffino, why do you afflict yourself with penance and prayer, since you are not among those predestined to eternal life? Believe me, I know whom I have elected and predestined; and if the son of Pietro Bernardone should tell you otherwise, do not believe him. Do not, in fact, ask him anything about this matter, for neither he nor anyone else knows but I, who am the Son of God. Believe me, you belong to the number of the damned and so does your father, the son of Pietro Bernardone, and his father too, and whoever follows him is damned and deceived."

The mind of Brother Ruffino became so darkened at these

words of the Prince of Darkness that he began to lose the love and faith he had had for St. Francis, and did not wish to tell him anything of the vision.

But what Brother Ruffino did not say to the holy father the Holy Spirit did, and St. Francis, seeing in spirit the danger of Brother Ruffino, asked Brother Masseo to bring him to him. And Brother Ruffino answered, grumbling: "What have I to do with Brother Francis?"

Then Brother Masseo, filled with divine wisdom, knowing that the devil is a liar, said to Brother Ruffino: "Don't you know that Brother Francis is like an angel of God who has enlightened many souls in this world, and from whom we have received the grace of God? I insist, therefore, that you come to see him, for I clearly see that you have been deceived by the devil."

And after Brother Masseo had said this, Brother Ruffino set off to see St. Francis. When he was not yet near, St. Francis began to shout: "O my bad little one, Brother Ruffino, whom did you believe?" and when Brother Ruffino came up to him, he told him in detail of the temptations of the devil from within and from without, making clear to him that he who had appeared was the devil and not Christ, and that he was in no way to listen to his admonitions. "But when the devil tells you that you are damned," said St. Francis, "do you answer, 'Open your mouth and I will empty my bowels into it.' This will be a sign to you that he is the devil, because as soon as you will have given him this answer, he will flee forthwith. And you should have known that he was the devil from something else, since he hardened your heart to all that is good, a work that is peculiarly his. But the Blessed Christ never hardens the heart of the faithful. On the contrary, He softens it, as He says through the mouth of the prophet, 'I will take away your heart of stone and give you a heart of flesh.' "

Then Brother Ruffino, seeing that St. Francis had told him in detail the whole story of his temptation, and made contrite by his words, began to weep copiously and to plead with St. Francis and to humbly acknowledge his fault in having kept his temptation from him. And so he remained comforted and consoled by the admonitions of the holy father, and all changed for the better. And finally St. Francis said to him: "Go, son, and confess, and do not abandon your habit of prayer. Know in all certainty that this temptation will be of great usefulness and consolation, and you will soon have a proof thereof."

Brother Ruffino returned to his cell in the woods, and while he was weeping and deep in prayer the Enemy came, assuming the form of Christ, and said to him: "O Brother Ruffino, did I not tell you not to believe the son of Pietro Bernardone and not to weary yourself in tears and in prayers, since you are damned? What good will it do to suffer so while you are alive when on dying you will be damned?"

And Brother Ruffino answered without hesitation: "Open your mouth and I will empty my bowels into it."

The devil, enraged, left immediately in tempestuous fury, with such a great upheaval of massive rocks from nearby Mount Subasio that the roar of falling stones could be heard for long after. In falling, the rocks collided with such force that they sparked a horrible fire through the valley, and their terrifying rumble made St. Francis come out of the shelter and look with great amazement at what was happening. The great landslide is still to be seen.

Then Brother Ruffino clearly recognized that it had been the devil who had deceived him: and returning to St. Francis, he again threw himself at his feet and acknowledged his fault. St. Francis comforted him with sweet words and sent him strengthened to his cell. There, in devout prayer, the Blessed Christ appeared to him, warming his heart with divine love, and said: "You did well, son, to believe Brother Francis, for he who had troubled you was the devil; but I am Christ, your teacher; and to make you quite certain of it I leave you this sign, that as long as you shall live you will feel neither sadness nor melancholy."

Having said this, Christ departed, leaving him in such joy and elevation of mind that day and night he was absorbed and lifted up in God. From that time on, he was so confirmed in grace and in the certainty of his salvation that he became completely transformed into another man, and had he been allowed, he would have remained day and night in prayer and contemplation.

That is why St. Francis said of him that Brother Ruffino was in this life canonized by Jesus Christ and that, except in his presence, he would not have hesitated to say "St. Ruffino" even though he was still among the living. In praise of Christ. Amen.

# CHAPTER XXX

*How St. Francis and Brother Ruffino, naked, preached in Assisi.*

Brother Ruffino, because of constant contemplation of God, was so absorbed in Him that he had become almost insensible and mute, and he spoke very rarely, for he lacked grace, passion, and ease in preaching. Nevertheless St. Francis once ordered him to go to Assisi and preach to the people whatever God inspired him to.

And Brother Ruffino answered: "Reverend Father, I beg you to excuse me and not to send me there, for as you know, I have no grace in preaching, and am simple and unlettered."

And St. Francis said: "Since you did not obey instantly, I order you in the name of holy obedience to go naked, with only your breeches, into a church in Assisi and there, stripped, speak to the people."

On hearing this order Brother Ruffino stripped himself and went naked to Assisi, entered the church, and after kneeling before the altar, ascended the pulpit and began to preach. Those present, children and grown-ups, began to laugh and say: "Now look, these friars have practiced so much penance that they are now quite out of their wits."

In the meantime, St. Francis, thinking over the quick obedience of Brother Ruffino, one of the most noble men of Assisi, and of the harsh order that he had given him, began to reproach himself: "Where did you get such presumption, son of Pietro Bernardone, wretched little man, to order Brother Ruffino, who is one of the most noble men of Assisi, to go naked and preach to the people like a madman? By, God, you will experience yourself what you have commanded others to do."

And thereupon, in great fervor of spirit, he too stripped himself and went to Assisi, taking with him Brother Leo, who brought his habit and that of Brother Ruffino. When the people of Assisi saw him, they mocked him as well, judging that both he and Brother Ruffino had gone mad out of an excess of penance. And St. Francis entered the church where Brother Ruffino was preaching these words: "O my dearest brethren, flee the world, leave sin behind, give unto others, if you wish to escape Hell. Observe the commandments of God, loving Him and your neighbor, if you wish to go to Heaven; and practice penance if you wish to possess the kingdom of Heaven."

Whereupon St. Francis, naked, went up into the pulpit and spoke so marvelously of the contempt of the world, of holy penance, of voluntary poverty, of the desire of the heavenly kingdom, and of the nakedness and humiliation of the passion of our Lord Jesus Christ, that all those present, a great number of men and women, began to weep aloud with great devotion. Not only there, but throughout all of Assisi that day the Passion of Christ was more lamented than it had ever been before.

And the people, edified and consoled by the words of St. Francis and Brother Ruffino, saw St. Francis dress Brother Ruffino and himself. And so, clothed once more, they returned to the shelter of the Portiuncola, praising and glorifying God, who had given them the grace to vanquish themselves, out of contempt for themselves, and to edify the sheep of Christ by good example, and to show them how to have contempt for the world. And the devotion of the people for them that day grew to the point that whoever could touch the hem of their habits considered himself blessed. In praise of the Blessed Christ. Amen.

## CHAPTER XXXI

*How St. Francis knew the virtues and the hidden vices of all of his friars, as was made evident in the cases of Brother Ruffino and Brother Elia.*

Just as our Lord Jesus Christ says in the gospel: "I know my sheep and they know Me," so the blessed father St. Francis, as a good shepherd, knew through divine revelation all the merits and virtues of his companions, and their defects as well. He knew how to furnish help for all by humbling the proud, exalting the humble, chastising vices, and praising virtues, as we read in the wonderful revelations that he had of the family of his first brothers.

Once, when St. Francis was in a shelter speaking of God

with the brothers, Brother Ruffino was not with them but was in the woods rapt in contemplation; and as St. Francis continued talking, Brother Ruffino came out of the woods and walked past them at some distance. St. Francis, seeing him, turned to his companions and asked: "Tell me, who do you think is the most holy soul that God has on earth today?"

And since they answered that they thought it was he, St. Francis said to them: "I, my dearest brothers, consider myself the most unworthy and abject man that God has put into this world. But do you see Brother Ruffino, who is now coming out of the wood? God has revealed to me that his soul is one of the three most holy souls in this world. With all certainty I tell you that I would not hesitate to call him St. Ruffino while he still lives, since his soul is confirmed in grace and sanctified and canonized in Heaven by our Lord Jesus Christ." But St. Francis never uttered these words in the presence of Brother Ruffino.

In a similar way, St. Francis' awareness of the defects of his friars was clearly made manifest in the case of Brother Elia, whom he often reproached for his pride; in the case of Brother Giovanni della Cappella, to whom he prophesied that he would hang himself; in the case of another friar, whom the devil held by the throat when he was corrected for disobedience; and in the case of many other friars whose secret defects and virtues he clearly knew through the revelation of the Blessed Christ. Amen.

## CHAPTER XXXII

*How Brother Masseo, through prayer, won from the Blessed Christ perfect humility.*

The first companions of St. Francis made every effort with all of their strength to be poor in terrestrial things and rich in the virtues through which one comes to true celestial eternal riches. And as a number of them were one day gathered together and speaking of God, one of them told this edifying story: "There was a man who was a great friend of God and had abundant grace in active and contemplative life, and together with this, a great and profound humility, for he considered himself a great sinner. This humility sanctified him and confirmed him in grace and made him grow more and more in virtues and gifts of God, and never let him fall into sin."

Brother Masseo, hearing such wonderful things of humility and knowing that it was a treasure of eternal life, began to be inflamed with such love and desire of this virtue that with great fervor, raising his countenance to Heaven, he strongly resolved and vowed never to rejoice in this world until he would perfectly experience that humility. And from that time on, he remained almost constantly closed within his cell, tormenting himself with fasts, vigils, prayers, and great weeping before God, to beg of Him this virtue with which that friend of God of whom he had heard was endowed, and without which he considered himself worthy of Hell.

Absorbed in this desire for many days, Brother Masseo went one day into the woods and there wept, sighed, and cried out, imploring from God this divine virtue; and since God gladly listens to the prayers of the humble and the contrite, a voice from Heaven spoke to Brother Masseo, calling him twice: "Brother Masseo, Brother Masseo."

And Brother Masseo, who knew in his heart that it was the voice of Christ, answered; "My Lord, my Lord."

And Christ said to him: "What would you give to have this grace that you ask?"

Brother Masseo answered: "Lord, I would give the eyes of my head."

And Christ said to him: "I want you to have that grace, and your eyes as well."

And having said this, the voice faded away, and Brother Masseo remained so filled with the grace of the desired virtue of humility and of the light of God that from that time on he was constantly rejoicing. Having become extremely humble, he considered himself the least of all the men of this world, and frequently when in prayer he would make a steady jubilant sound, like a soft dove, "ooh, ooh, ooh," and remain so with a happy countenance and a mirthful heart. When asked by Brother Jacopo da Fallerone why he never changed the tone of his rejoicing, he answered with great joy that when something goes well there is no need to change it. In praise of Christ. Amen.

## CHAPTER XXXIII

*How St. Clare, obeying the order of the Pope, blessed the bread on the table, and how there suddenly appeared a cross on those loaves.*

St. Clare, the most devoted disciple of the cross of Christ, and a noble flower of Messer St. Francis, was of such sanctity that not only bishops and cardinals but even the Pope enjoyed seeing her and often paid her personal visits. One of these times the Holy Father came to the convent to hear her speak of divine things, and when they were together discussing things of God, St. Clare had the tables set and bread placed on them for the Holy Father to bless. After the spiritual conversation, St. Clare, kneeling with great reverence, begged him to bless the bread on the table.

The Holy Father answered: "Most faithful Sister Clare, I want you to bless this bread and to make over it the sign of the cross, to which you have given yourself completely."

And St. Clare answered: "Most Holy Father, excuse me, for I would deserve strong reproach if before the Vicar of Christ, I, a common little woman, should presume to make such a blessing."

And the Pope replied: "So that it may not be judged presumption but rather meritorious obedience, I command you in the name of holy obedience to make the sign of the cross over these loaves and bless them in the name of God."

Then St. Clare, as a true daughter of obedience, with great devotion blessed those loaves with the sign of the holy cross. And marvelously there suddenly appeared engraven on all the loaves a beautiful sign of the cross. Some of the loaves were then eaten and others, because of the miracle, put away. When the Holy Father saw the miracle, he took some of the bread and, thanking God, departed, leaving St. Clare with his benediction.

At that time, Sister Ortolana, the mother of St. Clare, and Sister Agnesa, her sister, lived in that convent, and both of them, together with St. Clare, were filled with virtue and the Holy Spirit, as were many other holy nuns. St. Francis sent many sick persons to them, and they, with their prayers and the sign of the cross, made them well again. In praise of Christ. Amen.

## CHAPTER XXXIV

> *How St. Louis, King of France, came to visit Brother Egidio, and how they understood each other without speaking to one another.*

Once when St. Louis, King of France, was on a pilgrimage to visit sanctuaries throughout the world, he heard of the great fame of the sanctity of Brother Egidio, one of the first companions of St. Francis, and strongly resolved to visit him. And so he came to Perugia, where Brother Egidio was then living. Dressed like a poor nameless pilgrim, he came to the door of the friars' shelter, together with a few friends, and asked insistently for Brother Egidio, not telling the door-keeper who he was.

The doorkeeper then went to Brother Egidio and told him that a pilgrim was waiting for him at the door; and God revealed to Brother Egidio that the pilgrim was the King of France. Immediately and with great fervor, he left his cell and ran to the door. Without any questions and without their ever having seen each other, they knelt before each other with great devotion and embraced and kissed each other with tenderness, as if they had long been good friends. In all this they spoke not a word to one another but remained embraced in silence, in charitable signs of love. After staying that way for a long time without a word, they took leave of each other, and St. Louis continued on his journey and Brother Egidio returned to his cell.

When the King had left, a friar asked one of his companions who it was that had been so warmly embraced by Brother Egidio, and he answered that it was Louis, King of France, who had come to see Brother Egidio. And when he told the other friars they were disturbed that Brother Egidio had not said a word, and reproached him, saying: "Brother Egidio, why were you so ill-bred to such a king, who came from France to see you and to hear a good word from you, and why did you say nothing?"

Brother Egidio answered: "My dearest brothers, do not marvel that neither he nor I could say a word, because from the minute that we embraced, the light of divine wisdom showed his heart to me and mine to him. By the workings of God we looked into each other, knowing what I wanted to say to him and what he wanted to say to me better and with greater comfort than if we had spoken. Because of the inadequacy of all words, which cannot clearly express the secret mysteries of God, there would have been disappointment rather than comfort. Know, therefore, that the King left wonderfully comforted." In praise of Christ. Amen.

## CHAPTER XXXV

*How, when St. Clare was sick, she was brought to St. Francis' church on Christmas Eve for matins, and saw and heard all of the solemnities of the friars, and how this was brought about by the workings of God.*

Once, when St. Clare was so grievously ill that she could not go to recite the office in church with the other nuns, at the approach of the solemn feast of Christmas all the nuns went to matins and she remained alone in bed, unhappy at not being able to go with the others and to receive that spiritual consolation. But her bridegroom, Jesus Christ, not wishing to leave her disconsolate, had her miraculously transported to St. Francis' church and present at the entire office of matins there, and at Midnight Mass, and had her receive holy communion before having her transported back to bed.

When the other nuns returned to St. Clare after reciting the office in St. Damian's they said to her: "O Sister Clare, our mother, what great joy we have had this night of the holy nativity! If only you could have been with us!"

And St. Clare answered: "I give praise and thanks to my Blessed Lord Jesus Christ, my beloved sisters and daughters, for I was present, and more so than you, at the solemnities of this most holy night, and my soul rejoiced greatly, because of the intercession of my holy father Francis. Through the grace of my Lord Jesus Christ, I was present in the church of my holy father St. Francis, and I heard in body and in spirit the chant and the musical instruments, and there I even received holy communion. Rejoice, therefore, and thank God for the grace conceded to me." Amen.


## CHAPTER XXXVI

*How a vision of Brother Leo was explained to him by St. Francis.*


Once, when St. Francis was gravely ill and Brother Leo was caring for him, this brother, while praying beside St. Francis, was lifted up in ecstasy and brought in spirit before a great, broad, and turbulent river. Watching those who wanted to cross, he saw a number of friars weighted down with burdens starting to ford the stream, and they were thrown down immediately by the turbulence of the river and were drowned. A number of others got one-third of the way across, others halfway, and some almost reached the other side. All, because of the rush of the waters and the weights they were carrying, finally fell and drowned. When he saw this, Brother Leo had great compassion for them. Suddenly, as he was standing there, there came another great multitude of friars, without any kind of weight or burden, from whom holy poverty shone forth; and they entered the river and crossed it without danger. And after this vision Brother Leo came back to himself.

St. Francis, aware in spirit that Brother Leo had had a vision, called him and asked him what he had seen. When Brother Leo had told him of the vision in all its details, St. Francis said: "What you have seen is true. The broad river is this world. The brothers who drown in it are those who do not follow evangelical counsel, above all with respect to most noble poverty. Those who cross without danger are those friars who neither seek nor possess any earthly or carnal thing in this world, but having only modest dress and modest food, are content, following the naked Christ on the cross. And they joyfully and willingly carry the weight and gentle burden of Christ and of holy obedience and therefore, without difficulty, go from this temporal life to eternal life." In praise of Christ. Amen.

## CHAPTER XXXVII

*How a rich and courteous nobleman was converted by St. Francis and entered the Order.*

Late one evening, when the servant of Christ, St. Francis, came to the house of a great and powerful nobleman, he and his companion were well received, as if they were angels of Paradise, with great courtesy and devotion. Because of that courtesy, St. Francis looked upon the nobleman with love, considering that when they entered his house he had embraced them and kissed them, had washed their feet, dried them, and humbly kissed them, and had then lit a big fire and prepared a table with many good things.

As they were eating, the nobleman continued to serve them with a happy countenance. After St. Francis and his companion had eaten, the nobleman said: "See, Father, I offer you myself and all my belongings; should you ever need a tunic or a mantle or anything whatsoever, buy, and I will pay for it. You see that I am equipped to provide your every need, since through the grace of God I am in a position to do so. I have many temporal goods, and for love of Him who has given me these goods I gladly give them to His poor."

Seeing such courtesy and benignity, and hearing such generous offers, St. Francis felt such love for him that as they left, he said to his companion: "Truly this nobleman, who is so grateful to God and so loving and courteous to his neighbor and to the poor, would be good for our company. For you must know, my beloved brother, that courtesy is one of the virtues of God, who out of courtesy gives the sun and rain to the just and the unjust. Courtesy is the sister of charity, which puts out hatred and nourishes love. Since I have seen such divine virtue in this good man, I would gladly have him as a companion. I think, therefore, that we should come back to him some day to see if God has touched his heart, and whether he will join us in the service of God. In the meantime we shall pray to God to put this wish into his heart and to give him the grace to act on it."

And marvelously, a few days after St. Francis prayed thus, God put this desire into the heart of that nobleman. For St. Francis said to his companion: "Let us go, Brother, to that courteous nobleman, for I trust in God that this man, considering his courtesy in temporal things, will offer himself to us as our companion."

They left, and as they approached the house, St. Francis said to his companions: "Wait here a while, for first I want to pray to God that He will give a prosperous end to our quest, and that it may please Christ in virtue of His most holy passion to grant us poor little ones, us weak ones, that noble prey which we hope to take away from the world."

Having said this, the Saint began to pray in a place where he could be seen by the courteous nobleman. And, as it pleased God, as that man looked about, he saw St. Francis devoutly in prayer before Christ, who with great charity had appeared before him. As the nobleman stood there, he saw St. Francis lifted bodily from the ground and suspended for some time. On seeing this, he was touched by God and so inspired to leave the world that he forthwith left the palace and with great fervor ran toward St. Francis. Coming to him while the Saint was still in prayer, he knelt before him and insistently and devoutly begged him to receive him so that they might do penance together. Then St. Francis, seeing that God had answered his prayer, arose with great fervor and joy and embraced and kissed him, devoutly thanking God, who had given such a magnificent knight to his company.

And that nobleman asked St. Francis: "What will you have me do, holy father? For now I am prepared at your command to give my possessions to the poor and, together with you, to follow Christ, unburdened of every temporal good." And acting according to the commandment of St. Francis, he distributed his goods to the poor and entered the Order, living in great penance and sanctity of life. In praise of Christ. Amen.

## CHAPTER XXXVIII

*How St. Francis knew in spirit that Brother
Elia was damned and was to leave the Order,
and how he prayed God for him.*

Once, when St. Francis and Brother Elia lived in a
shelter of the brothers, God revealed to St. Francis that
Brother Elia was damned and was to abandon the Order.
Following this revelation, St. Francis felt a strong aversion
for him. He no longer spoke to him or with him; and if on
some occasion Brother Elia was coming toward him, he
would change his path and go elsewhere so as not to meet
him.

Brother Elia began to realize that St. Francis was dis-
pleased with him, and he wished to know the reason. One
day he approached St. Francis to speak to him about it.
When St. Francis sought to avoid him, Brother Elia held him
courteously by force and besought him to tell him why he
avoided his company and why he no longer spoke to him.

And St. Francis answered: "The reason is that God has
revealed to me that because of your sins you will abandon
the Order and you will die out of the Order; God, moreover, has revealed to me that you are damned."

On hearing this, Brother Elia said: "My reverend father, I implore you by the love of Christ that because of
this you do not cast me off, but like a good shepherd, in
imitation of Christ, find again and rescue the lost sheep,
which without you will perish. Pray to God for me. If it
pleases Him, He will revoke the sentence of my damnation, for it is written that God can change His sentence if
the sinner makes amends for his sins. I have such faith
in your prayers that if I were in the midst of Hell and you
were to pray for me, I would find some relief therein. I
implore you then to pray that God, who came to save
sinners, may in His mercy receive me, a sinner."

Brother Elia said this with great feeling and many tears,
and St. Francis, like a merciful father, promised and did
pray to God for him. And it was revealed to him that
God had granted his prayer, that the sentence of damnation was revoked, and that in the end the soul of Brother

Elia would be saved; but he would definitely leave the Order and die outside of it.

And so it came to pass. When King Frederick of Sicily rebelled against the Church and, together with all those who gave him aid or counsel, was excommunicated by the Pope, Brother Elia, considered one of the wisest men in the world, on being asked by King Frederick, took his place beside him and became a rebel against the Church and an apostate from the Order. He was excommunicated by the Pope and deprived of the habit of St. Francis; and while in the state of excommunication, he fell gravely ill. A brother of his, who had remained in the Order and who was a man of good and noble life, on hearing of his sickness, went to visit Brother Elia and among other things said to him: "My dearest brother, I am greatly grieved that you are excommunicated and outside of your Order and that you will die thus; but if you knew of some way in which I could save you from this danger I would gladly take the task upon myself." Brother Elia replied: "My brother, I see no other way, unless you go to the Pope and beg him, for the love of Christ and for His servant St. Francis, because of whose teachings I abandoned the world, to absolve me from excommunication and give back to me the habit of the Order."

The brother said that he would gladly do this for Brother Elia's salvation. He left him and went on foot to the Holy Father, begging him in all humility to concede this grace to his brother out of love of Christ and St. Francis. And as it pleased God, the Pope granted that if he returned and found Brother Elia still alive, he might absolve him from excommunication and let him wear the habit again. The brother left happily and returned to Brother Elia in great haste. He found him on the verge of death but still alive, and thus absolved him from the excommunication. He put the habit on him again, and Brother Elia passed out of this life, his soul saved because of the merits of St. Francis and his prayers, in which he had always had great trust. In praise of Christ. Amen.

## CHAPTER XXXIX

*How St. Anthony of Padua preached in a consistory before the Pope and cardinals, and marvelously so.*

That marvelous vessel of the spirit, St. Anthony of Padua, was one of the chosen disciples and companions of St. Francis. The Saint used to call him his bishop. On one occasion he preached in a consistory before the Pope and cardinals, and there were present men from many different nations: Greeks, Latins, Frenchmen, Germans, Slavs, Englishmen, and men of many other tongues. Aflame with the Holy Spirit, he so efficaciously, devoutly, subtly, and authoritatively preached the word of God that all those in the consistory, although they were of different tongues, clearly understood him as if he had spoken in their own tongues.

They were all taken aback, and it seemed to them that the ancient miracle of the Apostles on the day of Pentecost, by which in virtue of the Holy Spirit they spoke in many tongues, was being repeated; and they said to each other admiringly: "Doesn't he come from Spain? And how is it that we hear him speak our tongue?"

Similarly, the Pope, considering and meditating upon the profundity of his talk, said: "This man is in truth the Ark of the Convenant and a treasure house of Divine Scripture." In praise of Christ. Amen.

## CHAPTER XL

*How St. Anthony of Padua preached at Rimini to the fish in the sea, and how they miraculously heard him.*

The Blessed Christ showed on one occasion the great sanctity of His most faithful servant, St. Anthony, and how He wished His preaching and holy doctrine to be devoutly heard by animals as well as men. In a sermon to the fish he denounced the foolishness of heretical infidels, just as in the Old Testament God had denounced, through the mouth of a donkey, the ignorance of Balaam.

While in Rimini, where there were great numbers of heretics, St. Anthony sought to lead them back to the light of the true faith. He preached to them for many days, arguing to them about faith in Christ and in Holy Scripture. Since the heretics, however, not only refused consent to his holy words but, worse, as hardened and obstinate sinners, did not even wish to listen to him, St. Anthony, out of divine inspiration went one day to where the river empties into the sea, and there began to preach to the fish.

"Listen to the word of God, you fish of the sea and of the river, since the heretical infidels do not." And after he spoke thus, there came close to the shore such a multitude of large, small, and medium-sized fish as had never been seen before in that sea or river. They held their heads out of the water and, with great peace and docility and order, looked attentively towards St. Anthony.

Those closest to the shore were the smaller fish, and after them the middle-sized ones, and after them, where the water was deepest, the biggest fish. When they were arranged in this order, St. Anthony solemnly began to preach to them in the following manner: "My brother fish, you are greatly bound, to the extent that it is possible, to thank your Creator, who has given you such a noble element for your habitation, so that as it pleases you, you have sweet and salt waters and many places in which to take refuge from storms. And He has given you a clear and transparent element and food that will sustain you. God, your courteous and benign Creator, when He made you, ordered you to increase and multiply, and He gave you His blessing. Afterward, at the time of the great flood, when all other animals were dying, God preserved you alone without harm. Later He gave you fins that you might go where you willed. It was conceded to you by command of God to save the prophet Jonah, and after the third day to deposit him safely on land. You offered the coin to our Lord Jesus Christ, which He, poor little One, did not have for the tax. Later, you were, unique mystery, the food of the eternal King, Jesus Christ, before and after the Resurrection. Because of all these things, you ought to praise and bless God, who has given you more blessings than any other creatures."

At these and similar words and teachings of St. Anthony, the fish began to open their mouths and bow their heads and make other signs of reverence, praising God to the best of their ability.

Then St. Anthony, seeing such reverence among the fish for God the Creator, joyfully cried out: "Blessed be the eternal God, for the fish honor Him more than the heretics, and unreasoning animals hear His word better than infidels." And the more St. Anthony preached, the more the multitude of fish grew, and not one left the place he had taken.

The people of the city, among them the above-mentioned heretics, then ran to see the miracle, and seeing such a marvelous miracle, they became contrite and threw themselves at the feet of St. Anthony to hear his sermon; and then St. Anthony preached so well on the Catholic faith that he converted all those heretics and made them return to the true faith of Christ. And all the faithful present were filled with great joy, and were much strengthened and solaced in their faith. Later, St. Anthony, blessing the fish, gave them leave to go, and they all left with marvelously joyful movements, as did the people. And St. Anthony stayed at Rimini for many days, preaching and winning over many souls. In praise of Christ. Amen.

## CHAPTER XLI

*How Brother Simone of Assisi, through his great sanctity, freed a brother from temptation.*

In the early days of the Order, while St. Francis was still alive, there entered the Order a young man of Assisi called Brother Simone, whom God had adorned and gifted with such grace and contemplation and elevation of mind that for all of his life he was a mirror of sanctity, according to those who had been with him for a long time.

He was rarely seen outside of his cell, and if on occasion he spoke with the friars, he always spoke of God. This young man had no formal training in the schools, but nonetheless he spoke so deeply of God and of the love of Christ that his words seemed supernatural. Once he remained an entire night in the woods with Brother Jacopo da Massa, speaking of God and of divine love, and (as Brother Jacopo said to me) in the morning it seemed to both that the night had been very short.

Brother Simone had such gentle and sweet knowledge of the Holy Spirit that frequently when he sensed the approach of divine visitation he would lie down on his bed, for the gentle serenity of the Holy Spirit required from him not only the repose of the mind but also of the body. In those divine visitations he was frequently lifted up to God, and he would become insensible to corporeal things. Thus once, when he was lifted up in God and deaf to the world, burning within with divine fire, a friar, wishing to test whether what seemed to be actually was, took a burning coal and placed it on his bare foot. Brother Simone felt nothing, and although the coal remained there for some time until it burned itself out, it did not leave a mark on the foot.

When Brother Simone would sit down at the table, before taking bodily food, he would speak of God, giving himself and others spiritual food.

And due to this devout talk a young man from San Severino, who had been in the world a very vain and worldly type, with very delicate tastes, was converted. Brother Simone, receiving the young man into the Order, took the robes the young man laid aside and instructed him in the regulations of the Order.

But the devil, who tries to undermine goodness with every means at his disposal, then put such a strong stimulus and temptation of the flesh into the young man that he could in no way resist it. He went to Brother Simone and said: "Give me back the clothes that I wore in the world. I can no longer resist carnal temptation."

And Brother Simone, having compassion on him, said: "Sit down awhile, son, with me." And as he spoke to him of God, all temptation vanished.

And so whenever the temptation would return and he would ask for his clothes, Brother Simone would drive out that temptation by speaking of God. This happened many times. Finally one night the temptation became so strong that, unable to resist it in any way, he went to Brother Simone and strongly insisted on having his secular garb, since he could remain there no longer. Then Brother Simone, as was his custom, made him sit next to him, and as he spoke to him of God, the young man, because of melancholy and sadness, placed his head in Brother Simone's lap. Brother Simone, filled with compassion, raised his eyes to Heaven, praying to God for him, and God heard his prayer and lifted him up to Him.

When Brother Simone came back to himself, the young man felt himself completely freed from that temptation, as if he had never experienced it. The ardor of that temptation had been changed into ardor of the Holy Spirit, for in being close to the burning coal (that is, Brother Simone), the young man became himself aflame with the love of God and neighbor.

Once, when a criminal was captured and his eyes were to be put out, the young man, full of compassion, courageously went to the mayor and the council, and with tears and prayers asked that one eye be taken from him and the other from the evildoer, so that the criminal would not be completely deprived of his sight. The mayor and the council, seeing the fervent charity of the friar, pardoned both him and the criminal.

Another time, when Brother Simone was praying in the woods and receiving great comfort therefrom, a flock of crows began to molest him with their cries, and he ordered them, in the name of Jesus, to leave and never to return. The birds left and from that day on were not seen either there or in the surrounding region. And this miracle was manifest to all the district of Fermo, where the shelter was. In praise of Christ. Amen.

## CHAPTER XLII

*Of the many miracles performed by holy friars.*

The province of the Marches of Ancona was long ago as adorned with holy exemplary friars as the heavens are adorned with stars, and those friars, like the luminaries of the sky, have illumined with their example and their doctrine the Order of St. Francis and the world. There was the very old Brother Lucido, who truly shone in sanctity and glowed with divine charity, and whose glorious tongue, inspired by the Holy Spirit, reaped marvelous fruit in preaching. Another was Brother Bentivoglia of San Severino, who was seen by Brother Masseo of San Severino to be raised bodily in the air, while he was praying in the woods, and suspended there for a great length of time. Because of this miracle, Brother Masseo, then a country priest, became a Friar Minor, and he was of such sanctity that he performed many miracles in life and after death.

The above-mentioned Brother Bentivoglia once lived in Trevebonanti, dedicated to watching over and caring for a leper. When his superior ordered him to leave that place and go to another place fifteen miles away, not wishing to abandon the leper, with great charity he took him on his shoulders and carried him from daybreak to sunrise up to the place he had been sent to, Mount Sanvicino. The distance could not have been covered in that time even had he been an eagle, and all the countryside felt great marvel and admiration for this miracle.

Another famous friar was Brother Pietro da Montecchio, who was seen by Brother Servodeo d'Urbino, then his guardian in the old shelter of Ancona, suspended in the air about five or six cubits off the ground, near the foot of the crucifix of the church before which he had been praying.

This Brother Pietro was once keeping the fast of St. Michael the Archangel with great devotion; and on the last day of that fast, as he was praying in church, he was heard speaking with St. Michael the Archangel by a young friar who had carefully hidden himself under the main altar to spy out some sign of Brother Pietro's sanctity. And the young friar overheard the following words.

St. Michael said: "Brother Pietro, you have faithfully suffered for me and in many ways inflicted bodily pain on yourself. Now I have come to console you and I will intercede with God for any grace that you ask."

Brother Pietro answered: "Most holy prince of the celestial army and most faithful defender of divine honor, merciful protector of souls, I ask you the grace of forgiveness of my sins."

St. Michael answered: "Ask me some other grace, for this I will procure very easily."

And when Brother Pietro asked for nothing more, the Archangel concluded: "Because of the faith and devotion you have for me, I will procure this grace and many others for you."

Their talk lasted for some time, and when he had finished speaking the holy Archangel Michael departed, leaving Brother Pietro much solaced.

At the time of this holy Brother Pietro, there lived in the same place, in the shelter of Forano in the group of monasteries of Ancona, a Brother Corrado da Offida. One day Brother Corrado went into the woods to contemplate God, and Brother Pietro, without being seen, followed him to see what would happen. Brother Corrado began to pray most devoutly and with many tears to the Virgin Mary that she would grant him the grace, through her Blessed Son, to feel some of the sweetness that St. Simeon felt on the day of the Purification when he held the Blessed Saviour Jesus in his arms. And when he had offered this prayer, the merciful Virgin Mary granted his wish and the Queen of Heaven appeared with her Blessed Child in her arms. In a great splendor of light she approached Brother Corrado and placed her Blessed Child in his arms. And he, with great devotion, hugged Him and kissed Him and clasped Him to him, burning and melting with love and unutterable joy. Brother Pietro, who had seen everything from his hiding place, felt great sweetness and solace, too, and when the Virgin Mary had left Brother Corrado he hastily returned to the shelter so as not to be seen.

But when he saw Brother Corrado returning, happy and gay, he said to him: "O heavenly man, you have had much joy today."

And Brother Corrado replied: "What do you mean, Brother Pietro? What do you know of what happened to me?"

"I know, I know," said Brother Pietro, "how the Virgin Mary and her Blessed Son visited you."

Then Brother Corrado, who was truly humble, and wished to keep secret this grace of God, begged him to say nothing of it. And from that time on there was such love between the two that in all matters they showed one heart and one soul.

Once, in the shelter of Sirolo, Brother Corrado through his prayers freed a possessed woman. He prayed for her all of one night and then appeared to the mother of the possessed woman. The next morning he fled so as not to be found and honored by the people. In praise of Christ. Amen.

## CHAPTER XLIII

*How Brother Corrado converted a young friar
who was disturbing the monastery.*

Brother Corrado da Offida, admirable and zealous follower of evangelical poverty and of the Rule of St. Francis,
led such a religious life and obtained such merit with God
that both in his life and in his death he was honored by
Christ with many miracles.

Once, when still a stranger, he came to the shelter of
Offida and was begged by the friars in the name of God
and charity to admonish a young friar who was acting so
childishly and in so disordered a manner that he upset
both the young and the old of that monastery.

Brother Corrado, out of compassion for that young man
and in answer to the friars' request, called the young man
aside and in perfect charity spoke to him so persuasively
and with such holy counsel that by divine grace he forthwith changed in his habits from a child to a wise old man.
He became benign and solicitous and devout and peaceful
and humble, a student of every virtuous practice. Just as
formerly the entire monastery had been troubled by him,
so now everyone was content and comforted by him, and
everyone loved him greatly.

But as it pleased God, a few days after this change, the
young man died, bringing grief to the friars. After a few
days his soul appeared to Brother Corrado while he was devoutly in prayer before the altar of the monastery, and
hailed him as father. And Brother Corrado asked: "Who
are you?"

The answer was: "I am the soul of that young friar who
died a short while ago."

And Brother Corrado said: "O my dearest son, what has
become of you?"

And the answer was: "My most beloved father, through
the grace of God and your teaching I am well, for I am not
damned; but because of certain sins from which I did not
have time to sufficiently purge myself, I endure great pain in
Purgatory. I beseech you, Father, that just as out of pity

you came to my aid when I was alive, so now you give me succor in my sufferings by saying some Our Fathers for me, since your prayer is very acceptable in the sight of God."

Then Brother Corrado benignly consented to his request and recited an Our Father with the *Requiem aeternam;* and then that soul said: "O my dear father, I feel such solace and such refreshment! I beg of you to say another prayer."

And Brother Corrado said another, and the soul then said: "Father, when you pray for me I feel myself lightened; I beseech you not to stop praying for me."

Then Brother Corrado, seeing that his prayers did much, said a hundred Our Fathers for that soul. After he had finished, the soul said: "I thank you, my dearest father, in the name of God, for the charity you have shown toward me. Through your prayers I am freed from all punishment and I go forth to the heavenly kingdom." Having said this, the soul departed.

Then Brother Corrado, to give joy and comfort to the friars, told them of the vision in great detail. In praise of the Blessed Christ. Amen.

## CHAPTER XLIV

*How the Mother of Christ and St. John the Evangelist and St. Francis appeared to Brother Pietro and told him which of them felt the greatest pain in the Passion of Christ.*

Brother Corrado and Brother Pietro, two of the shining stars in the province of the Marches, lived together for a while in the district of Ancona in the shelter of Forano. Because their love and charity for one another was so great, it appeared that one heart and one soul was in them, and they had promised each other that whatever comfort the mercy of God might send them they would reveal it to one another in charity.

One day Brother Pietro was in prayer, devoutly meditating on the Passion of Christ. Since the most blessed Mother of Christ and His beloved disciple John and St. Francis were painted at the foot of the cross as crucified with Christ in spiritual suffering, he began to wonder which of the three had suffered more in the Passion of Christ: the mother who had borne Him, the disciple who had rested against His bosom, or St. Francis, who was crucified with Christ.

As he dwelt on this devout thought, the Virgin Mary appeared to him, together with St. John the Evangelist and St. Francis, attired in noble vestments of blessed glory. But St. Francis seemed more splendidly attired than St. John. Brother Pietro was very frightened by this vision but St. John comforted him, saying: "Fear not, dear brother, for we have come to comfort you and to help you in your doubt. Know, then, that the Mother of Christ and I, above all creatures, grieved over the Passion of Christ; but after us St. Francis suffered because of it more than any other creature, and that is why you see him in such glory."

And Brother Pietro asked him: "Most holy Apostle of Christ, why does the attire of St. Francis seem more beautiful than yours?"

St. John answered: "This is the reason, that in the world he wore more common and coarse garments than did I."

After saying these words, St. John gave to Brother Pietro a glorious robe he was holding and said to him: "Take this robe that I have brought for you."

Since St. John wished to dress him in this robe, Brother Pietro, amazed, fell to the ground and began to cry out aloud: "Brother Corrado, Brother Corrado, beloved, come, hurry, come see this marvel!" As he said these things the holy vision disappeared. When Brother Corrado came, he told him of the vision in great detail and they both thanked God. Amen.

## CHAPTER XLV

*How God revealed to Brother Giovanni della Penna that he was to make a long trip and then make his way to Him, and how he became a friar and remained for many years in the Order in great sanctity.*

While Brother Giovanni della Penna was still a child of the world in the province of the Marches, there appeared to him one night a very beautiful young man who called him and said: "Giovanni, go to St. Stephen's, where one of the Friars Minor is preaching. Believe his words and act on them, for I have sent him there. And when you have done this you are then to take a long journey, after which you will come to me."

The young man immediately arose and felt a great change in his soul. He went to St. Stephen's and found there a great multitude of men and women waiting to hear the sermon. The friar who was to speak was Brother Filippo, one of the first friars to come to the March of Ancona, when there were still very few shelters in the March.

Brother Filippo began to preach and did so devoutly, not with human wisdom but with the spirit of Christ, announcing the realm of eternal life.

The young man went up to Brother Filippo after he had finished the sermon and said to him: "Father, if it pleases you to receive me into the Order, I would gladly do penance and serve our Lord Jesus Christ."

Brother Filippo, seeing and recognizing in the young man a marvelous innocence and readiness to serve God, said to him: "Come to me on such-and-such a day at Recanati, and I will have you received." (A provincial chapter was to be held at Recanati.)

The young man, who was very pure, believed that this was to be the great journey after which, in keeping with the revelation received, he was to go to Heaven. He thought all this would come about as soon as he was received into the Order.

When he was received, seeing that this was not coming to pass, he became very anxious to go to Provence, since the Minister of the chapter had said that whoever wanted to go to that province in the name of holy obedience would receive permission. In his heart he thought that this would be the long journey that he was to make before he would go to Heaven. But he was ashamed to ask to be sent to Provence. Finally, trusting in Brother Filippo, who had first received him into the Order, he besought him to go in his name and ask permission that he might go to Provence. Brother Filippo, seeing his purity and his holy intentions, obtained permission, and Brother Giovanni with great joy set out, certain that at the end of the journey he would go to Heaven.

But as it pleased God, he remained in that province and in that expectation and desire for twenty-five years, living in great honesty and sanctity, giving good example, constantly growing in virtue and grace in the eyes of God and the people. He was greatly beloved by friars and laymen alike.

One day, as Brother Giovanni was devoutly in prayer, weeping and lamenting that his desire was not being fulfilled and that his pilgrimage in this life was too prolonged, the Blessed Christ appeared to him. The soul of Brother Giovanni melted within him and Christ said to him: "Son, Brother Giovanni, ask Me what you wish."

And he answered: "My Lord, I know of naught I want but You. I desire nothing else and I beseech You for one thing alone, that You forgive all my sins and give me the grace of seeing You once again when I need You still more."

Christ said: "Your wish is granted." And when he had said this He departed and Brother Giovanni remained all comforted.

Toward the end of that time the friars of the Marches, learning of the fame of his sanctity, persuaded the General to bid Brother Giovanni, in the name of holy obedience, to come back to the Marches. Brother Giovanni received the command with joy and set out, believing that at the end of the journey he would go to Heaven, according to the promise of Christ. But once back in the province of the Marches he lived there for thirty years, no longer recognized by any of his relatives, and waiting day by day for the mercy of God, that He might keep His promise.

During this time he filled the office of guardian with great diligence, and God worked many miracles through him. And among other gifts that he received from God was that of prophecy. Once, as he was leaving the shelter, one of his novices was attacked and so greatly tempted by the devil that, yielding to the temptation, he decided to leave the Order as soon as Brother Giovanni would return. Brother Giovanni, knowing through the spirit of prophecy that the novice had been tempted and had succumbed, immediately returned home and called the novice to him and told him to confess himself. But before he heard his confession he told him about his temptation in detail, as God had revealed it to him, and concluded thus: "Son, because you

waited for me and did not wish to leave without my benediction, God has granted you this grace, that you will never
leave, and you will die in grace in the Order." The novice
was then strengthened in good will. He remained in the
Order and became a holy friar. (Brother Giovanni told me,
Brother Ugolino, this story.)

Brother Giovanni was a happy and relaxed man who rarely
spoke. He was a man of great prayer, very devout, and
after matins, in particular, he would never return to his cell
but would remain in prayer until daybreak. One night as he
was in prayer after matins, the angel of God appeared to
him and said: "Brother Giovanni, the end of your life, which
you have awaited for so long, is near at hand, and in the
name of God I ask you to beg for whatever grace you wish.
I also offer you the choice of one day in Purgatory or
seven days' suffering in this world."

No sooner had Brother Giovanni chosen seven days' suffering in this world than he fell sick of many infirmities.
He had a high fever, and gout in his hands and feet, a pain
in his side, and many other ailments. But what hurt him
most of all was that a devil stood before him, and in his
hand he had a long scroll on which was written all the sins
that Giovanni had ever committed in word or deed. The
devil said to him: "Because of these sins which you have
committed by thought, tongue, and deed, you are damned to
deepest Hell."

And he could not remember any good that he had ever
done, nor that he was in the Order, nor that he had ever
been in it; and he believed that he was damned, as the
devil told him. When he was asked, therefore, how he was,
he answered: "I am not at all well, because I am damned."

When the friars heard this, they sent for an old brother
by the name of Brother Matteo of Mount Rubbiano, a holy
man and a great friend of Brother Giovanni.

Brother Matteo arrived on the seventh day of the sufferings and greeted Brother Giovanni and asked him how he
was. Brother Giovanni answered that he was not well, that
he was damned. Brother Matteo then said: "Have you forgotten that you have frequently confessed to me and that I
have completely absolved you from all your sins? Don't you
remember that you have served God in this holy Order for
many years? Don't you remember that the mercy of God
is greater than all the sins of the world and that our Saviour,

the Blessed Christ, paid an infinite price to redeem us? Take heart, then, for without doubt you are saved."

And with these words, which came at the end of the trials of Brother Giovanni, the temptation left him and there came comfort. And Brother Giovanni said with great joy to Brother Matteo: "Since you are tired and it is late, I beg of you that you go and rest."

Brother Matteo did not want to leave him but finally, because of his insistence, he left and went to rest, leaving Brother Giovanni alone with the friar who was caring for him. And now the Blessed Christ came with great splendor and soft fragrance, as He had formerly promised to appear to him when he would have greatest need, and healed all his ailments. Then Brother Giovanni, with his hands joined, thanking God that he had finished his journey in this wretched life with the happiest end, entrusted and gave back into the hands of Christ his immortal soul, passing from this life to eternal life in Christ, whom he had awaited and desired for many years.

Brother Giovanni is buried in the shelter of Penna San Giovanni. In praise of Christ. Amen.

## CHAPTER XLVI

*How Brother Pacifico saw the soul of his brother, Brother Umile, rise to heaven.*

In the province of the Marches, after the death of St. Francis, were two brothers in the Order. The name of one was Brother Umile, of the other, Brother Pacifico, and both were men of great sanctity and perfection.

Brother Umile was in the shelter of Soffiano and there died; the other, Brother Pacifico, was with another family of brothers at some distance from him.

As it pleased God, while Brother Pacifico was praying in a lonely place, he was lifted up in ecstasy and saw the soul of his brother, Brother Umile, then leaving his body, go straight to Heaven without any delay or hindrance.

It so happened that after many years the surviving Brother Pacifico was transferred to Soffiano, where his brother had died. At that time the friars, by petition of the nobility of Brunforte, moved their shelter from one place to another. Among other things, they moved the relics of holy men who had died in that shelter. When he came to the grave of Brother Umile, his brother, Brother Pacifico, took up his bones and washed them with good wine and then wrapped them in a white cloth and kissed them and wept over them with great reverence and devotion.

The other friars were shocked, finding no good example in this. It seemed to them that he, a man of great sanctity, was weeping for his brother out of worldly and sensual love, and that he showed more devotion for his own brother's relics than for those of other brothers who were no less saintly and worthy of reverence.

Brother Pacifico, aware of the evil murmurings of the brothers, humbly satisfied them by saying: "My beloved brothers, do not be disturbed that I have done for the bones of my brother what I have not done for the bones of others. Blessed be Christ, I have not been drawn, as you think, by carnal love. I have acted this way because when my brother passed from this life, as I was praying in a remote and distant place I saw his soul go straight to Heaven. I am certain, then, that his bones are holy and must be in Paradise; and if God were to have conceded similar knowledge of other friars to me, I would have shown their bones as much reverence." The friars, seeing his devout and holy motive, were much edified by him and praised God, who works marvels through His holy friars. In praise of Christ. Amen.

## CHAPTER XLVII

*How the Virgin Mary came to a sick friar and brought three jars of medicine.*

In olden times there was, in the shelter of Soffiano, a Friar Minor of such grace and sanctity that he seemed almost divine; and he was frequently lifted up to God.

Once, as this friar was absorbed and lifted up in God (for he had an outstanding gift of contemplation), birds of many kinds came to him and tamely rested upon his shoulders and his head, on his arms and on his hands, singing gloriously. He was a solitary man who rarely spoke, but when he was asked for anything he would answer so graciously and wisely that he seemed more angel than man. A man of great prayer and contemplation, he was held in great reverence by the friars.

When this virtuous friar, as it pleased God, fell mortally ill, he could eat nothing and he would not take any bodily medicine, but put all of his trust in the Blessed Physician, Jesus Christ, and in his Blessed Mother, from whom he merited through divine clemency to be mercifully visited and comforted. Stretched out on his bed and preparing for death with all his heart and with great devotion, he saw in a vision the glorious and Blessed Virgin Mary, Mother of Christ, together with a great multitude of angels and holy virgins, in marvelous splendor; and she approached his bed. Looking at her, the brother felt great joy and bodily comfort and humbly besought her to ask her beloved Son that through His merits He deliver him from the prison of the wretched flesh.

As he persisted in this prayer with many tears, the Virgin Mary answered him, calling him by name: "Do not fear, Son. He has already granted your request; and I am here to comfort you a while before you leave this life."

Beside the Virgin Mary there were three holy virgins who held in their hands three medicine jars of honey and syrup of incredible fragrance and sweetness. Then the glorious Virgin took and opened one of those jars, and the entire house was filled with that scent. Taking a spoonful of that medicine, she gave it to the sick brother, and he had no sooner tasted it than he felt such comfort and sweetness that his soul no longer seemed able to remain in his body.

He started to say: "No more, most gentle Mother, Blessed Virgin and saviour of mankind, no more; for I cannot bear such sweetness!" But the merciful and Blessed Mother continued to give that medicine to the sick brother and emptied the whole jar.

The Blessed Virgin then took the second jar and dipped in a spoon to give him some, and the friar sweetly complained, saying: "O most blessed Mother of God, if my soul is almost completely undone by the scent and sweetness of the first medicine, how will I be able to take the second? I beg of you, Blessed above all angels and above all saints, give me no more."

Our Lady answered: "Taste some, a little bit, of this second jar." And having given it to him, she said: "Now, my son, you have as much as you need. Take comfort, my son, for I shall soon come for you and I will take you to the Kingdom of my Son, which you have always desired and sought."

And when she had said this, she took her leave. The brother remained so comforted and solaced by the sweetness of that medicine that he survived for many days, satisfied and strong, without any bodily food. Some days later, conversing happily with the friars, with joy and jubilee he left this wretched life for the life of the blessed. Amen.

## CHAPTER XLVIII

*How Brother Jacopo della Massa saw in a vision a golden tree on which were all the Friars Minor in the world, and how he knew the virtues and vices of each and every one.*

God opened the door of His secrets to Brother Jacopo della Massa and gave him a perfect knowledge and understanding of Divine Scripture and of the future. He was of such sanctity that Brother Egidio of Assisi, Brother Marco da Montino, Brother Juniper, and Brother Lucido said of him that they knew of no one in the world who was greater in the eyes of God.

I had a great desire to meet this Brother Jacopo, because when I asked Brother Giovanni, a companion of Brother Egidio, to explain certain spiritual matters to me he had said: "If you wish to be informed on things of the spirit, speak with Brother Jacopo della Massa. Brother Egidio himself sought to be enlightened by him; and no one can add to or take away from the words of Brother Jacopo, since he has come to a knowledge of heavenly secrets, and his words are the words of the Holy Spirit. There is no man on earth whom I love to see as much."

Once, in the early days of the ministry of Brother Giovanni da Parma, as Brother Jacopo was praying, he was lifted up to God and remained for three days in ecstasy, unconscious and insensitive to all, so that the friars wondered whether he was dead. And as he was lifted up to God, God revealed to him what was to happen to our Order. When I heard about this, the desire of seeing him and speaking with him grew, and when, as it pleased God, I had occasion to speak to him I begged him thus: "If what I have heard of you is true, I beg you not to conceal it from me. I have heard it said that when for three days you were almost as if dead, among the other things that God revealed to you was a knowledge of what was to happen to our Order; and this has been told to me by Brother Matteo, Minister of the province of Marches, to whom you, out of obedience, revealed it." Then Brother Jacopo conceded that what Brother Matteo had said was true.

And what Brother Matteo had said was as follows: "I know, Brother, through the revelation of God, what will become of our Order. Brother Jacopo della Massa has manifested and said to me that after God revealed many things to him about the state of the Church Militant, he saw in a vision a beautiful and tall tree whose roots were of gold and whose fruits were men, all of them Friars Minor. Its main branches were distinct one from the other, as are the various provinces of the Order, and each branch had as many friars as there were in the province symbolized by that branch. And then he knew the number of all the friars in the Order and in each province, and their names, their ages, conditions, offices, ranks, standings, and the graces and faults of all. And he saw Giovanni da Parma at the highest point of the main trunk of this tree, and at the tips of the branches surrounding this central branch were the ministers of all the provinces. And after this he saw Christ seated on a great and pure-white throne, calling St. Francis to him and giving him a chalice filled with the spirit of life, saying, 'Go and visit your friars and give them to drink from this chalice of the spirit of life, for the spirit of Satan will rise against them and strike them, and many of them will fall and will not rise again.' And Christ gave St. Francis two angels to accompany him.

"And then St. Francis came to offer the chalice of life to his friars, and he began by offering it to Brother Giovanni da Parma, who, taking it, drank it all speedily and devoutly, and immediately became as resplendent as the sun. And St. Francis offered it to all the rest after him, and there were but few of them who took it and drank it all with due reverence and devotion. Those who took it devoutly and drank it all became as shining as the sun. Those who spilled it and did not drink it with devotion turned black and dark and misshapen, horrible to behold. Those who drank a part of it and spilled a part became in part luminous and in part dark, according to the amount they drank or spilled. But above all others, the above-mentioned Brother Giovanni was resplendent, for he had drunk the chalice of life to the last drop, and he had profoundly contemplated the abyss of infinite divine light, and in it had seen the tempest that would be unleashed against the tree to lash and snap its branches.

"Because of this foreknowledge, Brother Giovanni left the tip of the branch and, climbing down beneath all the branches, hid himself against the thick trunk of the tree and there remained pensive. And Brother Bonaventure, who had taken part of the chalice and had spilled part, climbed up that branch and into that place from which Brother Giovanni had climbed down. As he stood there the nails of his fingers became like iron points, as sharp as razors. And moving from the place to which he had climbed with great impetus and fury, he wanted to hurl himself against Brother Giovanni, to hurt him. But Brother Giovanni, seeing this, cried for help to Christ, seated on the throne. Christ heard him and called St. Francis and gave him a cutting, burning stone and said to him, 'Go, and with this stone cut the nails of Brother Bonaventure, with which he wishes to claw Brother Giovanni, so that he cannot hurt him.' And then St. Francis came and did as Christ had ordered him to.

"After this a great storm arose and the wind shook the tree so strongly that the friars fell to the ground. The first to fall were those who had spilled all the chalice of the spirit of life, and they were taken by demons to dark and pain-filled places. But Brother Giovanni, together with all the others who had drunk all of the chalice, were taken by the angels to the place of life and eternal light and splendor.

"And Brother Jacopo, as he saw this vision, was able to understand and discern in great detail the name and condition and the state of everyone. And the tempestuous wind continued to blow against the tree, and hurled it down and carried it away. No sooner had the storm blown over than there emerged, from the roots of this tree, which were all of gold, another tree. It also was of gold, and produced golden leaves and flowers and fruit."

But concerning this tree and its growth, height, beauty, scent, and virtue, it is better at the present time to be silent than to speak. In praise of Christ. Amen.

## CHAPTER XLIX

*How Brother Giovanni of Alverna was converted, and how Christ visited him in intimacy and love.*

Among other wise and holy brothers and sons of St. Francis, who according to Solomon are the glory of the father, there was in our times, in the province of the Marches, the venerable and holy Brother Giovanni da Fermo. Because of the length of time that he lived in the holy shelter of Alverna and because there he passed away from this life, he was also called Brother Giovanni of Alverna. He was a man of singular life and great sanctity.

As a child, Brother Giovanni sought with all his heart the way of penance, which cleanses the body and soul. While still very little, he began to wear a hairshirt and iron bands against his flesh, and to perform great acts of abstinence, especially when he was living with the canons of St. Peter's in Fermo, who lived sumptuously. He fled corporal ease and delights, and with rigid abstinence disciplined his body. Since many of his companions were against these practices and took away his hairshirt and in a number of ways hindered his abstinence, he, inspired by God, thought of leaving the world and those who loved it and offering himself completely in the habit of the crucified St. Francis to the crucified Christ. And this he did.

Having been received into the Order as a young boy and committed to the care of the master of novices, he became so spiritual and devout that at times when he would hear this Master speak of God, his heart would melt like wax near a fire; and the love of God so inflamed him that he was not able to stand still and endure it. He would get up and, as if drunk in spirit, would go about now through the garden, now through the woods, now through the church, talking as the flame and the impetus of the spirit moved him.

Time and divine grace made this angelic man grow constantly from virtue to virtue and in heavenly gifts, so that he was often lifted up and rapt in God. Many times was his soul raised to the splendor of the cherubim, to the ardor of the seraphim, to the joy of the blessed, to the embraces, overflowing with love, of Christ. This not only came about from spiritual experiences within, but received added confirmation from external signs reflected in his body. And the fire of divine love once set his heart ablaze in such a way that this flame burned in him for all of three years. During this time, when living on holy Mount Alverna, he received great solace and divine visitations and was often rapt in God.

But since God takes singular care of His children and gives to them at different times consolations and tribulations, prosperity and adversity, and since He sees that it is necessary to keep them in humility in order to quicken in them the desire for heavenly things, it pleased Him, after three years, to withdraw from Brother Giovanni the ray and flame of that divine love and to deprive him of every spiritual consolation. And so Brother Giovanni remained without light and without the love of God, disconsolate, afflicted, and grieving. In great anguish he would go about the woods talking out loud, calling out in words and tears and sighs for the beloved Bridegroom of his soul, who had left him and hidden Himself, and without whose presence Brother Giovanni's soul could find neither peace nor rest. But nowhere and in no way was he able to find his sweet Jesus nor to recover that taste of the love of Christ that he had once known. This tribulation lasted for many days and during that time he persevered with tears and sighs, praying to God that He mercifully give back to him the beloved Bridegroom of his soul.

Finally God was satisfied that He had sufficiently tested Brother Giovanni's patience and sharpened his desire. On a certain day, as Brother Giovanni in great affliction and tribulation was going about the woods, he sat down out of weariness next to a beech tree. He remained there, his face wet with tears, looking up toward Heaven; and suddenly Jesus Christ appeared before him in the path; but He said nothing. Brother Giovanni, seeing Him and knowing full well that He was Christ, immediately threw himself at His feet and with uncontrollable tears most humbly prayed to Him, saying: "Help me, my Lord, for without You, my most sweet Saviour, I am in darkness and in tears; without You, most meek Lamb, I am in anguish and suffering and fear; without You, most high Son of God, I am confused and ashamed; without You, I am stripped of every good, and blind, for You are Jesus Christ, true light of souls; without You I am lost and damned, for You are the life of souls and the life of lives; without You I am sterile and arid, for You are the fountain of every gift and every grace; without You I am utterly disconsolate, for You are Jesus, our redemption, love, and desire, comforting bread and wine, who gives joy to the hearts of angels and of saints. Enlighten me, most gracious Teacher and most merciful Shepherd, for I am Your lamb, though unworthily so."

But because the desire of holy men is fanned to greater love and merit when God delays in answering, the Blessed Christ departed without granting him his wish and walked away along that path without saying a word. Then Brother Giovanni got up and ran after Him and again threw himself at His feet, and with holy importunity held on to Him, and with devout tears prayed, saying: "O most sweet Jesus Christ, have mercy on me in my tribulations, grant my request out of the vastness of Your mercy and out of the truth of Your salvation. Turn Your face and Your loving gaze to me, for all the earth is filled with Your mercy."

And again Christ departed without speaking a word or offering any consolation; and He acted as does the mother toward the child when she makes him want her breast and makes him follow her weeping so that he will all the more willingly take it after. And so Brother Giovanni, with greater fervor and desire, followed Christ. As he caught up to Him, the Blessed Christ turned toward him and looked at him with a gracious and happy countenance, and opening His most holy and merciful arms, He tenderly embraced him. As he stretched out his arms Brother Giovanni saw rays of shining light issue forth from the most holy breast of the Saviour, and they lit up the entire wood and his own body and soul.

Then Brother Giovanni knelt at the feet of Christ, and the Blessed Christ, as He had done with Magdalen, benignly offered him a foot to kiss. Brother Giovanni, taking the foot with great reverence, bathed it in such tears that in truth he seemed another Magdalen and he devoutly said: "I beg of You, my Lord, that You do not look at my sins but, because of Your most holy Passion and the shedding of Your most precious blood, resurrect my soul in the grace of Your love; for this is Your commandment: that we love You with all of our heart and affection; and no one can keep this commandment without Your help. Help me, then, most beloved Son of God, so that I may love You with all my heart and with all my strength."

As Brother Giovanni spoke thus at the feet of Christ, his prayer was granted, and he had again from Christ that first grace of the flame of divine love, and felt himself consoled and renewed; and since he knew that the gift of divine grace had been given him again he began to thank the Blessed Christ and to devoutly kiss His feet. And then, as he stood up to look into the eyes of Christ, Jesus Christ extended His hands that Brother Giovanni might kiss them; and when Brother Giovanni had kissed them he came close and embraced and kissed Jesus, and Christ similarly embraced and kissed him. In that embrace and kiss Brother Giovanni sensed such a divine fragrance that if all the spices and scented things of the world were put together they would be vile in comparison to that fragrance. In that fragrance Brother Giovanni was rapt and consoled and illumined, and that scent lasted within him for many months.

From that time on, from his mouth, which had drunk from the fountain of divine wisdom in the holy breast of the Saviour, there came forth marvelous and celestial words that changed the hearts of those who heard them and yielded great fruit in souls. And for a long time after, on and around the path of the woods where the blessed feet of Christ had trod, whenever he would go there Brother Giovanni sensed that fragrance and saw that splendor.

When Brother Giovanni came back to himself after being so rapt, and when the bodily presence of Christ had disappeared, he remained so enlightened in soul, having seen into the abyss of divinity, that although he was not in human terms a learned man, he nevertheless marvelously expounded and resolved the most subtle and difficult questions of the Holy Trinity and of the profound mysteries of Holy Scripture. And many times after, speaking before the Pope and cardinals, kings, barons, teachers, and doctors, he astonished them all by the lofty words and profound judgments that he gave. In praise of Christ. Amen.

## CHAPTER L

> *How, as Brother Giovanni of Alverna was celebrating Mass the day after All Saints, he saw many souls rise to Heaven.*

Once, as Brother Giovanni was celebrating Mass the day after All Saints, offering it for the souls of the dead as the Church has decreed, he offered that most high Sacrament with such charity and such compassion (the souls of the dead desire that sacrifice, because of its efficacy, above all other good works that may be offered for them) that it seemed to him that he was melting with compassion and fraternal charity.

As he devoutly raised the body of Christ during the Mass, offering it to God the Father, he prayed that out of love for His blessed Son, Jesus Christ, who to redeem souls had hung on the cross, He would free the souls of the redeemed dead from the pains of Purgatory. And he suddenly saw an almost infinite multitude of souls leave Purgatory, like sparks from numberless fires in a blazing furnace. He saw them rise to Heaven by the merits of the Passion of Christ, who is daily offered for the living and the dead in that most holy Host, which is worthy of being adored for all eternity. Amen.

## CHAPTER LI

> *How, when Brother Jacopo da Fallerone was ill, Brother Giovanni of Alverna recommended him to God; and how his prayer was miraculously answered.*

When Brother Jacopo da Fallerone, a man of great sanctity, was gravely ill in the shelter of Mogliano in the district of

Fermo, brother Giovanni of Alverna, then living in the shelter of Massa, heard of his illness. Because he loved him as a dear father, he began to pray for him, devoutly beseeching God to make Brother Jacopo well, if it were for his good.

And as he was in devout prayer, he was lifted up in ecstasy and he saw in the air a great army of angels and of saints above his cell in the woods, in such radiance that all the surrounding country was lit up. And among these angels he saw the sick Brother Jacopo for whom he was praying, in robes of shining white. He also saw among them the blessed father St. Francis, adorned with the sacred stigmata of Christ and in great glory. He looked further and recognized holy Brother Lucido, and old Brother Matteo of Mount Rubbiano, and many other friars whom he had never seen or known in this life. As Brother Giovanni was looking at that blessed host of saints with great delight, it was revealed to him in all certainty that the soul of the sick friar was saved and that he was to die of that sickness, but not immediately, and that after his death he was to go to Paradise, although he would have to be purified for a short time in Purgatory. Brother Giovanni felt such joy for the salvation of that soul that he did not grieve at all over the death of the body, but with great sweetness of spirit he went about calling out to him silently: "Brother Jacopo, my sweet father; Brother Jacopo, my sweet brother; Brother Jacopo, most faithful servant and friend of God; Brother Jacopo, companion of the angels and sharer of the life of the blessed!"

In this joy and certainty, Brother Giovanni came back to himself and immediately left the shelter and went to visit Brother Jacopo at Mogliano. Finding him so worsened that he could barely talk, he announced to him the death of his body and the salvation and glory of his soul, as he had learned in all certainty through divine revelation. Brother Jacopo, joyous in countenance and soul, received him with great happiness and with a smiling face, thanking him for the good news he brought and commending himself to him fervently.

Then Brother Giovanni affectionately entreated him that after death he should appear to him and speak to him of his new state, and Brother Jacopo promised to do so if it pleased God. And having uttered these words, as the time of his

death approached, Brother Jacopo devoutly began to recite
the verse of the psalm: "In peace and in eternal life I shall
fall asleep, and I will rest." And when he had recited this
verse, with a happy and smiling countenance he passed from
this life.

When Brother Jacopo was buried, Brother Giovanni returned to the shelter of Massa, waiting for Brother Jacopo to
appear to him on the day he had promised to. As he
was praying that day, Christ appeared to him with a great
company of angels and of saints, and Brother Jacopo was
not among them. Brother Giovanni, marveling greatly, devoutly prayed to Christ for him.

The following day, as Brother Giovanni was praying in the
woods, Brother Jacopo appeared, accompanied by angels, all
radiant and joyful; and Brother Giovanni said to him: "O
my beloved father, why did you not come to me on the
promised day?"

Brother Jacopo answered: "Because I still needed to be
purified; but in the very hour that Christ appeared to you
and that you prayed to Him for me, Christ granted your
prayer and freed me from all punishment. And then I appeared to Brother Jacopo della Massa, the holy lay brother,
as he was serving Mass, and as the priest raised the consecrated Host, it converted and changed into the form of a
beautiful living Child. I said to him, 'Today I will fly up
to the kingdom of eternal life with this Child, and no one
may ascend there without Him.' "

And after he had said these words, Brother Jacopo disappeared and went to Heaven with all that blessed company
of angels, and Brother Giovanni remained much solaced.

Brother Jacopo da Fallerone died on the vigil of St. James
the Apostle during the month of July in the shelter of
Mogliano, where through his merits, divine goodness worked
many miracles after his death. In praise of Christ. Amen.

## CHAPTER LII

*How Christ showed, and made Brother Giovanni
of Alverna understand, the most high Holy
Trinity and all the holy and marvelous things that
Holy Church teaches of divinity.*

Since Brother Giovanni of Alverna had perfectly renounced every worldly temporal joy and delight and had
placed all his happiness and his hope in God, divine goodness gave him the gift of marvelous consolations and revelations, especially on the solemn feasts of Christ. Once, when
the solemnity of the feast of the Nativity was drawing close,
at which time in all certainty he expected solace from God
with a revelation on the sweet humanity of Jesus, the Holy
Spirit infused in him such great, boundless, and fervent love
for the charity of Christ, because of which He humbled
Himself to take on our humanity, that it really seemed to
him as if his soul had been drawn out of his body and
that he was burning like a furnace. Unable to endure this
ardor, he was in anguish and close to fainting; and because
of the rush of the Holy Spirit and because of the excess of
love, he cried out loud. And at the hour in which that
boundless fervor came upon him, and with it the strong and
certain hope of his salvation, he was sure that if he were
to die, he would not have to endure the pains of Purgatory
at all. This love lasted within him for a year and a half, although this boundless fervor was not constant, but came
during certain hours of the day.

And in these times he received many and marvelous visitations and consolations from God; and he was frequently
rapt up to God, as the friar who first wrote down these things
saw. One night, for example, he was raised and rapt up to
God and saw in Him the Creator, all created celestial and
earthly things, and all their perfections, degrees, and hier-
archies. Then he clearly knew how each thing represented its
Creator and how God is above and beneath and outside and
beside all created things. Then he knew one God in three
Persons and three Persons in one God, and that infinite
charity which made incarnate the Son of God through

obedience to the Father. And finally he knew in that vision that there was no other way in which the soul can ascend to God and have eternal life except through the Blessed Christ, who is the Way, the Truth, and the Life of the soul. Amen

## CHAPTER LIII

*How Brother Giovanni of Alverna fainted while consecrating the Body of Christ during the celebration of Mass.*

Once when Brother Giovanni was in the shelter at Mogliano, as the friars who were present there recount, an admirable event took place. The first night after the octave of St. Lawrence, and within the octave of the Assumption of our Lady, after he had recited matins in church with the other brothers, there came upon him the chrism of divine grace. He went into the garden to meditate on the Passion of Christ and to prepare himself to celebrate Mass, which it was his turn to sing that morning, and as he meditated on the words of consecration of the Body of Christ, and considered the infinite charity of Christ, who not only wished to redeem us with His precious blood but, even more, wished to leave us as food for our souls His most worthy Body and Blood, the love of sweet Jesus grew in him with such fervor and gentleness that his soul could not endure it. He cried out and, as if drunk in spirit, kept saying to himself: *"Hoc est corpus meum"*; and saying these words he seemed to see the Blessed Christ with the Virgin Mary and a multitude of angels. And as he pronounced these words he was enlightened by the Holy Spirit in all the profound and lofty mysteries of that most high Sacrament.

And when the dawn came, he entered the church with great fervor of spirit, constantly repeating those words, not thinking himself seen or heard by anyone; but there was a friar in prayer in the choir who saw and heard all. And being unable, because of the abundance of divine grace, to restrain his fervor, he continued to cry out aloud, and did so until the hour came to celebrate Mass. Then he went to put on his vestments and went to the altar.

As he celebrated Mass, the further he proceeded the more

his love of Christ grew, and together with it that fervent devotion that imparted to him an ineffable experience of God, which he himself could not or would not later describe in words. And fearing that his fervor and experience of God might grow to the point where he would have to stop celebrating Mass, he was greatly troubled and did not know what to do—whether to go on with the Mass or to wait. Something similar had happened to him once before, however, and the Lord had then tempered his fervor so that he had been able to finish the Mass. He trusted, therefore, that he could do so once again, and with great awe he continued with the Sacrament.

Coming to the Preface of the feast of Our Lady, the divine illumination and gracious tenderness of the love of God increased to the point that having come to the *Qui pridie* he could barely endure the sweetness. Finally, when he came to the act of Consecration, he said half of the words over the Host (that is, *"Hoc est . . ."*), and could in no way say more, but kept repeating the same words, *"Hoc est . . ."* The reason he could go no further was that he saw and felt the presence of Christ with a multitude of angels, and he could not endure such majesty; and he saw that Christ would not enter into the Host, nor would the Host be transubstantiated into the Body of Christ, unless he said the other half of the words, that is, *"corpus meum."* While Brother Giovanni was fixed in this anxiety and unable to go further, the guardian and the other brothers, and even many laymen who were in church to hear Mass, approached the altar and remained there, frightened by the actions of Brother Giovanni; and many of them wept out of devotion.

At last, after a long period of time, that is, when it pleased God, Brother Giovanni said aloud, *"corpus meum."* Immediately the form of the bread vanished and there appeared in the Host the Blessed Jesus Christ crowned and in glory; and He showed him the humility and charity that made Him incarnate of the Virgin Mary and that makes Him come every day into the hands of the priest when the Host is consecrated. And Brother John was raised up in sweetness of contemplation, and as he elevated the Host and the consecrated chalice he was lifted outside of himself. As his soul was suspended from bodily feeling his body fell back; and if he had not been held up by the guardian, who was behind him, he would have fallen to the ground. And the friars and the laymen who were in the church, both men and women, rushed up to him and he was carried into the sacristy as if dead, because his body was as cold as a dead person's and the fingers of his hands were so stiff that they could barely be straightened out or moved. He remained in this condition, rapt in God, until tierce, and this was during the summer.

And because I, present when all this occurred, desired greatly to know what God had worked through him, no sooner was he himself again than I went to him and begged him out of the charity of God to tell me all. And because he trusted me he told me all, and in detail. And among other things he told me that as he was consecrating the Body and Blood of Jesus Christ, and even before, his heart was as liquid as molten wax and his flesh seemed to be without bones, so that he could barely lift his arms or hands to make the sign of the cross above the Host or the chalice. He also told me that before he became a priest God had revealed to him that he was to faint at Mass; but since he had celebrated many Masses and that had never happened, he thought that the revelation was not of God. Nonetheless, about fifty days before the Assumption of Our Lady, on which feast the prophesied event occurred, God had revealed to him that it would happen about the time of the feast of the Assumption, though later he had forgotten this revelation. Amen.

# FIVE
## CONSIDERATIONS
## ON THE STIGMATA
## OF ST. FRANCIS.

In this part we shall devoutly consider the glorious stigmata that our blessed father, Messer St. Francis, received from Christ on the holy Mount Alverna. Since the stigmata were five, like the five wounds of Christ, this treatise will be divided into five parts.

The first will describe how St. Francis came to the holy Mount Alverna.

The second will describe the life and the conversations that he held with his companions on this holy mountain.

The third will describe the seraphic apparition and the impressing of the stigmata.

The fourth will describe how St. Francis came down from Mount Alverna after receiving the stigmata, and how he returned to St. Mary of the Angels.

The fifth will describe certain divine apparitions and revelations concerning the glorious stigmata, which were made after the death of St. Francis to holy friars and other devout persons.

> *On the first consideration; that is, how Messer Orlando da Chiusi gave Mount Alverna to St. Francis as a gift.*

With respect to the first consideration, one must know that when St. Francis was forty-three years old, in the year 1224, he was inspired by God to leave the Valley of Spoleto and go with Brother Leo, his companion, to Romagna.

On the way he passed the foot of the castle of Montefeltro, where a great banquet and festival were being held to honor the knighting of one of the counts of Montefeltro. St. Francis, hearing of the festivities that were taking place and knowing that many noblemen were gathered there from many different towns, said to Brother Leo: "Let us go to this feast, for with the help of God we shall gather some spiritual fruit."

Among the noblemen who had come to this tournament there was a great and rich nobleman of Tuscany by the name of Messer Orlando da Chiusi di Casentino. Because of the wonderful things that he had heard of the sanctity and miracles of St. Francis, he had great devotion to him and a very strong desire to see him and hear him preach.

St. Francis arrived at this castle, entered, and went to the square where a crowd of these noblemen had gathered; and in great fervor of spirit he climbed up on a low wall and began to preach, using as the theme of his sermon these words in the vulgar tongue: "So great the good I have in sight, that every pain I count delight." And inspired by the Holy Spirit, he preached devoutly and profoundly, illustrating this thought with many sufferings and martyrdoms of holy Apostles and Martyrs, with the harsh penances of holy confessors, with the many tribulations and temptations of holy virgins and of other saints.

Everyone stayed with his eyes and his soul fixed on St. Francis, listening as carefully as if an angel of God were speaking. Among those present was Messer Orlando, whose heart was touched by God through the marvelous sermon of St. Francis; he resolved to see him after the sermon and speak to him concerning his own soul.

And so, after the sermon, he drew St. Francis aside and said to him: "Father, with your help I would like to put my soul in order."

St. Francis answered: "It would please me greatly, but this morning go and honor your friends, who have invited you to the feast, and eat with them. After you have eaten, we shall speak together as long as you wish."

Messer Orlando accordingly went to eat, and after eating, returned to St. Francis and talked with him about his spiritual life.

At the end of the talk Messer Orlando said to St. Francis: "I have in Tuscany a most holy mountain called Mount Alverna. It is very solitary and wild and altogether fitting for someone who desires a solitary life or for one who would do penance in a place apart from all. If it pleases you, I would gladly give it to you and your companions for the well-being of my soul."

Hearing this generous offer of something that he greatly desired, St. Francis felt great joy, and thanking and praising first God and then Messer Orlando, said: "Messer, when you will return home I will send you some of my companions and you will show them that mountain. If they find it fitting for prayer and for penance, I accept your charitable offer from this moment on."

And when he had said this, St. Francis left, and after completing his journey, he returned to St. Mary of the Angels. Similarly Messer Orlando, after he had celebrated the solemnities of that feast, returned to his castle, the castle of Chiusi, about a mile away from Alverna.

When St. Francis returned to St. Mary of the Angels he sent two of his companions to Messer Orlando, who greeted them with great joy and charity. He was glad to show them Mount Alverna, and sent fifty armed men with them that they might be protected against wild animals. And so accompanied, these friars climbed up the mountain and studied it meticulously. Near the summit they came to a level part of the mountain very appropriate for contemplation, and they chose that place for themselves and for St. Francis. With the help of the armed men who were with them, they made a few huts from the branches of trees and accepted, in the name of God, the mountain of Alverna and the shelter for friars on this mountain.

They then departed and returned to St. Francis. They told him how the shelter they had chosen on Mount Alverna was most appropriate for prayer and contemplation.

On hearing the news, St. Francis rejoiced greatly, and praising and thanking God joyfully, said to the friars: "My sons, we are approaching the forty-day fast of St. Michael the Archangel. I firmly believe that it is the will of God that we pass this Lent on Mount Alverna, which has been prepared for us by Divine Providence, so that in honor and glory of God and His glorious Mother, the Virgin Mary, and of the holy angels, with our penances we may merit from Christ the grace to consecrate this blessed mountain."

St. Francis then took with him Brother Masseo da Marignano of Assisi, a man of great wisdom and eloquence; Brother Angelo Tancredi da Rieti, a man of very noble birth who in the world had been a knight; and Brother Leo, a man of great simplicity and purity, whom St. Francis dearly loved and to whom he revealed his every secret. With these three brothers, St. Francis began to pray, and after the prayer, he asked that he and his chosen companions be remembered in the prayers of the friars who stayed behind. He then left with those three, in the name of the crucified Jesus Christ, to go to Mount Alverna.

On the way St. Francis called one of those three companions, Brother Masseo, and said to him: "You, Brother Masseo, will be our guardian and superior during this journey as long as we travel and stay together; and during this time we will either recite the office, or speak of God, or keep silence. From now on we will not take thought for food or drink or sleep. When it will be time to rest and sleep, we will beg a bit of bread and stay and rest in that place which God will prepare for us." And the three companions bowed their heads and, making the sign of the cross, started on the way.

The first evening they came to a shelter of friars and there they rested; the second evening, in part because of the bad weather and in part because of their tiredness, unable to reach any shelter of the friars or any castle or house, and night coming fast upon the bad weather, they took refuge in an abandoned church, and rested there.

As his companions were sleeping, St. Francis began to pray, and as he persevered in prayer, there appeared in the early hours of the night a great multitude of fierce demons, with great noise and confusion, molesting him and waging battle against him. One took him from one side, another from the other. One pulled him up, another down. One threatened him with one thing, another reproached him for another. In many ways they sought to distract him from prayer but because God was with him, they could not. And when St. Francis had endured this attack at length, he began to cry out aloud: "O damned spirits, since you can only do what the hand of God allows you to do, I tell you that in the name of the Omnipotent God you may do to my body what God allows and I will gladly endure it, for I have no greater enemy than my body. If, therefore, you wish to avenge yourselves on my enemy, you do me a great service."

Then the demons with great force and fury took him and began to drag him through the church and to do him even greater violence than before. And St. Francis then began to shout and cry out: "My Lord Jesus Christ, I thank you for the great love and charity that You show toward me, for it is a sign of great love when the Lord punishes His servant for all his defects in this world, so that he will not be punished in the next. And I am joyfully disposed to endure all the punishments and adversities that You, my God, wish to send me for my sins."

Then the demons, confused and overcome by his constancy and patience, departed. St. Francis, in fervor of spirit, left the church and entered a nearby wood and there threw himself into prayer and, beating his breast and weeping, sought to find Jesus Christ, the beloved bridegroom of his soul. And when he finally found Him in the depths of his soul, he reverently prayed to Him as to his Lord, answered to Him as to his Judge, prayed to Him as to his father, spoke to Him as to his friend. During that night and in that wood, his companions, who had awakened and were listening and watching what he was doing, saw and heard him tearfully and devoutly pray for divine mercy for sinners. They also saw him weep and cry out aloud over the Passion of Christ, as if he were bodily present. During that same night they saw him pray with his arms folded in the form of a cross, raised from the ground for a long period of time, surrounded by a luminous cloud.

And so he passed that entire night in this holy devotion, without sleep. The following morning his companions, knowing that because of the fatigue of the night and the lack of sleep St. Francis was very weak and could hardly walk, went to a poor farm laborer of those parts and asked him, out of the love of God, to lend them his donkey for Brother Francis, their father, who could no longer go on foot.

When this laborer heard Brother Francis mentioned, he asked: "Are you of those brothers of Francis of Assisi, of whom people speak so well?" The friars answered that they were and that they were truly asking for the donkey for him. Then this good man with great devotion and solicitude prepared the donkey and led it to St. Francis and reverently helped him to mount; and they went on, the laborer following them after the donkey.

And after they had gone on a while, the peasant said to St. Francis; "Tell me, are you Brother Francis of Assisi?"

St. Francis answered that he was.

"Try, then," said the peasant, "to be as good as you are

believed to be by the people, because they have great faith in you; do not deceive them."

When he heard these words St. Francis did not feel indignant at being admonished by a peasant and did not say to himself; "What sort of fool is this who admonishes me?" as many haughty ones who wear the habit today would say. He immediately leaped down from the donkey, knelt down before the peasant, kissed his feet, and humbly thanked him for having deigned to admonish him in charity. Then the peasant, together with the companions of St. Francis, lifted him from the ground with great devotion, set him back on the donkey, and proceeded on their way.

When they were halfway up the mountain, since it was very hot and the climb was tiring, the peasant became very thirsty and began to call after St. Francis; "Poor me, I am dying of thirst; if I do not get something to drink immediately I will faint."

St. Francis stepped down from the donkey and began to pray, and stayed on his knees with his arms raised to Heaven for a long time until he knew that God had granted his request. He then said to the peasant: "Hurry, run over to that stone, and there you will find living water that Jesus Christ in this hour, out of His mercy, has made spring from it."

The peasant ran to the place that St. Francis pointed out to him and found a beautiful spring gushing forth from the hard rock. He drank copiously and was comforted, and it was quite evident that that spring was brought forth miraculously by God in answer to the prayers of St. Francis, because neither before nor after was a spring of any kind to be found within any distance from that place. After this, St. Francis and his companions and the peasant thanked God for the miracle and continued on their way.

As they approached the foot of Mount Alverna, it pleased St. Francis to rest a while under an oak that was near the path and is still there now. As he sat under it St. Francis studied the nature of the place and the surroundings, and as he was looking out over the valley there came a great multitude of many diverse birds who showed great joy and happiness by their singing and the beating of their wings. They surrounded St. Francis. Some alighted on his head, some on his arms, some on his shoulders, some on his lap, and some at his feet. His companions and the peasant, seeing this, marveled.

And St. Francis joyfully said: "I believe, my dearest brothers, that it pleases our Lord Jesus Christ that we live on this solitary mountain, since our sisters and brothers the birds show such happiness at our coming."

And after he had said these words, they walked farther up and they finally came to the place his companions had first chosen.

And so much for the first consideration, of how St. Francis came to the holy mountain of Alverna.

> *On the second consideration; that is, how St. Francis lived with his companions, how he struggled with the devil, and how God visited them.*

The second consideration treats of the way of life of St. Francis with his companions on Mount Alverna.

When Messer Orlando heard that St. Francis had come up to dwell on Mount Alverna with three companions he was extremely happy. On the following day, together with many people from his castle, he came to visit St. Francis; and they brought with them bread and wine and other necessary things for him and his companions.

When they came to the top of the mountain they found St. Francis and his companions in prayer, and Messer Orlando went over to them and greeted them. Then St. Francis stood up and with great joy and charity received Messer Orlando and those with him, and afterward spoke to him at length. After St. Francis had thanked him for his visit and the gift of the holy mountain, he begged him to have a small cell made at the foot of a very beautiful beech tree that was a stone's throw from the friars' shelter, because that place seemed to him conducive to prayer. And Messer Orlando had that done immediately. Since night was approaching, however, and the time had come for them to leave, St. Francis preached to them a while.

Before leaving, Messer Orlando called St. Francis and his companions aside and said to them; "My dearest brothers, I do not want you to suffer any bodily need in this wild place because that would distract you from things of the spirit. I want you, on all occasions, to send unhesitatingly to my house for your every need. If you were not to do so I

should consider it an offense." Having said this, he left with
his company and returned to the castle.

Then St. Francis had his companions sit down, and he
taught them the way of life they or whoever would wish to
live the religious life of the hermit should follow. Among
others things he specifically laid upon them the observance
of holy poverty, saying: "Do not so dwell on the charitable
offer of Messer Orlando that you will offend our lady, Lady
Poverty. Know for certain that the more we shun poverty,
the more the world will shun us and the more we will suffer.
But if we strongly embrace poverty, the world will follow us
and will nourish us generously. God has called us to this
holy Order for the salvation of the world and has placed
this pact between us and the world; that we give a good
example to the world and that the world provide us with our
necessities. Therefore let us persevere in our holy poverty,
for it is a way of perfection, a guarantee of eternal riches."

And he finished with the words: "This is the way of life I
impose on myself and on you. Now, because I see death
approaching, I mean to stay in solitude and gather myself
in God, and weep before Him for my sins. Brother Leo, when
it seems time to him, will bring me some bread and some
water. Under no circumstances are you to let a layman come
to me, but do you answer for me." Having said these words, he
gave them his benediction and went to the cell under the
beech tree; and his companions remained in the shelter
with the firm resolve to observe the commandments of St.
Francis.

A few days later, as St. Francis was beside the hut, looking
at the contour of the mountain and marveling at the great
crevices and openings in the boulders there, he began to
pray; and God revealed to him that those astounding crevices
were miraculously opened there at the time of the Passion
of Christ, when, in the words of the Evangelist, the very
stones were ripped asunder.

And God willed that these crevices appear especially on
Mount Alverna to signify that on this mountain the Passion
of our Lord Jesus Christ was to be renewed, in the spirit because of the Saint's compassionate love, and in his body
through the stigmata. No sooner had St. Francis received this
revelation than he closed himself within his cell in contemplation, seeking to understand the mystery of this revelation.

From that time on, because of constant prayer, St. Francis

began to taste more frequently the sweetness of divine contemplation. He was often lifted up to God, so that he was seen by his companions lifted bodily into the air and his spirit swept up to God. In these mystical raptures God revealed to him not only things present and future but even the secret thoughts and desires of the friars, as St. Francis' companion Brother Leo experienced that very day.

Brother Leo, being sorely tempted by the devil, had a great desire for some words written in the very hand of St. Francis. He felt that if he had them, the temptation would leave him in part or completely; and though he had this desire, out of reverence and shame he did not mention it to St. Francis. But that which Brother Leo did not reveal, the Holy Spirit did. St. Francis therefore called him, and had pen, ink, and paper brought. In his own hand he wrote a laud of Christ, according to the desire of the brother, and at the end signed it with the mark of the Tau and said to Brother Leo: "Here, my dearest brother, take this note and guard it diligently until death. May God bless you and keep you and guard you against every temptation. Do not be troubled because you are subject to temptations, for the more you are besieged by temptations the more I consider you a servant and friend of God and the more I love you. For truly I tell you that no one is to consider himself a perfect friend of God until he has passed through many temptations and tribulations."

When Brother Leo received this note with great devotion and faith, all temptation immediately left him, and returning to the shelter he joyfully told the companions of the grace God had shown him in having him receive that note from the very hand of St. Francis. The friars put the paper aside and guarded it carefully; and they worked many miracles with it.

From that hour on, Brother Leo, with great purity and good intention, began earnestly to study the life of St. Francis. And because of his purity, he many times earned the grace to see St. Francis swept up to God and raised bodily from the earth—at times to the height of three arm-lengths, at times four, on occasion as high as the tip of the beech tree, and once so high in the sky and so surrounded by radiance that he could barely see him. And what did this simple friar do when St. Francis was lifted off the ground just high enough so that he could reach him?

He would approach softly, embrace him, and kiss his feet, saying tearfully: "My God, have mercy on me, a sinner, and through the merits of this holy man let me find Your grace."

And on one occasion among others, as he was beneath the feet of St. Francis when the Saint was so high above the ground that he could not touch him, he saw a scroll written in golden letters descend from the heavens and alight on the head of St. Francis, and on it was written: "Here is the grace of God." And after he had read it, he saw it go up to Heaven again.

Because of the gift of grace that was in him, St. Francis was not only rapt up to God in ecstatic contemplation but was even at times comforted with angelic visions. One day, as St. Francis was meditating on his death and on the condition of his Order in years to come, he asked: "Lord God, after my death what will befall Your poor little family, which You have graciously entrusted to me, a sinner? Who will comfort it, who will correct it, who will pray for it?"

And as he was asking these questions there appeared an angel sent by God, who comforted him, saying: "In the name of God I tell you that the Rule of your Order will last until Judgment Day. There will be no sinner so great that if he loves your Order with all his heart he will not find mercy with God; and no one who persecutes your Order out of malice will be able to live long. Moreover, no very evil person in your Order, if he does not correct his life, will be able to persevere long in the Order. Therefore, do not become sad if you see in the Order some brothers who are not good, who do not observe the Rule as they should; and do not think that this Order will fail. There will always be many who will perfectly observe the life of Christ's gospel and the purity of the Rule and they, after this corporal life, will go to eternal life without passing through Purgatory. Others will observe it less perfectly, and before they go to Paradise they will go to Purgatory, but God, because of your merits, will shorten the time of their purgation. But as for those who do not observe the Rule at all, have no concern for them, says God, because He has no concern for them." And the angel departed and St. Francis remained much comforted and consoled.

As the feast of the Assumption of Our Lady approached, St. Francis sought a more solitary and secret place in which he could in greater seclusion offer the forty-day fast of St. Michael the Archangel, which began with the feast of the Assumption. He called Brother Leo and said: "Go and stay at the door of the oratory of the shelter of the brothers. When I call, come."

Brother Leo did so, and St. Francis stayed a while and then cried out loudly.

When Brother Leo heard him call him, he went to him and St. Francis said to him: "Son, let us find a more secret place, where you cannot hear when I call you."

And when they had searched, they saw on the side of the mountain, on the southern side, a secret and very appropriate place for his purpose; but they could not get to it because there was a deep and terrifying crevice before it. However, with a great effort they placed a log there as a bridge and thus passed over to it.

St. Francis then called for the other brothers and told them how he intended to pass the Lent of St. Michael in that solitary place and asked them to build a little hut for him there, so that if he were to cry out they would not hear him. Then St. Francis said to them: "Go to your shelter and leave me here alone, because with the help of God I hope to pass this fast without noise or distraction. Let none of you come to me. You, however, Brother Leo, will come once a day to me with a bit of bread and water and you will come during the night before matins. You will come silently, and when you are at the other side of the bridge you will say, '*Domine, labia mea aperies.*' And if I answer you, pass over, come to the cell, and we shall recite matins together. If I do not respond, leave at once."

And St. Francis said this because at times he was so lifted up to God that he could not hear or feel anything bodily. After this talk St. Francis gave them his blessing and they went back to their shelter.

When the feast of the Assumption came, St. Francis began to fast with harsh abstinence, abusing the body and comforting the spirit with fervent prayer, vigils, and discipline. In these prayers, which made him grow in virtue, he prepared his soul to see divine mysteries and splendors, and his flesh to sustain cruel battles with demons, against whom he often fought bodily.

And one time among others during that fast, St. Francis left his cell in fervor of spirit and went nearby to pray in a hollowed rock up very high, near a terrifying and fearful precipice. There the devil suddenly came to him with the sound of tempest and avalanche in a form terrible to behold, and struck him and sought to make him fall. St. Francis, having nowhere to flee, and unable to endure the fiendishly cruel expression of the devil, immediately turned his hands and face and his whole body to the rock and entrusted himself to God, groping with his fingers for something to which he could hold fast. As it pleased God, who never allows His servants to be tempted beyond their powers, the stone to which he was clinging immediately and miraculously hollowed itself out in the form of his body, receiving him as if he had pressed his hands and face into liquid wax. And so the stone was left with the imprint of the hands and face of the Saint; and thus with the help of God he was saved from the devil.

But what the devil could not then do to St. Francis, that is, to hurl him down, he did sometime later, after the death of St. Francis, to one of his dear and devoted friars. One day, in the very same place, the friar, out of devotion to St. Francis and the miracle there performed, was arranging some logs so that it would be possible to go there without danger. As he was carrying on his head a large log that he wanted to set there, the devil pushed him down. But God, who had saved St. Francis from falling, through his merits protected the devout friar in his fall. As he cried out to St. Francis in his fall, St. Francis suddenly appeared to the friar, held him, and placed him gently on the rocks without cut or bruise. The other brothers, having heard the friar's cry as he was falling and believing him to be dead and his body mutilated because of the height of the fall and the jagged rocks, had taken a stretcher and with great sorrow and tears had gone to the other side of the mountain to look for the remains of his body in order to bury them. While descending the mountain, they were met by the brother who had fallen, and he was singing aloud the *Te Deum laudamus*. And he told the marveling brothers in great detail how St. Francis had saved him. Then all the friars went with him to the shelter, singing the *Te Deum* with great fervor, praising and thanking God for the miracle that He had worked for His friar.

As St. Francis, then, was continuing his fast, he fought many battles with the devil, receiving at the same time many consolations from God, not only angelic visitations but also the ministrations of wild birds. During the entire fast a falcon who had made a nest near the cell woke him up every night before matins with his song and with the fluttering of wings, and would not leave until St. Francis rose to recite matins. When St. Francis was more tired than usual, or weak or sick, the falcon, like a discreet and compassionate person, would sing later. And St. Francis took great pleasure in this bird because the falcon's solicitude put idleness to flight and prodded him to prayer. During the day the falcon would remain tamely at his side.

But because St. Francis was greatly weakened by his great abstinence and as a result of his battles with the Devil, he sought to comfort his body with the spiritual food of the soul. He thus began to meditate on the limitless glory and joy of those blessed in eternal life, praying to God to concede him the grace of tasting a bit of that joy.

As he meditated thus, an angel, with a viola in his left hand and the bow in his right hand, appeared to him in great splendor. St. Francis, astonished, looked at him. The angel made an upward stroke on the viola and an ineffable melody sweetened the soul of St. Francis, suspending it from all bodily feelings. The Saint later told his companions that he wondered, had the angel then made the downward stroke, whether his soul, out of unbearable sweetness, would not have left his body.

And this concludes the second consideration.

> *On the third consideration; that is, how the glorious stigmata of the Blessed Christ came to St. Francis.*

With respect to the third consideration, that is, the seraphic apparition and the impression of the stigmata, one must know that one evening, as the feast of the most Holy Cross was approaching in the month of September, Brother Leo went to the usual place at the usual hour to recite matins with St. Francis. He stopped before crossing the bridge and said, as usual, "*Domine, labia mea aperies.*" When St. Francis did not answer, Brother Leo did not turn back, as St. Francis had ordered, but with good and holy intention crossed the bridge and quietly entered into the cell of the Saint; and not finding him, he thought that he might be somewhere in the woods, in prayer.

And so, by the light of the moon, he went quietly looking through the woods. Finally he heard the voice of St. Francis, and coming closer, he saw him kneeling, his face and arms raised to Heaven, and saying fervently: "Who are You, my most sweet God, and what am I, lowliest worm and most useless servant?" And he repeated these words again and again, and said nothing else.

Brother Leo marveled greatly at this, and raising his eyes and looking up to Heaven, he saw a most beautiful flaming torch come down and rest on the head of St. Francis; and a voice came out of the flame and spoke to St. Francis, but Brother Leo did not understand the words.

Seeing this and considering himself unworthy of remaining so close to the holy site of that admirable vision, and fearing, moreover, to offend or distract St. Francis from his consolation if he were heard, he quietly drew back and waited at some distance to see the end of it. And watching intently, he saw St. Francis stretch out his hands three times to the flame and finally, after a long time, he saw the flame turn back to heaven. Made happy and confident by the vision, Brother Leo returned to his cell.

Since he was excited and not very careful, St. Francis heard the sound of his feet on the leaves and called out, ordering him to wait and not move. Brother Leo obediently stood still and waited for him in great fear; and he was in such fear that, as he said later to his companions, he would rather have had the earth swallow him than wait for St. Francis, whom he expected to be angry with him; for Brother Leo took great care never to offend the Saint so as never to be deprived of his company.

Coming up to him, St. Francis asked: "Who are you?"

And Brother Leo, trembling, answered: "I am Brother Leo, my father."

And St. Francis said to him: "Why did you come here, Brother Lamb? Did I not tell you that you should not spy on me? Tell me, in the name of holy obedience, whether you saw or heard anything."

Brother Leo answered: "Father, I heard you speak and say many times, 'Who are You, oh my most sweet God, and what am I, lowliest worm and most useless servant?'" And kneeling before St. Francis, Brother Leo accused himself of disobedience, and with many tears asked forgiveness. Then he reverently begged that St. Francis explain the words he had heard and tell him of those he had not heard.

St. Francis, seeing that God had revealed or conceded to humble Brother Leo the grace to see certain things because of his simplicity and purity, deigned to reveal and explain to him what he asked, and he said: "Know, Brother Lamb of Jesus Christ, that when I was speaking those words you heard, two lights were being shown to my soul: one, the knowledge of myself, the other the knowledge of the Creator. When I was saying, 'Who are You, my most sweet God?' I was then in a light of contemplation in which I saw the abyss of the infinite goodness and wisdom and power of God; and when I was saying, 'What am I, etc.' I was in the light of contemplation in which I saw the tearful depths of my own wretchedness and misery. That is why I was saying, 'Who are You, Lord of infinite goodness and wisdom and power, who deigns to visit me, an abominable, vile worm?' God was in the flame that you saw, and He spoke to me under the form He assumed when He spoke to Moses.

"Among other things that He said to me, He asked me to give Him three gifts, and I answered, 'Lord, my Lord, I am all Yours. You know well that I have only the tunic and the cord and the cloth that warms my legs, and these three things are also Yours. What then can I offer and give to Your Majesty?'

"Then God said to me, 'Look in your lap.'

"I looked there and I found a golden ball and offered it to God, and I did so three times, as God had ordered. I then knelt three times and blessed and thanked God, who had given me something to offer. And then I suddenly understood that those three offerings signified holy obedience, lofty poverty, and resplendent charity, which God through His grace has granted me to observe so perfectly that in no way does my conscience reproach me.

"When you saw me put my hand in my lap and offer these three virtues to God, symbolized by the three golden balls that God had placed in my lap, God strengthened my soul, because of which I always praise and magnify Him with my heart and tongue. These are the words that you heard, and the thrice raising of the arms that you saw. But see to it, Brother Little Lamb, that you no longer spy on me. Return to your cell with the blessing of God and have solicitous care for me; for in a few days God will do such great and marvelous things on this mountain that all the world will marvel, for He will do new things such as He has done to no creature in this world."

And after these words, he had the book of the gospels brought to him, because God had revealed to him that in opening the Gospels three times he would know what God would do with him. When the book was brought to him, St. Francis began to pray; and after the prayer he had Brother Leo open the book three times in the name of the most Holy Trinity. And as it pleased Divine Providence, all three times there appeared before him passages on the Passion of Christ. He understood, then, that as he had followed Christ in his life, so he was to follow Him and conform to Him in the afflictions and sorrows of the Passion before he was to pass from this life.

And from that time on, St. Francis began to taste more fully the sweetness of divine contemplation and visitations. And among such visitations was one, in this form, that prepared him to receive the sacred stigmata. The day before the feast of the Holy Cross in the month of September, as St. Francis was praying alone in his cell, the angel of God appeared to him and said: "I exhort you to prepare yourself in humility and patience to submit to what God wills to do with you."

St. Francis answered: "I am prepared to endure patiently whatever my Lord wishes to do to me." And the angel departed.

On the following day, the day of the feast of the Holy Cross, in the morning, before daybreak, St. Francis began to pray in front of the entrance of his cell, turning his face toward the east and praying in these words: "O my Lord Jesus Christ, I beg of You to concede me two graces before I die. One, that I will feel in my body and soul while still living, and as much as possible, that suffering which You, dear Jesus, endured in Your most bitter Passion. The second is that I will feel in my heart, as much as possible, the love with which You, the Son of God, were aflame, so as to willingly suffer for us sinners." And remaining in this prayer for a long time, he understood that God would grant his wish, and to the extent that He could grant it to a simple creature, both prayers would be answered.

Having received this promise, St. Francis began to contemplate devoutly the Passion and the infinite charity of Christ; and the fervor of devotion so grew in him that he was transformed into Christ through love and compassion. As he remained in this contemplation, that same morning he saw coming toward him a Seraph with six fiery resplendent wings, approaching him in swift flight. The Saint could make Him out and saw clearly that he had the likeness of a Crucified Man, and His wings were so placed that two were above the head, two were arched in flight, and the other two covered His entire body.

Seeing this, St. Francis was greatly frightened, and at the same time filled with joy and pain and wonder. He took great joy in the gentle aspect of Christ, who appeared to him so tenderly, and he savored that intimacy. But on the other hand, seeing Him crucified on the cross, he felt a limitless compassion. He greatly marveled at this extraordinary and amazing vision, realizing that the sufferings of the Passion contrasted with the immortality of the seraphic spirit. As he wondered, it was revealed to him that the vision was shown to him in such a form so that he would know that he was to be completely transformed into a likeness of the crucified Christ, not by a bodily martyrdom but through spiritual fire.

During this admirable vision it seemed that the entire mountain of Alverna blazed with a splendid light, which lit up all the surrounding mountains and valleys as if the sun were shining. And the shepherds who were keeping watch in those parts, seeing the mountain aflame and a great light all around, were greatly frightened, as they later told the brothers; and they said that the flame had lasted on Mount Alverna for more than an hour. Similarly, because of the splendor of that light, which shone through the windows of the houses nearby, a group of muleteers on their way to Romagna, thinking that the sun had risen, got up and saddled and loaded their beasts, and as they were on their way they saw that light die and the natural sun rise in the heavens.

In this seraphic vision, Christ revealed certain secret and profound things to St. Francis that the Saint did not want to reveal to anyone during his lifetime. (He did so, as it is later shown, after his death.) Christ said: "Do you know what I have done to you? I have given you the stigmata, the signs of My Passion, so that you will be My standard-bearer. And just as I, on the day of My death, descended into Hell and freed all the souls I found there by virtue of My stigmata, so I concede to you that every year, on the anniversary of your death, you may go to Purgatory and there free, by virtue of your stigmata, all the souls of your three Orders: that is, the Friars Minor, the Sisters, and the Third Order, and even others who were devoted to you. Bring them to the glory of Paradise, so that you will conform yourself to Me in death as you have in life."

When this admirable vision left him, St. Francis felt a great burning in his heart, the flame of the love of God. And Christ left in his flesh a marvelous image and trace of His Passion. For suddenly in the hands and feet of St. Francis there began to appear the marks of nails such as he had just seen in the body of the crucified Christ who had appeared to him in the form of a Seraph. The hands and feet seemed to have been pierced through the center by nails, the heads of which protruded from the palms of the hands and the soles of the feet; and their points came out the other side of the hands and feet and were twisted and bent back into the flesh, so that one could put a finger through that bent part of the nail as through a ring; and the heads of the nails were rounded and black. Similarly, on his right side there opened a spear wound, red and bloody, which often bled and made his habit and his leg cloths bloody.

Before his companions learned from him what had happened, they had noticed that he never uncovered his hands or his feet, and that he could not put his feet on the ground. Later, when they washed his habit and his leg cloths and found them bloody, they fully understood that in his hands and in his feet and in his side he had impressed on him the image and likeness of our Lord Jesus Christ crucified.

And although St. Francis sought to conceal those glorious stigmata so clearly impressed on his flesh, the Saint also recognized that he could hardly conceal them from the companions close to him. He feared, though, to speak the secrets of God, and was in great doubt as to whether or not he should reveal the seraphic vision and the impressing of the holy stigmata.

Finally, for reasons of conscience, he called some of his closest brothers to him and discussed this problem with them in general terms, not alluding directly to what happened but asking their advice. Among those friars was one of great sanctity, Brother Illuminato. Truly illumined by God and understanding that St. Francis must have seen marvelous things, he said: "Brother Francis, know that God shows you His secrets not for you alone but even more for others; and therefore you are right in feeling that if you hide what God has revealed to you for the benefit of others, you are at fault." Then St. Francis, moved by these words, with great awe told them in detail of the vision, adding that Christ, who had appeared to him, had revealed to him certain truths that he was not to divulge while he still lived.

And although those holy wounds, inasmuch as they were impressed by Christ, gave his heart great joy, they nevertheless gave intolerable pain to his flesh. Out of necessity he chose Brother Leo, who was the simplest and the purest among others and to whom he had revealed all, to see and touch and bandage with strips of cloth those holy wounds, to lessen the pain and to stop the bleeding. He let these strips of cloth be changed frequently, even every day when he was very ill, but not during the period from Thursday evening to Saturday morning. He did not want any human remedy or medicine to mitigate the pain of the Passion of Christ, which he carried about in his body, during the time when our Lord and Saviour Jesus Christ had for us been taken and crucified, had died and been buried.

It happened at times that when Brother Leo changed the cloth on the wound in his side, St. Francis, because of the pain that he felt as the bloody cloth was being removed, would put his hand to the chest of Brother Leo; and in the touch of those holy hands, Brother Leo felt such sweet devotion in his heart that he would almost faint.

In conclusion, with respect to this third consideration, when St. Francis finished the fast of St. Michael the Archangel he prepared himself, following a divine revelation, to return to St. Mary of the Angels. And he called Brother Masseo and Brother Angelo and, after many words and holy teachings, entrusted to them that holy mountain, telling them that he had to return with Brother Leo to St. Mary of the Angels. Taking his leave of them and blessing them in the name of the crucified Jesus, he yielded to their pleas and extended to them his most holy hands adorned with the glorious stigmata, so that they might see, touch, and kiss them. Leaving them greatly solaced, he departed and went down the holy mountain. In praise of Christ. Amen.

*On the fourth consideration; that is, how St.
Francis left Alverna and, on the way to St. Mary
of the Angels, worked numerous miracles.*

As for the fourth consideration, one must know that after
the love of Christ had perfectly transformed St. Francis to
the true image of the crucified Christ, and after the Saint had
completed the forty-day fast in honor of St. Michael the
Archangel on the holy mountain of Alverna, he descended
the mountain. He took with him Brother Leo and a devout
peasant, on whose donkey the Saint rode because he could
not go on foot on account of the nails in his feet.

Since the shepherds had spoken of seeing Mount Alverna
all aflame and that this was a sign that God had performed
a great miracle for St. Francis, the fame of his sanctity
had spread throughout the countryside. Therefore the people
of the surrounding parts, hearing that the Saint was passing
through, came to see him; and men and women, young
and old, with great devotion sought to touch him and kiss
his hands. Unable to deny himself to the devotion of the
people, the Saint nevertheless did try to conceal the holy
stigmata; he put thick bandages over the wounds on his hands
and then covered the hands with his sleeves, extending only
his uncovered fingers to be kissed.

But although he sought to conceal the signs of the glorious
stigmata and to flee every occasion for worldly glory, it
pleased God to work many miracles to His own glory by
virtue of the stigmata, particularly on the journey from
Mount Alverna to St. Mary of the Angels, and later in many
parts of the world during the Saint's life and after. Thus, their
hidden and marvelous virtue, and the great charity and
mercy of God toward him on whom He had wondrously bestowed the stigmata, were manifest to the world in clear and
evident miracles, some of which we will here mention.

As St. Francis approached a house on the outskirts of
Arezzo, there appeared before him, weeping aloud, a woman with her child in her arms. The child was eight years old
and had been suffering from dropsy for four years, and his
stomach was so swollen that when he was standing he could
not see his feet. This woman placed her son before St. Francis
and pleaded that he pray to God for him. The Saint began to
pray and, after the prayer, placed his hand on the stomach of the child. Immediately the swelling went away and he

was made well and given back to his mother. She received him with great joy and took him home with her, thanking God and St. Francis; and she gladly showed her cured child to all of those who came to her house to see him.

That same day St. Francis passed through the hamlet of San Sepolcro, and before he approached the castle, crowds from the castle and from the houses came toward him, many of them with olive branches in their hands, shouting: "Here is the Saint, here is the Saint!" And the people devoutly wanted to touch him, and they pressed about him on all sides. But he moved on, his soul lifted up and rapt in God; and although he was touched and pushed and pulled by the people, he heard nothing that was said or done around him, nor did he notice that he was passing by that castle or that particular district.

When he had passed through the hamlet and the crowds had gone back to their homes, near a house for lepers more than a mile past the hamlet he came to himself, as if returning from another world, and asked his friend: "When will we be near the hamlet?" His soul had been fixed and rapt in the contemplation of heavenly things, and he had not heard terrestrial sounds nor had he been aware of changes in time and place and persons. And this happened many other times, as his companions could attest.

That evening St. Francis came to the shelter of Mount Casale, where there was a brother so cruelly afflicted and so horribly wracked by the pain of sickness that his illness seemed more a tribulation and torment from the devil than a natural infirmity. At times he would throw himself on the ground, trembling and foaming at the mouth, and then all the joints of his body would stiffen or flail about or bend. Other times he would touch the nape of his neck with his heels, leap upwards, and soon after fall supine. Seated at the table and hearing from the friars of this wretchedly sick brother, who had no hope of being cured, the Saint had compassion on him. He took a piece of the bread that he was eating and made the sign of the cross over it with his holy stigmatized hands and sent it to the sick brother, who no sooner ate it than he was perfectly cured and no longer suffered from that illness.

On the following morning St. Francis sent two of the brothers from that shelter to Alverna, and with them the peasant who had come along with him, walking behind the donkey that he had loaned to St. Francis. The brothers went with the peasant, and when some of the people from near Arezzo saw them from a distance they were very joyful, thinking that it was St. Francis, who had passed there two days before. One of their women, who had been in labor for three days and could not give birth, was dying, and they thought that if St. Francis could place his holy hands on her, she would be delivered of her child and would be well again. But as the friars approached, the people realized that St. Francis was not among them and they were very sorrowful; but where the Saint was bodily absent, his power was not, because their faith was not wanting. Wondrous thing! The woman was dying and her countenance already bore the traces of death, but the people asked the friars if they had anything that had been touched by the most holy hands of St. Francis. The friars sought to remember and looked about diligently, but could find absolutely nothing that St. Francis had touched with his own hands except the halter of the donkey on which he had ridden. The people took this halter with great reverence and devotion and placed it on the body of the pregnant woman, calling on the name of St. Francis and entrusting her to his care. And no sooner was the halter placed on her than she was freed from all danger and she gave birth easily, happily, and well.

After St. Francis remained a few days in this place, he left and went to Città di Castello. There, many townspeople brought before him a woman who had been possessed for a long time, and they humbly prayed him to free her, for she had been troubling the quarter with her painful cries, ghastly shrieks, and doglike howls. St. Francis first prayed and then made the sign of the cross on her and ordered the devil to leave her; and the devil did so, and the woman was left sound in body and mind.

And as the fame of this miracle spread among the people, another woman with great faith brought her child to him. The child was sick with a cruel sore and his mother devoutly pleaded with St. Francis to make a sign over him with his hands. St. Francis, seeing her devotion, took this child and lifted up the bandage on the sore and blessed him, making the sign of the cross three times over the sore. With his own hands he fixed the bandage in place again and gave the child back to his mother; and since it was evening, she put him to bed. In the morning she went to take the child from the bed and found the bandage off. She looked at him and found him perfectly healed, as if he had never had a sore, except that where it used to be, the flesh had grown in the shape of a red rose. This rose was more an evidence of the miracle than a remnant of the sore, because it remained there for the boy's whole life and made him think often and devoutly of St. Francis, who had cured him.

At the request of the townspeople, St. Francis lived there for a month, and he worked many miracles during that time. He then left to go to St. Mary of the Angels with Brother Leo and another good man who loaned him a donkey on which to ride. Because of the poor roads and the great cold, although they traveled all day, they were unable to reach a place of shelter for the night. Forced by the dark and the bad weather, they found shelter under the brow of an overhanging rock and waited for the snow to stop and for day to come.

The good man who had brought the donkey could not sleep because of the cold, for he was not warmly dressed, and there was no way to make a fire. And he began to complain quietly to himself. Crying from the cold, he almost murmured against St. Francis, who had led him to this place. St. Francis heard him and had compassion on him. In great fervor of spirit, he extended his hand to the man and touched him. Wondrous thing! No sooner had he touched him with the hand that had been warmed and aflame with seraphic fire than all cold left the man, and he felt such warmth within him and without that he thought he was near the mouth of a burning furnace. Instantly solaced in body and soul he fell asleep, and according to what he said later, he slept that whole night until morning more comfortably between the rocks and the snow than he had ever slept in his own bed.

They walked all of the next day and arrived at St. Mary of the Angels. When they were close, Brother Leo looked up, and turning toward the shelter of St. Mary, he noticed a beautiful cross with the figure of the Crucified One go before St. Francis, who was walking in front of him. And the cross moved with St. Francis, going when he went and stopping when he stopped. Such radiance shone from that cross that it lit up not only St. Francis' face but all the road around him. And the light lasted until St. Francis entered the shelter of St. Mary.

When they arrived, St. Francis and Brother Leo were received by the brothers with great joy and charity. And from that time on, until his death St. Francis lived most of the time in the shelter of St. Mary. The fame of his sanctity and of his miracles continued to spread throughout the Order and throughout the world, although he, out of profound humility, concealed as much as he could the gifts and graces of God and called himself a great sinner.

Brother Leo marveled greatly at this and once foolishly thought to himself: "This man calls himself a great sinner in public. He came to this Order already a man, and he is greatly honored by God, but nevertheless he never in private confesses himself guilty of sins of the flesh; could he be a virgin?" Since he had a strong desire to know the truth of the matter but did not dare ask St. Francis, he had recourse to God and insistently prayed to Him to find out. Because of his many prayers he was heard, and in a vision he was assured that St. Francis was truly a virgin in the body. In this vision he saw St. Francis on a high and lofty place that no one could ascend to, and he was told that that lofty and excellent place represented the excellence of the virginal chastity of St. Francis, which was appropriate in the flesh that was to be adorned by the sacred stigmata of Christ.

At the time St. Francis, aware that the stigmata were sapping his strength and that he could no longer direct and rule the Order, hastily called for a General Chapter. When the chapter was convened, he humbly excused himself to his brothers for the physical weakness that kept him from attending to the direction of the Order. He could not renounce the position of General because that was a papal appointment, and therefore he could not quit that office nor substitute another in his place without the express approval of the Pope. But he did install Brother Pietro Catani as his Vicar, entrusting the Order to him and to the provincial ministers with all possible affection.

Then St. Francis, comforted in spirit, raised his eyes and hands to Heaven and said: "To you, O Lord, I entrust my family, which You have until now committed to my care. Because of my infirmities, of which You know, my most gentle Lord, I can no longer care for it. I entrust my family to the provincial ministers; let them account to You on the

Day of Judgment if any brother will perish either because of their negligence or bad example or excessively harsh correction."

The words in which he excused himself for his sickness were, as it pleased God, understood by the brothers at the chapter as a reference to the stigmata, and none of them could hold back their tears of devotion. And from that day on, he left the care and the rule of the Order in the hands of his Vicar and the provincial ministers, and he said: "Now, since I have relinquished the care of the Order because of my infirmities, I am bound only to pray God for our Order and to give good example to the brothers. And I know in truth that if this infirmity were to leave me, the most good that I could do for my Order would be to pray constantly that God govern, defend, and preserve it."

Now, although after receiving the stigmata St. Francis sought to hide them as well as he could and went about with his hands and feet covered, he could not prevent many friars from noticing them and touching them, especially the wound on his side, which he did his utmost to conceal. A brother who was caring for him induced him to remove his habit so as to shake off the dust, and when the Saint had done so the brother clearly saw the wound in his side. Quickly touching it with his hand, he felt with three fingers the size and depth of the wound. His Vicar, in a similar way and about the same time, also saw the wound.

But Brother Ruffino, a very great contemplative, of whom St. Francis once said that there was no more saintly person in the world, and that because of that sanctity he loved him and wanted to please him in everything, had the surest knowledge of the stigmata. This Brother Ruffino had a threefold confirmation of the stigmata and the special wound in the side. In the first place, he washed St. Francis' breeches, which were so long that by pulling them up the Saint could cover the wound on his right side. Looking at them very carefully, Brother Ruffino found that the breeches were always bloody on the right side, and he realized that that was due to blood flowing from that side. When St. Francis became aware that he was spreading out the breeches to see the blood, he reproached him. Another time, as Brother Ruffino was rubbing St. Francis' back, he ran his hand near the wound in his side and inserted his fingers into it, so that St. Francis cried out in great pain: "God forgive you, Brother

Ruffino, why did you do that?" And a third time, Brother Ruffino insistently asked St. Francis to exchange habits with him in the name of charity. And the loving father accepted, drawing off his habit with difficulty and exchanging with Brother Ruffino, who clearly saw the wound in St. Francis' side as he took one off and put on the other.

Similarly, Brother Leo and many other brothers saw the stigmata of St. Francis during his lifetime. And although their sanctity and simple, honest words made them worthy of belief, nevertheless, in order to remove all doubts, these friars swore on the Holy Book that they had clearly seen the stigmata.

Some cardinals who were very close to him also saw them, and out of reverence for the stigmata of St. Francis, they composed beautiful and devout hymns and antiphons and prose works.

The Supreme Pontiff, Pope Alexander, preaching to the people and all the cardinals, among whom was the holy Brother Bonaventure, who was a cardinal, said and affirmed that he had seen the holy stigmata of St. Francis with his own eyes during the Saint's lifetime.

And Lady Jacopa dei Settesoli of Rome, who was the most important woman in Rome at this time and extremely devoted to St. Francis, came to see the Saint before his death; and after his death she too saw the stigmata and kissed them many times with great reverence. She had come from Rome to Assisi because of a divine revelation as to the imminent death of St. Francis, and it came about in the following way.

A few days before his death St. Francis was sick in Assisi in the palace of the bishop where he was with a number of his companions; and there, in spite of his illness, he frequently sang lauds in praise of Christ. And one of his companions said to him: "Father, you know that these people have great faith in you and consider you a holy man. For them to believe that you are what they think you to be, you should in this affliction think of death and, since you are so gravely ill, weep rather than sing. You must know that your singing and ours, which you force upon us, can be heard by many, inside and outside the palace, and because of you this palace is guarded by many armed men, who could be scandalized by your singing. I think, therefore," said this brother, "that it would be well if you left here and we all returned to St. Mary of the Angels, because we are not comfortable here among laymen."

St. Francis answered: "My dear brother, you know that two years ago, while we were still in Foligno, God revealed to you the date of my death, and He also revealed it to me. He told me that a few days from now, during this illness, the set time will be expired, and He also assured me of the remission of my sins and the blessedness of Paradise. Until the time of that revelation I used to weep at the thought of death and of my sins, but since that revelation I have been so filled with joy that I can no longer weep. I sing and will continue to sing to God, who has given me His grace and has assured me of the glory of Paradise. But I do consent, and it pleases me, to leave this palace. But you must find some way of carrying me, because my sickness does not allow me to walk."

Then the friars took him in their arms and carried him, accompanied by many townspeople. And as they came to a hostel on the way, St. Francis said to those who were carrying him: "Put me on the ground and have me face the city."

And they did, and he turned his face toward Assisi and blessed it with many benedictions, saying: "May God bless you, holy city, because through you many souls will be saved, and many servants of God will reside in you, and from you many will be chosen for the kingdom of eternal life." And after he had said these words he had himself carried up to St. Mary of the Angels, and on arriving there, they took him to the sick room, and there he rested.

Then St. Francis called one of his companions to him and said: "My dearest brother, God has revealed to me that I will live with this sickness until a given day. You know that Lady Jacopa dei Settesoli, a most devout friend of our Order, would be exceedingly sorrowful if she heard of my death and she had not been present. Let her know, therefore, that if she wants to see me alive she must come immediately."

The brother answered: "You speak well, Father; considering the great devotion that she has for you, it would be wrong for her not to be present at your death."

"Go, then," said St. Francis, "and bring ink, paper, and pen, and write as I tell you."

And St. Francis dictated the following words: "To Lady Jacopa, Servant of God, from Brother Francis, little poor one of Christ, greetings and fellowship in the Holy Spirit, and in our Lord Jesus Christ. Know, my dearest, that the Blessed Christ, out of His grace, has revealed to me the end of my life, which will come shortly. And therefore, if you wish to see me alive, set out after reading this letter and hasten to St. Mary of the Angels; for if you do not come by that day you will no longer find me alive. Bring with you some rough cloth in which to wrap my body and the wax needed for burial. I also beg of you to bring to me some of those things to eat that you used to give me when I was sick in Rome."

As this letter was being written, God revealed to St. Francis that Lady Jacopa was coming to him and was approaching the shelter, and had with her all those things he had asked for in that letter. St. Francis accordingly told the brother who was writing the letter not to write further, because it was no longer necessary, and to put aside the letter. And the brothers marveled greatly that he did not want to finish the letter or send it. As they stood thus, there was a loud knocking at the door of the shelter and St. Francis sent the doorkeeper to open it; and on opening the door, he saw Lady Jacopa, the Roman noblewoman, with two of her senator sons and a great company of men on horseback.

They entered, and Lady Jacopa went straight to the sick room and to St. Francis. He found great joy and solace in seeing her, and so did she in seeing him alive and able to talk. Then she explained to him how God had revealed to her, as she was praying in Rome, the imminent approach of his death, and how he was to send for her and ask her for those things that she had brought with her; and then she brought those things to St. Francis and gave him some to eat.

After he had eaten and felt much better, Lady Jacopa knelt at the feet of St. Francis, and taking his feet, marked and adorned with the wounds of Christ, she kissed them with great devotion and bathed them in tears. And the friars who were standing nearby thought that in truth they were seeing Magdalen at the feet of Jesus Christ, and no one could draw her away.

Finally, after a long time, they led her away and took her aside, and they asked her how she had come so rapidly and how she had all the things necessary for the life and burial of St. Francis. Lady Jacopa answered that as she was praying in Rome one night, she heard a voice from Heaven say: "If you wish to find St. Francis alive, go to Assisi without delay. Take with you those things that you used to give him when he was sick, and those needed for burial." "And," she said, "I have done so."

Lady Jacopa stayed until St. Francis left this life and was buried, and at his burial she and her company paid him great honor, and paid for all that was needed. She then returned to Rome and a short time after died a holy death. Out of devotion to St. Francis she chose St. Mary of the Angels as her burial place, and wished to be brought there; and it was done according to her wishes. In praise of Christ. Amen.

### How many persons saw the stigmata of St. Francis.

At the death of St. Francis, not only Lady Jacopa and her sons and her company saw and kissed the glorious stigmata of St. Francis, but so did many citizens of Assisi. Among them was a great and famous nobleman by the name of Messer Jeronimo, who was as doubtful and skeptical as the Apostle Thomas had been toward Christ. In order to satisfy himself and others, in the presence of the brothers and laymen he daringly moved the nails in the hands and feet and rudely handled the wound in Francis' side. Thus he saw and was a witness to that truth, swearing on the Bible that he had seen and touched those wounds.

St. Clare and her sisters, who were present at his burial, also saw and kissed the glorious stigmata.

The glorious confessor of Christ, Messer St. Francis, passed from this life on Saturday, the third of October, in the year of the Lord 1226, and he was buried on Sunday. That year was the twentieth after his conversion, when he had begun to practice penance, and the second year after the impressing of the stigmata.

He was canonized in 1228 by Pope Gregory IX, who came personally to Assisi to canonize him. In praise of Christ. Amen.

And this suffices for the fourth consideration.

> *On the fifth consideration; that is, how a number of apparitions appeared to holy persons with respect to the sacred stigmata of St. Francis.*

The fifth and last consideration treats of a number of apparitions, revelations, and miracles that God worked and manifested after the death of St. Francis, in confirmation of his stigmata and of the day and hour that Christ impressed them on him.

It should be known that in the year 1282, on the third day of the month, Brother Filippo, Minister of Tuscany, by command of the Minister General, Brother Buonagrazia, asked Brother Matteo da Castiglione of Arezzo, a man of great sanctity, to tell what he knew of the day and the hour in which the holy stigmata were impressed by Christ on the body of St. Francis; for Brother Filippo had heard that Brother Matteo had received a divine revelation concerning this.

Brother Matteo, ordered in the name of holy obedience, answered thus: "Last year, in May, as I prayed one day in the cell of the shelter of Alverna where the Seraph is said to have appeared to the Saint, I devoutly beseeched God to reveal to someone the day, the hour, and the place in which the holy stigmata were impressed on the body of St. Francis. As I persevered in prayer beyond the usual hour for sleep, St. Francis appeared to me in a great light and said to me, 'Son, what are you praying to God for?' And I told him why. And he said to me, 'I am your father, Francis; do you recognize me?' 'I do, Father,' I said.

"Then he showed me the stigmata in his hands and feet and the wound on his side and said, 'The time has come in which God wishes His glory to be manifest, and wishes the brothers to know what they made no effort to know in the past. Know, then, that He who appeared to me was not an angel but Jesus Christ in the form of a Seraph, who with His hands impressed upon my body these five wounds as He received them in His body on the cross.

"'And it came about in the following way: the day before the feast of the Exaltation of the Holy Cross an angel appeared to me and told me in the name of God to prepare myself patiently for what God wished to do to me. And I answered that I was prepared to receive whatever it pleased God to do. On the following morning, that is, the morning of the feast of the Holy Cross, which fell that year on a Friday, I left my cell at daybreak with great fervor and came to pray in this very place where you are now, a place where I often prayed. As I prayed, there suddenly appeared from Heaven, amid a great rush of wind, a crucified Youth in the form of a Seraph with six wings. I humbly knelt in His wondrous presence and began to contemplate devoutly the boundless love of the crucified Jesus and the infinite pain of His Passion, and the sight of Him wrought such compassion in me that I seemed to feel that suffering in my very own body; and in His presence this entire mountain was as resplendent as the sun. And the vision hovered closer to me, and remaining in front of me, told me secret words that I have revealed to no one; but the time in which they will be revealed is now approaching. After some time, Christ departed and returned to Heaven, and I found myself marked with these wounds. Go,' said St. Francis, 'and be sure to tell these things to your Minister, for this is the work of God and not of man.' And when he had said this, St. Francis blessed me and returned to Heaven with a great multitude of resplendent youths."

Brother Matteo said he had seen and heard all of these things awake, and not in a dream, and when he was asked to do so out of holy obedience, he swore that it was so to the Minister General in his cell in Florence. In praise of Christ. Amen.

On another occasion a holy and devout brother, reading in St. Bonaventure's life of St. Francis the chapter on the stigmata, greatly wondered what those secret words might be that St. Francis had said he would not reveal to anyone while he still lived, the words that the Seraph had spoken to him. And this brother said to himself: "St. Francis did not want to tell us those words while he was still living, but if he were devoutly prayed to now, after his bodily death, he might tell us."

And from that time on, the devout brother began to pray God and St. Francis to reveal those words to him. Having persevered in this prayer for eight years, in the eighth year his wish was granted in the following way.

One day after mealtime, and after thanksgiving had been offered in church, as he was praying to God and St. Francis more devoutly than usual and with many tears, he was called by another friar, who told him in the name of the guardian to accompany him to town for some needs of the monastery. Not doubting at all that obedience is more meritorious than prayer, he had no sooner heard the order of the superior than he left his prayer and humbly went with the brother. And as it pleased God, in this act of prompt obedience he merited that which he had not merited with long prayer.

As soon as they came out of the door of the shelter, they met two foreign brothers who seemed to come from distant lands. One of them was young, the other old and thin; and both of them, because of the weather, were wet and splattered with mud. The obedient friar, having great compassion for them, said to his traveling companion: "My dearest brother, if we can delay our errand a bit, I beg you to let me first wash their feet, for these friars need to be greeted lovingly. I will wash the feet of this old friar, who has greater need of it, and you may wash those of the younger, and then we will go on our errand."

The brother yielded to the charity of his companion, and they turned back and greeted the strangers with great charity, and took them into the kitchen so that they could be warmed and dried; and they sat around the fire, with eight other brothers of the shelter.

After staying near the fire awhile, they took them aside to wash their feet, as they had planned. As the obedient and devout friar was washing the feet of the older brother and removing the mud, which was quite thick, he looked and saw the mark of the stigmata on the feet. Immediately, in amazement and joy, he hugged him tightly, crying out: "Are you Christ or St. Francis?"

The friars who were around the fire got up when they heard this and came to see, with great fear and reverence, the glorious stigmata; and the old brother granted their wish and allowed them to clearly see, touch, and kiss the stigmata. And as they continued to marvel in joy, he said to them: "Do not question and do not fear, my beloved brothers and sons. I am your father, Brother Francis, who according to the will of God founded three Orders. The brother who was cleaning my feet has been praying to me for eight years, and today more fervently than ever, to reveal to him those secret words that the Seraph said to me when I received the stigmata. I did not wish to reveal those words while I was still living, but today, at the command of God, because of his perseverance and the prompt obedience that made him leave the sweetness of prayer, I am sent by God to reveal to you what he has asked of me."

And turning to that brother, St. Francis said as follows: "Know, then, my beloved brother, that as I was on Mount

Alverna, absorbed in the memory of the Passion of Christ, I received the stigmata on my body from Christ in the seraphic apparition, and Christ said to me: 'Do you know what I have done? I have given you the marks of My Passion so that you will be My standard-bearer. Just as I on the day of My death descended into Limbo and took and brought to Heaven, by virtue of My stigmata, all the souls that I found there, similarly do I concede to you from this time on, so that you will be like Me in death as in life, that after having passed from this life you may on the anniversary of your death go to Purgatory and, in virtue of your stigmata, take out all the souls of your three Orders (that is, the Friars Minor, the Sisters, and the Third Order) and bring them to Heaven.' And as long as I lived in the world I did not reveal these words." And after having said these words, St. Francis and his companion immediately disappeared.

Later, many brothers heard all this from the eight brothers who were present at this vision and heard these words of St. Francis. In praise of Christ. Amen.

⌇

St. Francis once appeared on Mount Alverna to Brother Giovanni of Alverna, a man of great sanctity, as he was praying; and he stayed and spoke to him for a long period of time. Finally, before leaving, he said to him: "Ask of me what you wish."

And Brother Giovanni said: "Father, I beg that you tell me what I have sought to know for a long time; that is, what you were doing and where you were when the Seraph appeared to you."

Brother Francis answered: "I was praying in that place where the chapel of Count Simone da Battifolle is now, and I was asking two graces from my Lord Jesus Christ. One, that He concede to me that while still living I might feel in my body and in my soul, as much as possible, the pain that He had felt at the time of His anguished Passion. The second grace that I sought was to feel in my heart that unbounded love with which He burned, so as to suffer such anguish for us poor sinners. And God told me that He would grant my prayers to the extent that it was possible to concede them to creatures, and this promise was fulfilled in the stigmata."

Then Brother Giovanni asked him whether those secret words which the Seraph had told him were those the above-mentioned brother had reported, and which he claimed to have heard from St. Francis in the presence of eight brothers. St. Francis answered yes, that this was as the brother claimed.

Brother Giovanni then made bold to ask, considering the generosity of the Saint: "Father, I earnestly entreat you to allow me to see and kiss your glorious stigmata, not from any doubt of mine but because I have always desired to."

And St. Francis freely showed them to him and held them out to him, and Brother Giovanni clearly saw, touched, and kissed them.

Finally he asked him: "Father, how much solace did your soul feel when you saw the Blessed Christ coming to you and impressing upon you the sign of His most sacred Passion? Would to God that I could feel a bit of that sweetness!"

St. Francis replied: "Do you see these nails?"

And Brother Giovanni answered: "Yes, Father."

"Touch once more," said St. Francis, "the nail that is in my hand."

Then Brother Giovanni, with great reverence and with fear, touched that nail, and as he did so there came from it such perfume as a wisp of smoke from incense gives off. And the scent filled the body and soul of Brother Giovanni with such sweet joy that he was forthwith rapt up to God in ecstasy and became insensible to all things; and he remained thus from that time, tierce, until vespers. Brother Giovanni never spoke to anyone but his confessor about this vision and loving talk with St. Francis, until the time of his death; but at that time he revealed it to many brothers. In praise of Christ. Amen.

In the province of Rome a saintly and devout brother had this wondrous vision: a very dear friend of his, a brother, died one night and was buried the following morning outside the entrance of the chapter room; the surviving brother went into a corner of that room to pray for the soul of his dead friend. Persevering in tearful prayer while all the other brothers had retired to their cells at noon, he suddenly heard a great bustling about in the cloister outside. In great fear he looked toward the burial place of his friend and saw on the threshold of the chapter room St. Francis, and behind him a great multitude of brothers gathered around the grave.

He continued to look intently, and saw in the midst of them a fiercely burning flame, in the center of which was the soul of his dead friend. He looked around the cloister and saw Jesus Christ walking around it with a great company of angels and saints, and as he looked at all this with great wonder, he saw that whenever Christ passed before the chapter room St. Francis bowed, with all the brothers present, and said: "I beg of You, most holy Father and Lord, in the name of that ineffable charity which You showed for mankind with Your incarnation, to have pity on the soul of my brother, who is burning in that fire."

And Christ did not answer but walked on. When He came back a second time and walked past the chapter room, St. Francis knelt down with his brothers, as before, and prayed thus: "I beg of You, merciful Father and Lord, out of the boundless charity that You showed mankind when You died on the cross, to have mercy on my brother."

And again Christ passed on and did not grant his wish, and went around the cloister for the third time, and passed before the chapter room. Then St. Francis knelt down as before and showed Him his hands and feet and side and said: "I beg of you, merciful Father and Lord, in the name of the great pain and solace that I felt when You impressed these stigmata upon my flesh, to have mercy on the soul of my brother, who is in the fire of Purgatory."

And marvelously, when Christ was prayed to a third time by St. Francis, in the name of his stigmata, He stopped, considered the stigmata, and granted the Saint's wish, saying: "To you, Brother Francis, I concede the soul of your brother."

By this action He honored and testified to the glorious stigmata of St. Francis; for He clearly signified that the souls of his brothers in Purgatory are released from pain and brought to the glory of Paradise just as easily by virtue of the stigmata of St. Francis as by virtue of His own, in keeping with the words that Christ spoke when he impressed the stigmata on St. Francis.

And when Christ finished speaking, the fire in the cloister disappeared and the dead brother came to St. Francis, and with him and with Christ and with all that blessed, glorious company, went to Heaven. His friend, the brother who had prayed for him, seeing him freed from punishment and brought to Paradise, rejoiced greatly. Later he told the other brothers the story of the vision, and together they praised and thanked God. In praise of the crucified Christ. Amen.

A noble knight of Massa di Santo Piero by the name of Messer Landolfo, who was a devout follower of St. Francis and who received the habit of the Third Order from the Saint's hands, was assured of the death of St. Francis and of his glorious stigmata in the following way.

As St. Francis lay dying, the devil entered into a woman of that castle and cruelly tormented her. He made her speak so learnedly that she defeated in debate all the wise and erudite men who came to dispute with her. After leaving her free for two days, the devil came back the third day and afflicted her more cruelly than before. When Messer Landolfo heard about this he went to the woman and asked the devil within her why he had left for two days and then on his return tormented her more grievously than ever.

The devil answered: "When I left her, I met together with all of my companions in these parts and hastened to the death of the beggar Francis to argue with him and take his soul. But he was surrounded and defended by a great multitude of angels, greater than we in numbers; and so, when his soul was brought straight to Heaven and we turned back confused, I then paid back this wretched woman for the two days' liberty I had granted her."

Then Messer Landolfo adjured him in the name of God to tell the truth of the sanctity of St. Francis, who, he had said, was dead, and of St. Clare, who was living.

The devil answered: "I shall tell you, whether I wish to or not, the truth. God the Father was so indignant at the sins of this world that it seemed that in a short time He was to pass sentence on men and women and exterminate them all, if they did not correct themselves. But Christ, praying for sinners, promised to renew His life and Passion in one man; that is, in the poor and beggarly St. Francis, through whose life and doctrine He would bring many to the way of truth and penance. And now, to show the world what He wished to do with St. Francis, He has willed that the stigmata of His Passion, which He impressed on the Saint's body while he was still living, be seen and touched by many in his death. Similarly, the mother of Christ promised to renew her virginal purity and humility in a woman; that is, in St. Clare, so that by her example she would snatch many thousands of women from our hands. And so God's anger was mitigated by these promises, and He delayed His sentence."

Then Messer Landolfo, wishing to know with certainty whether the devil, who is the father of lies, was speaking the truth, and especially with respect to the death of St. Francis, sent one of his servants to St. Mary of the Angels in Assisi to find out whether St. Francis was living or dead. The servant arrived there, confirmed all, and returned to assure his lord that St. Francis had passed from this life at the very day and hour that the devil had mentioned. In praise of Christ. Amen.

Leaving aside all the miracles of the stigmata of St. Francis that are mentioned in the *Legenda* of St. Bonaventure, in conclusion of the fifth consideration it should be known that Pope Gregory IX, as he later acknowledged, once had doubts as to the wound in the side of St. Francis. One night St. Francis appeared to him and, raising his right arm a bit, showed the wound on his side and asked him for a vessel. When the Pope had a vessel brought, St. Francis had it placed under the wound on his side, and it truthfully seemed to the Pope that the vessel was filled to the very brim with the blood mixed with water that flowed from the wound.

And from that time on, all doubt left him, and with the advice of all the cardinals, he affirmed the stigmata of St. Francis and gave to the brothers a special privilege with a papal decree; and he did this at Viterbo in the eleventh year of his pontificate. The following year he granted a still more generous privilege. In addition, Pope Nicholas III and Pope Alexander both granted further privileges, and decreed that whoever would deny the stigmata of St. Francis might be dealt with as a heretic.

And let this suffice for the fifth and last consideration of the glorious stigmata of our holy father St. Francis. May God grant us the grace to follow his life in this world, so that by virtue of his glorious stigmata we will merit salvation in Paradise. In praise of the Blessed Christ. Amen.

# THE LIFE OF BROTHER JUNIPER

## CHAPTER I

*How Brother Juniper cut off the foot of a pig in order to give it to a sick man.*

Brother Juniper was one of the first companions and most elect disciples of St. Francis. He was a man of deep humility and of great fervor and charity, of whom St. Francis once said, speaking to his companions: "He who overcomes himself and the world, as does Brother Juniper, is a good Friar Minor."

Once, as Brother Juniper, inflamed with the love of God, was visiting a sick brother at St. Mary of the Angels, he asked him with great compassion: "Is there anything I can do to help you?"

The sick brother answered: "It would be a great solace to me if you were to get me a pig's foot."

Brother Juniper quickly answered: "Trust me. I will get it for you immediately."

And he left and took a knife—I believe it was a kitchen knife—and in great fervor of spirit he went into the field where there were pigs grazing, threw himself on one of them, cut off his foot, and fled, leaving the pig with a truncated leg. Once back, he washed and prepared and cooked the foot, going to great pains to prepare it well, and with great love brought this foot to the sick friar. And the sick friar ate it with great appetite, to the great joy and solace of Brother Juniper, who with great delight, in order to hearten and cheer the sick friar, told him in detail of how he had attacked the pig.

In the meantime, the swineherd who had been watching the pigs and who had seen this brother cut off the pig's foot, told his master about it with great bitterness. When the master learned about this, he came to the shelter of the brothers and vehemently called them hypocrites, thieves, counterfeiters, connivers, and evildoers. The man's reproaches drew forth St. Francis and all his brothers, and the Saint humbly apologized for his brothers' conduct, of which he had been ignorant, and in order to placate the man, promised to make good for the damage done. But the man's anger was not assuaged by St. Francis. With great ire and rudeness and threats he left the brothers, accusing them repeatedly of maliciously cutting off the pig's foot. He refused to accept apologies or reparation, and left in a fury.

And St. Francis, filled with prudence, wondered in his heart, as did many of the other friars: "Could Brother Juniper have done this out of indiscreet zeal?" He immediately had Brother Juniper called, and asked him: "Did you cut off a pig's foot in the wood?"

Brother Juniper, not like a person who had committed a fault but as one who had performed a great act of charity, joyfully answered: "My sweet father, I did in truth cut off a foot from a pig. I will tell you why, my father, if you will listen with sympathy. Out of charity one day I went to visit Brother so-and-so, who was sick . . ." And then he went on to tell him the entire story, concluding: "And I tell you that, considering the consolation and joy that our brother had from that foot, I think that if I had cut off a hundred feet from a hundred pigs I am sure that God would have approved."

St. Francis answered, and his words showed a zeal for justice: "O Brother Juniper, why did you make us the object of great scandal? The man has a right to complain and to be furious with us. Perhaps even now he is going about the city, taking away our good name because of your misdeed; and he has good reason. Therefore, I command you in the name of holy obedience to run after him and catch up with him. Throw yourself on the ground before him, acknowledge your guilt, and promise satisfaction to the point where he will no longer have cause to complain about us—for what you did was rash."

Brother Juniper was quite surprised at this admonition, although the brothers present marveled that he did not seem the least upset about it. But Brother Juniper believed that temporal things are of no value unless they are charitably shared with a neighbor, and so he answered: "Fear not, my father. I will repay him and I will satisfy him. And why should he be so upset, since this pig, whose foot I have cut off, belonged more to God than to him, and since great charity came of it?"

And so he began to run, and he caught up with the angry man, who had lost all patience; and he explained to him how and why he had cut off the pig's foot. He did so with fervor, exaltation, and joy, as if he had rendered the owner of the pig a great service and merited an ample reward from him. The owner, overcome with anger and fury, insulted Brother Juniper, calling him a mad and stupid little thief, and the worst type of villain.

Brother Juniper showed no concern for the insulting words. Although he took delight in those injuries, he thought that the man had not understood him well, because the story was for him occasion for joy and not wrath; consequently, he repeated the story and embraced the man and kissed him, telling him that all this had been done out of charity. He also begged him for the rest of the pig with such charity, simplicity, and humility that the man, in a change of heart, with many tears threw himself at Brother Juniper's feet. Acknowledging the harm done to the brothers and the insults given to them, he went and took this pig, killed it and cooked it, and with great devotion and many tears brought it to St. Mary of the Angels and gave it to those holy brothers to eat as compensation for the wrong done them.

St. Francis, considering the simplicity and patience of holy Brother Juniper in adversity, used to say to his companions and those surrounding him: "Would to God, my brothers, that I had a vast thicket of such junipers." In praise of Christ. Amen.

## CHAPTER II

*How Brother Juniper used his great power against the devil.*

The demons could not endure the deep humility and innocence of Brother Juniper, and this was demonstrated by the following incident. A possessed person, contrary to all his usual ways, began to run away from the main road and crisscrossed the surrounding territory for seven miles.

When his relatives, who had followed him with great concern because of his strange behavior, asked him why he acted thus, he answered: "The reason is this: since that foolish Brother Juniper was passing by that road, I knew that I could not endure his presence nor wait for him, and I fled to these places." When his relatives sought to confirm this story they found that, precisely as the devil said, Brother Juniper had come along at that hour.

This is why St. Francis, when he was asked to cure the diabolically possessed, would say, if the devils did not immediately leave at his command: "If you do not leave this creature immediately I will call Brother Juniper against you." Then the devil, fearing the presence of Brother Juniper and unable to endure the virtue and humility of St. Francis, would leave immediately.


## CHAPTER III

> *How Brother Juniper, by the wiles of the devil, was condemned to the gallows.*


Once, when the devil sought to frighten Brother Juniper, to scandalize him and to make him suffer, he appeared to a very cruel tyrant by the name of Niccolao, then warring on the city of Viterbo, and said: "My lord, guard your castle carefully. Soon a great traitor will be sent here by the people of Viterbo, to kill you and set the castle on fire. And I offer you the following signs as truth of what I say: he will be dressed as a poor man, his clothes torn and patched, his cowl torn and hanging down from his shoulders; he will carry an awl with him, with which to kill you, and a flint with which to set the castle on fire. If what I say does not prove to be true, deal with me as you will."

Niccolao was quite terrified by these words, because he thought that he who gave him this information was trustworthy. He ordered the sentries to be particularly careful, therefore, and commanded that if a man answering this description were to appear he should be brought before him immediately.

At about this very time, Brother Juniper, who because of his perfection had leave to go about without a companion, came along, all alone.

He had met some young people who made fun of him, but had not been upset by it. He had rather induced them to make even more fun of him.

When he came to the door of the castle, the guards saw him completely disarrayed, with his habit torn and unkempt —for out of love of God, he had given away much of it to the poor. He did not look at all like a Friar Minor, and therefore was angrily brought before the tyrant Niccolao. They searched him for weapons and found in his sleeve an awl, which he used to mend his sandals, and a flint, which he carried to start a fire, because he often suffered spells of weakness when he would dwell at length in woods and deserts.

Niccolao, seeing that he fit the description given by the accusing devil, ordered a rope to be placed around his neck and tightened. This was done with such cruelty that the rope cut into the flesh. He then put him on the rack and had his arms and body stretched without mercy. When Brother Juniper was asked who he was, he answered: "I am a very great sinner." When asked whether he sought to betray the castle and hand it over to the people of Viterbo, he answered: "I am the greatest of traitors and unworthy of any good." When asked if he wanted to kill the tyrant Niccolao with that awl and to burn down the castle, he answered: "That and many worse things I would do, if God would permit it."

Niccolao, overcome by wrath, asked nothing more. Without further delay, and with great fury, judging Brother Juniper as a traitor and murderer, he ordered him tied to the tail of a horse and dragged up to the gallows, there to be hanged.

During all this, Brother Juniper made no excuses for himself, nor did he show any desperation; but as a person who contented himself in adversity out of the love of God, he showed great joy.

When the order of the tyrant was executed and Brother Juniper was tied by the feet to the tail of a horse and dragged along the ground, he neither reproached the people nor lamented. Like a lamb led to slaughter, he went with great meekness. He was not recognized, and so all of the people ran in a festive and cruel spirit to see the spectacle and the hanging.

But as God willed, a good man who had seen Brother Juniper taken and condemned ran to the shelter of the Friars Minor and said: "In the name of God, I beg you to come immediately, for a poor man has been taken and quickly sentenced and led to death. Come, so that at least he can put his soul into your hands. He seems a good person to me, for having been taken to the gallows without the time to confess, he shows no fear of death or for the salvation of his soul. Come, come immediately."

The guardian, who was a merciful man, left immediately. When he came to the place, the crowd of people come to see the execution was so great that he could not make his way through it. The guardian stood by, waiting, and as he did so he heard a voice saying: "Stop, poor evil ones, stop. You are hurting my legs." When he heard this voice, the guardian suspected that it might be Brother Juniper, and he pushed his way through the crowd and removed the blindfold from the man's face.

He recognized that it was indeed Brother Juniper, and out of pity, began to take off his own habit and put it on Brother Juniper.

But Brother Juniper, with a happy countenance, almost laughing, said: "O guardian, you are fat, and it would be too embarrassing to see you naked. I won't let you."

Then the guardian with many tears begged the executioner and the people to wait a bit while he went to see the tyrant to intercede for Brother Juniper. The executioners, believing that the guardian must be a relative, agreed to wait.

When the guardian came before the tyrant Niccolao, he wept bitterly and said: "Lord, I am so stunned and disconsolate that my tongue will serve me poorly. The gravest sin and the greatest evil that was ever committed since antiquity has been committed today and in this town. I think it has been done out of ignorance."

Niccolao listened patiently and replied: "What is this great wrong and evil that has been committed today and in this town?"

"My lord," the guardian said, "one of the most holy brothers in the Order of St. Francis, to which you are singularly devoted, has been judged and cruelly sentenced by you, and I am certain unjustly."

"Now, tell me," replied Niccolao, "who this man is, for perhaps by not knowing him I have committed a great wrong."

"The man you have condemned to death," the guardian said, "is Brother Juniper, the companion of St. Francis."

The tyrant Niccolao, who had heard of the fame and holy life of Brother Juniper, was amazed. Pale and stunned, he immediately ran with the guardian to Brother Juniper and untied him from the tail of the horse. And in front of all those present, he threw himself on the ground before Brother Juniper, acknowledging his wrong in the harm and insults he had done to this holy brother, and adding: "I truly believe that evil days are about to fall on me, for I have tortured this holy man without reason. Because of my evil life, God will soon allow me to die an evil death, even though I have acted in ignorance."

Brother Juniper freely forgave the tyrant Niccolao, but God did permit Niccolao to end his life a few days later with a very cruel death.

And Brother Juniper departed, leaving the people edified. In praise of Christ. Amen.

## CHAPTER IV

*How Brother Juniper gave to the poor whatever he could, out of the love of God.*

Brother Juniper had such compassion for the poor that when he saw anyone poorly dressed or naked, he would immediately remove his habit or the cowl from his cloak and give it to him. The guardian, therefore, ordered him under obedience to give neither his habit nor any part of it to any poor man.

It happened that a few days later Brother Juniper met a poor man, almost naked, who begged him for alms, out of the love of God. "I have nothing to give you," said Brother Juniper with compassion, "except my habit, and my superior has ordered me, in the name of obedience, not to give it or any part of it to anyone. If you were to strip it from my back, however, I would not oppose you."

The man he was speaking to was not deaf, and he immediately stripped Brother Juniper of his habit and, leaving him naked, went off with it. When Brother Juniper returned to the shelter he was asked where his habit was; and he answered: "A good man took it from me and went away with it."

As the virtue of compassion grew in him, he was not content with giving his habit, but he also gave to the poor books, vestments, cloaks, and whatever he could get his hands on. The friars, for this reason, did not leave anything in sight, because out of love of God, Brother Juniper would give all to the poor. In praise of Christ. Amen.

## CHAPTER V

*How Brother Juniper took certain little ringlets from the frontal of the altar and, out of the love of God, gave them away.*

One Christmas, Brother Juniper was in Assisi, and he was meditating before the monastery altar, which was very beautifully adorned and decorated. The sacristan asked him to guard the altar while he went out to eat, and Brother Juniper consented. As he was praying thus, a poor woman came, asking for alms in the name of God. And Brother Juniper said to her: "Wait a bit and I will see if I can give you something from this very ornate altar." The altar had a golden frontal, very rich, with little silver ringlets of great price. "These ringlets," Brother Juniper said, "are superfluous." and he took a knife and cut them off the frontal and gave them to the poor woman.

The sacristan, after having eaten three or four mouthfuls, remembered the ways of Brother Juniper and began to dread that out of charity he might do something scandalous to the richly decorated altar. He immediately rose from the table, and rushed to the church to see if anything had been taken from the altar; and when he saw where the frontal had been cut and the ringlets removed, he was greatly upset. Brother Juniper, seeing him troubled, said: "Do not trouble yourself over those ringlets. I gave them to a poor woman in very great need. Here they served no purpose except that of worldly and vain display."

Greatly upset, the sacristan left the church, running through the city hoping to come upon the woman; but he did not find her, nor did he come upon anyone who had seen her. When he came back, he took the frontal and in great exasperation went to the Minister General, who was then in Assisi, and said: "Father General, I ask that you pass judgment on Brother Juniper, who has ruined this frontal, the most magnificent we had in the sacristy! Look how he has mutilated and ruined it, stripping it of its ringlets, which he says he gave to a poor woman in need."

"It was not Brother Juniper who did this," the General answered, "but your madness, for by now you should know his ways. I marvel that he did not give away everything on the altar. I will correct him, nevertheless, for this failing." And at a gathering of all the brothers of the chapter he harshly reproached Brother Juniper about the ringlets, and in doing so, became so furious that he became hoarse from straining his voice.

Brother Juniper had no concern at all for those words, since he took delight in insults and in being mortified, but he did worry over the General's anger and began to think of some remedy for it. After having been severely taken to task by the General, he went into the town and ordered a good dish of *farinata,* a special kind of porridge with butter. Late at night, when he came back, he lit a candle and, taking the dish of *farinata* with him, went to the cell of the General and knocked.

The General opened, saw Brother Juniper with the candle in one hand and the dish in the other, and softly asked: "What is all this?"

Brother Juniper answered: "My father, when you reproached me for my shortcomings today, I noticed that you strained yourself, and that your voice became hoarse. I thought of something to help you and had this *farinata* made for you. I beg of you, eat it. It will help your chest and throat."

"Do you know what time of night it is," the General replied, "that you go about disturbing others?"

Brother Juniper answered: "See, I had it made for you. I beg of you, let us not argue. Eat it, and it will help you a good deal."

Upset by the lateness of the hour and the insistence of Brother Juniper, the General ordered him to leave, insisting that that was not the hour to eat and that Brother Juniper was a vile and wicked man.

Considering that neither prayer nor polite persuasion had succeeded, Brother Juniper said: "My father, since you do not wish to eat this *farinata* that I had made for you, at least do me the favor of holding the candle, and I will eat it."

Then the General, as a pious and devout person, took into account the piety and simplicity of Brother Juniper and all that he had done out of love, and replied: "Now, since you are so inclined, let us eat together, you and I." And they both ate the dish of *farinata*, drawing more nourishment from their devotion than from the food. In praise of Christ. Amen.

## CHAPTER VI

*How Brother Juniper kept silence for six months.*

Once Brother Juniper resolved to keep silence for six months in the following way: the first day out of love of the Heavenly Father; the second day out of love of Jesus Christ, His Son; the third, out of love of the Holy Spirit; the fourth, out of reverence for the most holy Virgin Mary. And so in sequence, every day out of the love of some saint, he kept six months of silence without talking.

## CHAPTER VII

*How to resist temptations of the flesh.*

One day when Brother Egidio, Brother Simone of Assisi, Brother Ruffino, and Brother Juniper were speaking of God and the salvation of the soul, Brother Egidio asked the others: "What do you do against the temptations of the sins of the flesh?"

Brother Simone replied: "I consider the wretchedness and the filth of the sins of the flesh, and I feel such abomination as a consequence that I am freed from the temptation."

"I," Brother Ruffino said, "throw myself stretched out on

the ground and remain so in prayer, praying for the clemency of God and the mother of Jesus Christ until I feel myself completely freed."

And Brother Juniper replied: "When I feel the tempest of devilish carnal impulse, I immediately run and lock the door to my heart, and to make that fortress secure, busy myself with holy meditations and desires. When the carnal impulse comes and knocks at the threshold of the heart, I answer from within, 'Stay outside. The inn is all filled. There is no room for anyone else.' In this way no carnal thought can enter into my heart, and the temptation, defeated, leaves and goes far from me."

Brother Egidio answered, saying: "Brother Juniper, I am with you, for we cannot fight the enemy flesh but only flee it. Treacherous carnal appetite is a strong enemy and makes himself strongly felt within and without the senses. Not to flee is to be overcome. That is why to fight in any other way is rarely to win the struggle. Flee, then, this vice, and you will be victorious." In praise of Christ. Amen.

## CHAPTER VIII

*How Brother Juniper mortified himself in praise of God.*

Once Brother Juniper, wishing to mortify himself utterly, stripped himself naked. Having made a bundle of his clothes and put them on his head, he entered Viterbo and went to the public square to be mocked and laughed at.

As he remained there naked, young men and children, who thought him out of his mind, treated him badly, throwing mud and stones at him and scornfully pushing him about, now here, now there. And Brother Juniper remained there, mocked and suffering, for a good part of the day. Then, still naked, he returned to the monastery.

When the brothers saw him thus, they were extremely upset, and especially because the whole city had seen him naked and with his bundle on his head. They all reproached him harshly and with threats. One said: "Let us put him in jail." Another: "Let us hang him." Still another: "No punishment is enough for the scandal he has made of himself and the entire Order."

And Brother Juniper, with great joy and humility, replied: "You speak well. I am worthy of all these punishments and much more." In praise of Christ. Amen.

## CHAPTER IX

*How Brother Juniper, in order to mortify himself, went on a seesaw.*

On his way to Rome, where the fame of his sanctity was already widespread, Brother Juniper was awaited by many Romans who, out of devotion, were coming to meet him; and Brother Juniper, seeing all these people come, had the idea of turning their devotion to scorn.

There were two boys there who had placed one long piece of wood at right angles to another, and they were seesawing up and down. Brother Juniper went there, took one of the boys from his place, and sat down and started to go up and down.

Meanwhile, the people who had gone out to see him came upon the scene and marveled to see him on the seesaw; nevertheless, they greeted him with great devotion and waited until he should have finished playing on the seesaw so that they might accompany him with honor to the monastery.

And Brother Juniper, who was enjoying the seesaw, did not appear very concerned with their greetings and reverence or their waiting. After a great while, a number of those waiting began to tire, and said: "What kind of a stupid sheep is he?" Others, knowing his ways, increased their devotion to him, but nonetheless all of them went off and left Brother Juniper on the seesaw.

And after they had all left, Brother Juniper was quite consoled because many had mocked him. He then continued on his way, entered Rome, and with great meekness and humility came to the monastery of the Friars Minor. In praise of Christ. Amen.

## CHAPTER X

*How Brother Juniper once cooked for the friars enough food for fifteen days.*

One time when Brother Juniper was in a very small shelter, all the other brothers, for good reasons, had to leave, and Brother Juniper alone remained behind. The guardian said: "Brother Juniper, we are all going out. Have something ready for us to eat when we return."

"I will gladly do so," Brother Juniper replied. "Leave it to me."

And when the brothers had all gone out, Brother Juniper said to himself: "What a bother it is that a brother must lose time in the kitchen, far from prayer! Since I have been left behind to cook this time, I will cook so much that all the brothers, and even if there were more, will have enough for fifteen days."

In this spirit, he went to town and got a number of big pots to cook in, and fresh and dried meat, chicken, eggs, and a great amount of herbs and wood, and then began to cook everything together—the chickens with their feathers, the eggs with their shells, and many other things.

When the brothers returned, one of them, quite aware of the simplicity of Brother Juniper, walked into the kitchen and saw this confusion of large pots and many fires. He sat down and looked about in wonderment, not saying a word, but noticing with what zealous energy Brother Juniper was cooking. Because the fire was so strong and Brother Juniper could not get close to skim the tops of the pots, he had taken a long board and tied it tightly to his body, and with that board he was leaping about from one pot to another, a joy to behold.

Looking at all this with great delight, the brother left the kitchen, and when he saw the other friars he said: "I tell you, Brother Juniper is preparing a wedding feast!" The brothers thought he was joking.

Then Brother Juniper took the pots off the fire and rang for the brothers to come in and eat.

When the friars sat down at the table, Brother Juniper,

all red from the effort and from the heat of the fire, came into the refectory with all that he had cooked, and said: "Eat heartily, and then let us all go to pray. Let no one think further of the problem of cooking. I have cooked enough today to last us fifteen days"; and with that he put the mess of food in front of the brothers.

It was such that no starving pig in the countryside around Rome would have eaten it, but Brother Juniper praised the meal, seeking to persuade others to eat it. And seeing that the brothers were not eating, he said: "These chickens are good for the brains. This food provides moisture for the body. All this is good food."

While the brothers wondered devoutly at the devotion and simplicity of Brother Juniper, the guardian, exasperated at such lightheadedness and frivolous conduct and so much waste, harshly reproached Brother Juniper. And Brother Juniper immediately threw himself on his knees before the guardian and humbly acknowledged his fault to him and all the brothers, saying: "I am a very wicked man. A certain man committed a certain sin, and his eyes were put out; but I am more worthy of punishment than he. Another was hanged because of his evil doing; but I deserve even more because of the wicked things I have done. And now I have wasted the goods of God and of the Order." And weeping and lamenting, he left and did not show himself further to any brother that day.

And the guardian said: "My beloved brothers, I would wish that every day this brother would waste such goods as we might have, as he has just done, if it served for his and our edification. It is his great simplicity and charity that has made him do this." In praise of Christ. Amen.

## CHAPTER XI

*How Brother Juniper once went to Assisi to be reproached.*

In the days that Brother Juniper lived in the valley of Spoleto, he once heard that a great feast was to be celebrated in Assisi, and since many people were devoutly going there, he decided to go there too. And he took off all his clothes and went naked through Spello and through the heart of the city, until he came to the monastery. The friars, scandalized and upset, reproached him harshly and called him mad and foolish, a subverter of the Order of St. Francis, and worthy of being chained as a madman.

The General, who was then in the shelter, had all the brothers and Brother Juniper come to him, and in the presence of all, he berated him. He concluded his hard words, given in a spirit of justice, by saying: "Your wrongs are such that I do not know what fitting penance to impose on you."

"Father," Brother Juniper replied as one who delighted in reproach, "let me suggest it. As I came naked to this place, let me return naked to the point from which I set out to come to this feast."

In praise of Christ. Amen.


## CHAPTER XII

*How Brother Juniper was rapt in ecstasy as Mass was being celebrated.*

Once, as Brother Juniper was attending Mass devoutly, he was raised up to God for a long period of time, leaving the place where the other friars were. When he came back to himself, he asked fervently: "O my brothers, who in this world feels himself so noble that he would not willingly carry a basket of dung all through the world to gain a house filled with gold?" And he added: "Poor us! Why will we not endure a little shame so as to win a blessed life?"


## CHAPTER XIII

*Of the sadness of Brother Juniper at the death of his friend, Brother Amazialbene.*

Brother Juniper had a friar friend, by name of Amazialbene, whom he loved dearly. This friend had the virtue of great patience and humility. Even though he were beaten all day, he would not complain nor answer a single word.

He was often sent to places where friars were hard to get along with, and they usually treated him badly; but he endured all this with great patience and did not reproach them.

This Brother Amazialbene, who would weep or laugh at the order of Brother Juniper, as it pleased God, died one day. When Brother Juniper heard of his death, he felt such sadness as he had never in the course of his life felt for any earthly thing.

And he showed the bitter grief in him, saying: "Poor blind me, deprived of all my good. All the world is undone with the death of my sweet and beloved Brother Amazialbene!" And he added: "If it were not for the arguments I would have with my brothers, I would go to his tomb and make two bowls out of the skull. In his memory and devotion, I would eat always from one, and when thirsty or inclined to drink, drink from the other one."

To the glory of Christ. Amen.


## CHAPTER XIV

*Of the hand that Brother Juniper saw in the air.*

One day when Brother Juniper was praying (and perhaps he was thinking of doing great things) he thought he saw a hand in the air and heard a voice that spoke as follows: "O Brother Juniper, without this hand, you can do nothing."

And he immediately stood up and, looking up to Heaven, said in a loud voice, as he went walking through the monastery: "That is quite true, that is quite true!" And he said this over and over again.

To the glory of Christ. Amen.

# THE LIFE OF THE BLESSED BROTHER EGIDIO, COMPANION OF SAINT FRANCIS

## CHAPTER I

*How Brother Egidio and three companions were received into the Order of Friars Minor.*

Because the example of holy men can break the hold of transitory delights on devout listeners and because it can incite a desire for eternal salvation, I shall speak of the working of the Holy Spirit in holy Brother Egidio, in honor of God and His most reverend Mother, holy Lady Mary.

While still in secular garb, touched by the Holy Spirit, he began by himself to meditate on how he could please God in all ways. At this same time St. Francis, the new herald of God, through the example of his life, his humility, and his penance, but two years after his conversion had drawn and persuaded Messer Bernardo, a man rich with marvelous prudence and the goods of the world, together with Pietro Cattani, to follow evangelical poverty. Because of the counsel of St. Francis and out of the love of God, they distributed all their temporal goods to the poor and took on the glory of penance and evangelical perfection and the habit of the Friar Minor. With great fervor they promised to observe the Rule all their lives, and they did so perfectly.

Eight days after their conversion and the distribution of their goods to the poor, on the feast of St. George in the year of Our Lord 1209, Brother Egidio, still in secular garb, witnessed both the scorn of these noble gentlemen of Assisi for worldly things and the awe and admiration of the whole countryside for them. Aflame with the love of God, he went in great haste to the church of St. George, now the site of the convent of St. Clare, to pray. After praying, he felt a great need to see St. Francis and he went toward the lepers' hospital near which the Saint and Brother Bernardo and Brother Pietro Cattani lived in a humble shack. He came to a crossroad, and not knowing which road to take, he prayed to Christ, the precious Guide, who led him straightaway to that humble shack. St. Francis was just coming out of the wood after praying, and he wondered why Egidio had come to him; and Egidio knelt before the Saint and humbly requested if he might join his company, out of the love of God.

St. Francis, considering the holy countenance of Brother Egidio, said: "My dearest brother, God has shown you abundant grace. If the Emperor were to come to Assisi and were to make a citizen his knight or secret counselor, ought that person not rejoice? How much more then should you rejoice that God has chosen you as his knight and beloved servant, who will observe the perfection of the holy gospel! Remain firm and constant in your vocation, for God has called you."

And he took him by the hand, led him to the shack, and called Brother Bernardo, to whom he said: "Messer, the Lord God has sent us a good brother. Let us all rejoice in the Lord. Let us all eat in charity." And after having done so, St. Francis went with Egidio to Assisi to find cloth for his habit.

On the way they met a poor little woman who asked for alms, out of the love of God. St. Francis had nothing to offer the poor woman, and he turned to Brother Egidio and said: "Out of the love of God, my dearest brother, let us give her this cloak." And Brother Egidio gladly removed his cloak and gave it to the woman. And she flew straightway to Heaven, leaving Brother Egidio joyful and astonished.

And St. Francis, having found the cloth and made the tunic, received into the Order Brother Egidio, who was to become one of the most glorious contemplatives the world has ever seen.

After receiving Brother Egidio into the Order, St. Francis soon after went with him to the March of Ancona, singing with him, joyously praising the Lord of Heaven and earth. The Saint said to Brother Egidio: "Brother, our Order will be like the fisherman who throws his net into the water, pulling in a multitude of fish, keeping the largest and throwing the smaller back into the sea."

Brother Egidio greatly marveled at this prophecy, because the Order was then composed of only three brothers and St. Francis. And although St. Francis did not publicly preach to the people, he did admonish and correct the men and women he met on the way, saying with love and simplicity: "Love and fear God and make penance for your sins." And Brother Egidio would say: "Do what my spiritual father tells you to, for he speaks well." In praise of Christ. Amen.

## CHAPTER II

> *How Brother Egidio went to St. James of Compostela.*

With the permission of St. Francis, Brother Egidio once went to the church of St. James the Elder in Galicia, and during all that time, because of the great poverty of that region, he did not eat once. And so one evening, after begging and finding no one to give him charity, he came across by chance a few beans that had been left behind in a garden; and he gathered them and they were his meal. He slept there during the night, because he gladly lived in solitary places removed from people so as to better attend to prayers and vigils. And he was so comforted by God in that meal that he could not have satisfied his hunger as well had he eaten more.

Continuing on his journey, he found an old man who asked him for alms, out of the love of God. The charitable Brother Egidio had nothing but his habit; he cut off his cowl and gave it to the poor man, and he walked on this way, without his cowl, for twenty days.

And coming through Lombardy, he was called by a man. Believing that he would receive alms, he went willingly; but the man placed dice in his extended hand and asked him if he wanted to play. Brother Egidio humbly answered: "May God forgive you, son."

And going about in the world, he was much mocked and he received such taunts peacefully. In praise of Christ. Amen.

## CHAPTER III

> *How Brother Egidio lived when he went to the Holy Sepulcher.*

With the permission of St. Francis, Brother Egidio went to visit the Holy Sepulcher of Christ, and coming to the port of Brindisi, he stayed there for a number of days, for no ship was ready to sail. Since Brother Egidio wished to live by his labor, he bought a jug, filled it with water, and went about the city crying out: "Who wants water?" And for this work he received bread and the things necessary for life, for himself and his companion. Then he crossed the sea and with great devotion visited the Holy Sepulcher of Christ and other holy places.

And on the way back, he stayed in the city of Ancona for a few days. Since he was accustomed to working for a livelihood, he made bags woven of reeds and sold them, not for money but for bread for himself and his companion. He also buried the dead for the same price. And when he could not do so, he turned to the table of Our Lord, asking for alms from door to door. And so with much work and poverty, he made his way back to St. Mary of the Angels. In praise of Christ. Amen.

## CHAPTER IV

> *How Brother Egidio praised obedience more than prayer.*

Once a friar was praying in his cell, and his guardian ordered him in obedience to go and beg for alms. Whereupon he immediately went to Brother Egidio and said: "My father, I was praying and the guardian ordered me to go and beg for bread. It seems to me that it is better to remain in prayer."

Brother Egidio answered: "My son, you have not known or understood what prayer is. True prayer is doing the will of your guardian. It is a sign of great pride on the part of one who has placed himself under the yoke of holy obedience to oppose it in order to do his own will, even though it may seem to him that in doing so he is doing more good. The perfectly obedient brother is like a rider of a mighty horse, and because of its strength, he can move fearlessly along the road. On the contrary, the disobedient brother, given to complaints and reproaches, is like a rider of a skinny, skittery horse, and he is easily either taken or killed by his enemies.

"I tell you that if a man were so devout and of such elevation of thought that he could speak with angels, and if during this conversation he were called by his guardian, he should immediately break off the conversation with the angels and obey his guardian." In praise of Christ. Amen.

## CHAPTER V

### *How Brother Egidio lived from his labors.*

Once when Brother Egidio was in a monastery in Rome, he wished to earn a livelihood by working with his hands, as he had done since entering the Order. And this is how he did it. In the morning he would attend Mass with great devotion, and then he would go to a wood eight miles outside of Rome and would bring from there on his back a bundle of firewood, selling it in exchange for bread and other things to eat.

On one of these occasions, as he was coming back loaded down with wood a woman asked to buy it from him, and when the price was agreed upon, he brought it to her house. In spite of the agreed price the woman, seeing that he was a friar, gave him much more than had been agreed upon; whereupon Brother Egidio said: "Good woman, I do not want to be overcome by the vice of avarice, and I do not want more than the price agreed upon." So that he not only did not take more, but took only half of the stipulated price and left; and because of this, the woman had great respect and devotion for him.

Brother Egidio worked for pay, always in the spirit of holy honesty. He would help to gather olives and to press grapes. One day as he was in the square a man wanted someone to shake down nuts from a tree, and was trying to find someone to do it for a price. The man he approached refused because the tree was quite a distance away and difficult to climb. Brother Egidio said: "If you give me a part of the nuts, my friend, I will come with you and shake them down."

The offer being accepted, Brother Egidio left with him; and after making the sign of the cross, he climbed up the high nut tree and with much trepidation began to strike the branches with a stick.

After it was all done, the part that fell to him was so great that he could not carry it in the skirt of his robe. He removed his habit, and having tied the sleeves and hood, made a sack of it, thus remaining naked except for his breeches. And having filled his tunic with nuts, he carried them on his back to Rome, where with great joy, out of love of God, he gave them to the poor.

At the time of the wheat-cutting season, Brother Egidio would go with other poor men to glean, and if anyone offered him a handful of wheat he would answer: "My brother, I don't have a barn in which to put it," and most of the time he would give away the gleanings for the love of God.

Brother Egidio rarely helped anyone for the entire day, for he always stipulated that he should have time to recite his office, and for mental prayer.

Once Brother Egidio went to the fountain of St. Sixtus for the monks. A man asked him for drink, and Brother Egidio answered: "And how will I then bring a jug full of water to the monks if I give you a drink?"

The man, upset and angered, insulted Brother Egidio; and Brother Egidio, very troubled, brought the water to the monks. He then took another jug and immediately returned to the fountain. Finding the man still there, he said: "My friend, take this and drink as much as you want. Do not be upset, because it seemed wrong to me to bring to those holy monks water from which another had drunk."

The man, contrite and won over by the charity and humility of Brother Egidio, acknowledged his fault and from that time on held him in great devotion. In praise of Christ. Amen.

## CHAPTER VI

*How Brother Egidio was miraculously assisted
in time of great need when, because of a heavy
snowfall, he could not go out for alms.*

When Brother Egidio was in Rome, living with a cardinal,
as Lent approached and he lacked the mental quiet that he
desired, he said to the cardinal: "My father, with your permission I should like to go with my companion, and for
my peace pass this Lent in a solitary place."

And the cardinal answered: "Good, my beloved brother,
and where would you wish to go? There is a great famine in
the land and you are not yet accustomed to it. Remain at
my court, for it is a privilege for me to provide for your
needs, out of love of God."

Brother Egidio, however, wished to leave, and he left
Rome and went to a high mountain where there had formerly
been a castle. There he found an abandoned church by the
name of St. Lawrence, and he and his companion entered
therein and prayed and meditated.

They were not known and consequently were not given
reverence and devotion, and that is why they endured great
want; moreover, a heavy snowfall fell at this time and
lasted for several days. They could not leave the church,
they had nothing of their own to eat, and nothing was sent
to them; and they remained confined to the church for three
days.

Brother Egidio, seeing that he could not work for a living
nor go out for alms, said to his companion: "My beloved
brother, let us call out to Our Lord, that out of His mercy
He will care for us in our extremity and need. Long ago
when monks in great necessity cried out to God, Divine
Providence helped them."

And in imitation of those monks they began to pray with
all their hearts that God might succor them. God, who is
extremely merciful, considered their faith and devotion and
simplicity and helped them in the following way.

A passerby, looking at the church where Brother Egidio
and his companion were staying, was inspired by God and
said to himself: "Perhaps there are some good souls doing

penance in that church, and because of the heavy snowfall, they cannot find the necessities of life and might possibly be dying of hunger." And urged on by the Holy Spirit, he said: "And now I want to find out in all certainty whether or not my fears are well-founded."

He took some loaves of bread and a jug of wine, and he set out toward the church and with great difficulty came to it; and there he found Brother Egidio and his companion devoutly in prayer. They were so ravaged by hunger that they seemed more dead than alive. He had great compassion for them, and refreshing and consoling them, he returned and told his neighbors about the plight of those brothers, and begged and persuaded them to do something, for the love of God. Many, imitating him, brought them bread and wine and other necessary things to eat, and during all that Lent they arranged among themselves that the two brothers should always be provided for in their needs.

Considering such great mercy and charity, Brother Egidio said to his companion: "My dearest brother, up to now we have prayed to God that He might help us in our need, and He has answered our prayer. Let us give Him thanks and glory, and pray for those who have helped us with their alms, and for all Christian peoples."

And God conceded so much grace to Brother Egidio because of his fervor and devotion that many, imitating Brother Egidio, left this blind world; and many others, who were not inclined to become friars, did great penance in their homes. In praise of Christ. Amen.


## CHAPTER VII

*Of the day of the death of holy Brother Egidio.*

At matins on the eve of the feast of St. George, having worn the habit of St. Francis for exactly fifty-two years, the soul of Brother Egidio was received by God into the glory of Paradise.

## CHAPTER VIII

> *How a holy man, as he was praying, saw the soul of Brother Egidio ascend to eternal life.*

A good man, who was praying when Brother Egidio left this life, saw his soul, together with a multitude of souls then emerging from Purgatory, rise to Heaven. And Jesus Christ came to meet the soul of Brother Egidio, and with a great multitude of angels and all those souls, with sweet melody took it to Paradise. In praise of Christ. Amen.

## CHAPTER IX

> *How, through the merits of Brother Egidio, the soul of a friend of a Dominican friar was freed from the pains of Purgatory.*

At about the time that Brother Egidio fell ill of the sickness of which he was to die a few days later, a friar of St. Dominic also fell deathly ill. The Dominican friar had a friar friend and he, seeing him approaching death, said to the dying brother: "My brother, if God allows it, come to me after death and tell me where you are." The sick man answered that he would do so if it were possible.

Brother Egidio died the same day as the friar, and after his death the dead Dominican appeared to the living one and said: "It was the will of God that I should fulfill my promise."

And the living Dominican said to the dead: "What has become of you?"

The dead one answered: "All is well, because I died on the same day in which a Friar Minor by the name of Egidio died. Because of his great sanctity, Jesus Christ conceded that all the greatly tormented souls in Purgatory, and I was among them, should be taken to Paradise; and by the merits of holy Brother Egidio I was freed from those pains." And having said this, he immediately disappeared.

That friar did not reveal the vision to anyone. He became ill, and immediately thereafter, fearing that God had struck him down because he had made no revelation of the virtue and glory of Brother Egidio, he sent for the Friars Minor, and five friars came to him; and having gathered them together with the brothers of the Order of Preachers, he revealed that vision to them with great devotion. Going over the matter carefully, they found that the two men had died on the same day.

## CHAPTER X

*How God gave special grace to Brother Egidio; and of the year of Brother Egidio's death.*

Brother Bonaventura of Bagnoreggio used to say of Brother Egidio that God had given and conceded him special grace for all those who turned to him with devotion in spiritual matters. He performed many miracles in life and death, as it is said in the stories written of him. He left this life to his glory in 1262, on the day of the feast of St. George, and is buried in Perugia in the shelter of the Friars Minor.

# THE SECOND RULE
# OF THE FRIARS MINOR

*I Rule and Life of the Friars Minor.*

This is the Rule and life of the Friars Minor: to observe the gospel of our Lord Jesus Christ, to live in holy obedience, without any temporal or personal goods, and in chastity. Brother Francis promises obedience and reverence to Pope Honorius and his canonically elected successors and to the Holy Roman Church. The brothers are held to obey Brother Francis and his successors.

*II Concerning those who wish to lead this life, and how they are to be received.*

If a person wishes to adopt this life and for this reason comes to our brothers, let them send him to the provincial ministers, to whom alone is conceded the power to receive brothers. Let the ministers examine the person with true diligence as to the Catholic faith and the sacraments of the Church. And if that person holds to all these beliefs and wishes to truly adhere to them and observe them to the very end; and if he is not married, or, if married, his wife is already in a convent, or if he has permission from his bishop and has taken a vow of continence (and the wife is of such an age that no suspicions can arise); then, according to the words of the Holy Gospel, let him be instructed to go and sell all his goods and give them with great deliberation to the poor of God. And if he has nothing to give, then his good will is enough. Let the ministers and brothers take care not to be solicitous for the temporal goods of that person, so that he can liberally dispose of his possessions as God inspires him to. If the ministers are asked for advice in this matter, let them send the person to someone with the fear of God who will advise that person how to properly dispose of his goods to the poor.

At this point let the applicant be given the habit of a novice: that is, two tunics without a hood, a cord, breeches, and a long cape down to the belt, or of another length as may be decided by the ministers in accordance with the will of God. At the end of a year of novitiate let the applicant be received for obedience, promising on his part always to observe this life and Rule. In no way is the applicant to be allowed to leave the Order, in keeping with the mandate of the Pope, for the gospel says: "He who puts his hand to the plow and looks backward is not worthy of the Kingdom of God." As for those applicants who have already promised obedience, let them have a tunic with a hood, and one without a hood if they so wish. Let those who need it have footwear. Let all the brothers be clothed in very poor vestments and patch them with sackcloth and similar scraps, with the blessing of God. And I admonish them and beseech them not to have contempt for nor to judge those whom they see dressed in rich and colored attire, who are accustomed to fine food and beverages, but rather all the more let each one judge himself and have contempt for himself.

### III Concerning the Divine Office and fasting, and how brothers are to go about the world.

The clerics will say the office according to the order of the Holy Roman Church, except for the Psalter, of which they may use an abbreviated version. Let the lay brothers say twenty-four Our Fathers for matins, five for lauds, seven for prime, tierce, sext and none, twelve for vespers, seven for compline. Let them also pray for the dead.

Let them fast from All Saints until Christmas. Those who are willing, let them fast for forty days starting from Epiphany, a fast consecrated by Our Lord's holy voluntary fast, and may those who do so be blessed by the Lord Our God and may those who do not so wish not be obliged to do so. But all are obliged to observe the other regular Lenten fast until the Resurrection of our Lord Jesus Christ. At all other times they are to be obliged to fast only on Friday. In times of manifest necessity, the brothers are not bound to bodily fasting.

I counsel, beseech, and urge my brothers in the name of

Jesus Christ that when they go about the world they be not contemptuous, "nor dispute with words," nor judge others; but let them be humble and peaceful and modest, meek, self-effacing, speaking gently with all, as is proper. Let them say before entering any house: "Peace to this house." And as the Holy Gospel says, it is licit for them to eat whatever food is placed before them.

> *IV How St. Francis forbade the brothers to accept money or any form of wealth whatsoever, and the advice he gave them.*

I command all brothers not to receive money or its equivalents under any circumstances for themselves or through an intermediary. For the necessities of sick brothers or others in need, or for clothing, let the ministers alone and with them the guardians, through spiritual friends solicitously assist them (according to the place, time, and cold of the season), doing what they believe necessity requires—provided, as has been mentioned, they do not accept money or its equivalents.

> *V Concerning the way the friars are to work.*

Let those brothers to whom God has given the grace of being able to work, work faithfully and with devotion in such a way that, casting out sloth, the enemy of the soul, they do not hamper or lessen the spirit of devotion and prayer to which the rest of their time is to be devoted. As a reward for their labors, let them have for themselves and the brothers the corporal necessities, except money or its equivalents. Let them receive their reward with humility, as becomes the servants of God and the followers of most holy poverty.

> *VI The commandment of Francis to his brothers to own nothing, and how they are to beg for alms, and deal with sick brothers.*

The brothers are to own nothing, neither place, nor house, nor anything at all; but as "strangers and pilgrims" in this world, serving God in poverty and humility, they are to go out begging for alms without shame, because for us our Lord

Jesus Christ took the form of a poor man in this world. This is that sublime glory of the highest poverty, which, my dearest brothers, heirs of the kingdom of God and worthy of it, invested you and made you poor in the things of this world and adorned you with virtue. Let this be your reward, which leads to the "land of the living," and approaching which, my most beloved and dear brothers, you should want nothing else under the sun, in the name of Jesus Christ.

And wherever brothers are found together, let them be affectionate with one another and confidently tell one another of their needs, since as a mother nourishes and feeds her son, how much more ought one to love and nourish one's spiritual brother. And if any of the brothers fall ill, the friars must serve him as they themselves would wish to be served.

### VII Of the penance to be imposed on friars who sin.

If any brother fall into mortal sin because of diabolical instigation, let him recur to the provincial minister alone for those sins for which he is to be corrected, and let such a brother have such recourse as rapidly as possible. Those ministers, if they are priests, will impose a severe penance mercifully; if the ministers are not priests, let them have other priests of the Order impose penance, according to the will of God, as will seem best to them. And the ministers must take care not to give way to wrath nor become agitated for the sins of anyone, for wrath and agitation in ourselves and in others impedes charity.

### VIII On the election of the Minister General of the fraternity, and the Pentecostal Chapter.

Let all the brothers of this Order choose one from among them as Minister General and servant of all the fraternity, and let them steadfastly obey him. On his death, let the election of his successor be made by the provincial ministers and the guardians in the Pentecostal Chapter, at which time the provincial ministers must meet at a designated place for the election of a Minister General; and let a chapter be convened once every three years, or sooner or later as will be determined by the above-mentioned Minister. And if it seems for some time to most provincial ministers and custodians that the Minister General does not measure up to his task for the common good and service of the brothers, let the brothers with the right to elect, elect another Minister and custodian in the name of God. After the Pentecostal Chapter, the ministers and custodians may each, if it seems useful to them, convene local chapter meetings in their own provinces.

> *IX Francis orders the preaching friars not to preach in the diocese of any bishop without his permission.*

Let no brother preach in the diocese of any bishop unless he be so instructed by the bishop. Let no brother, above all, preach to the people if he is not first examined and approved by the Minister General of this fraternity and given permission to do so. I admonish and beseech the brothers themselves that in their sermons their words be pondered and chaste, for the good and edification of the people. Let them show the people vices and virtues, punishment and glory, with few words; for "the Lord God made His words brief on the earth."

> *X On the admonishment and punishment of brothers, and how they are to show humility and not seek to excuse themselves.*

Let the brothers who are ministers and servants of the other brothers visit and correct their brothers, and humbly and chastely punish them, and order them to do nothing against their consciences and our Rule. Let the brothers who are subject to them remember that out of the love of God they have abandoned their own will, because of which I strongly order them to obey their ministers, as they have promised, in all that is not contrary to their consciences and our Rule. And wherever there are brothers who know that they cannot observe the spiritual Rule, they must and ought to have recourse to the ministers. And the ministers are to receive them in charity and kindness and show them much warmth, so that those brothers who come to them may speak and act as lords do with servants; for this is the way it must be, that the ministers must act as the servants of all the brothers.

I admonish and beseech all the brothers in the name of

Jesus Christ to guard themselves against all pride, vainglory, jealousy, avarice, care and concern for this world, deceit, and slander. And those who do not know how to read and write, let them show no concern for it, and above all seek and desire the spirit of the Lord and His help; let them always pray to Him with a pure heart, and show humility and patience in persecutions and illness, loving those who persecute and reproach and dispute with them, for the Lord says: "Love your enemies and pray for those who persecute you and slander you. Blessed are those who suffer persecution for justice's sake, for theirs is the Kingdom of Heaven, and he who will persevere to the end will be saved."

> *XI Concerning the commandment of St. Francis that the brothers are not to enter a convent of nuns.*

I firmly command all the brothers to have no dealings with women or have anything to do with them that might arouse suspicion; and let them not enter the convents of nuns except those to which the Apostolic See has granted a special permission. Nor are the brothers to be godfathers for men or women, so that no scandal may arise therefrom.

> *XII Concerning those who will go among the Saracens and other infidels.*

Whoever among the friars, led by divine inspiration, will wish to go among the Saracens and other infidels, let them ask permission from their provincial ministers. Let the ministers give permission to no one except those whom they consider qualified to go.

Again in the name of obedience, I order the ministers to ask the Pope to designate one of the cardinals of the Holy Roman Church to act as governor, protector, and corrector of this Order, so that, always subject to and at the feet of this holy Church, and confirmed in our Catholic faith, we may observe the poverty and humility of the holy gospel of our Lord Jesus Christ, as we firmly promised to.

# THE TESTAMENT.

The Lord God gave me, Francis, this way of doing penance —I was a sinner and found it hard to look at lepers, and the Lord God led me among them, and I was merciful to them. As I left them, what had previously seemed bitter turned into sweetness of body and soul. And then, soon after, I left the world.

And the Lord God gave me such trust in churches that I, a simple person, would adore and say: "We adore You, Lord Jesus Christ, here and in all the churches everywhere in the world, and we bless You for having redeemed the world with Your Holy Cross."

Then the Lord gave me, and continues to give me, such faith in priests who live according to the form of the Holy Roman Church and in its Order that even if they were to persecute me, I would have recourse to them. And if I had the wisdom of Solomon and came across the poorest priests in the world, I would not want to preach in their parishes against their wishes. I want to fear and love and honor them and all the priests as my lords. I do this because I can corporeally see the most High Son of God, and His body and blood, in no other way than in the form that priests receive this Body and wisely administer It to others. I wish to honor these most holy and sacred mysteries above all else, and have them kept in a precious place.

And whenever I come across His most holy name and His words in unappropriate places, I wish to remedy it, and I wish others to do so and to gather up and put His name and words in a fitting place.

And we must honor all theologians and those that administer holy and sacred words, and hold the theologians in reverence as those who minister us life and spirit.

And later when the Lord God gave me brothers in charge,

no person showed me what to do; the High God alone revealed to me that I was to live according to the form of the Holy Gospel. With a few and simple words I had what I was to do written down, and the Pope gave it his approval.

And all those who were received into the Order and were to lead this life gave all that they had to the poor. They were happy with one tunic, patched within and without, with a cord and breeches. And they did not own anything more.

We clerics said the office like other clerics, and the lay brothers recited the Our Father. We willingly stayed in churches, simple and subject to all.

I worked with my hands, and still wish to do so—and I want all the other brothers to work steadfastly at some honest task. As for those who do not know how, let them learn, not out of any desire to receive a salary for their work but only to set a good example and cast out sloth. When we do not receive any wages for our work, let us have recourse to the table of Our Lord and go begging from door to door.

God has revealed to me the greeting we are to use, and the way we are to say: "May the Lord give you peace."

Let the brothers see to it that they do not receive, on any account, churches and houses made for them, if these are not in keeping with holy poverty—in accordance to what we promised in the Rule—and let them always adhere to these injunctions and live in this world like strangers and pilgrims.

I also command all brothers, wherever they may be, that none of them dare ask for any letter from the Roman court— to ask themselves or through intermediaries—for any church, for any place, for preaching, or even for protection against persecution. Wherever they may not be well received, let them flee to another land and with the blessing of God do penance.

I firmly wish to obey the Minister General of the fraternity and the guardian whom it shall please him to give me, and to do what he would have me do. I wish to be so held in his hands that I cannot do anything or act against his will and wishes, since he is my lord.

And although I am a simple person and infirm, I always want a cleric nearby who will perform the office with me, as it is provided in the Rule.

Let all the brothers be obligated to obey their guardians in this fashion and recite the office according to the Rule. As for those who will not recite the office according to the Rule, or who in some way wish to change it, or who are not Catholics—let all the brothers, wherever they may be, out of obedience, in encountering any such person take that brother to the nearest custodian of the place where they found him. The custodian, out of obedience, is to firmly watch over the brother brought to him, keep him bound day and night in such a way that he cannot be taken away from him, and hand him over to the Minister. The Minister, out of holy obedience, will send for brothers to watch over the brother day and night as a bound prisoner until they hand him over to the Cardinal of Ostia, the lord, protector, and corrector of this fraternity.

Let no brother say: "This is another Rule," because this testament is a remembrance and an admonition and exhortation which I, brother Francis, your little one and servant, make to you, my blessed brothers, so that the Rule that we have promised Our Lord may be kept better and in a more Catholic spirit.

And let the Minister General and all the other ministers and custodians, out of holy obedience, neither add nor take away from my words. Let them always, in all the future chapters to be held, read this testament together with the Rule.

I firmly command all my brothers, lay and clerics, out of holy obedience, to put no gloss on the Rule or on these words in any way by saying: "This is how it is to be understood." As the Lord God had me, a simple person, simply and clearly put down the Rule and these words, so in a similar way you are to observe these words, without gloss, in spirit and in practice, until the end.

And may each one of you who does so be filled in Heaven with blessings from the Most High Father, and on earth with the blessing of His Most Beloved Son, together with the Holy Spirit and all the powers of Heaven and all the saints.

I, brother Francis, your little one and servant, in every way and as much as it is possible for me, confirm you, within and without, in this most holy blessing. Amen.

# BIBLIOGRAPHICAL NOTE

Of the many Italian editions of the *Fioretti,* the best are those of: Benvenuto Bughetti, O.F.M., ed. (Florence, Adriano Salani, 1925; there is also a more recent edition) and of Mario Casella, ed. (Florence, G. C. Sansoni, 1946). The edition of G. L. Passerini (Florence, G. C. Sansoni), the basis of this translation, is also good, and so are those of Arnaldo della Torre, ed. (Turin, Paravia & Co., 1909), and of Fausta Casolini, ed. (Milan, Casa Editrice Giacomo Agnelli, 1926).

Among the essential work done on *Fioretti* is that of B. Bughetti: "Concetti fondamentali sui *'Fioretti di san Francesco'*" (*Archivum Franciscanum Historicum* 19, 1926, 321–33); "Bibliographica" (*AFH* 20, 1927, 386–407); "Intorno ai Fioretti di San Francesco" (*Frate Francesco* 4, 1927, 235–57); "Una parziale nuova traduzione degli *Actus* accoppiata ad alcuni capitoli dei *Fioretti"* (*AFH* 21, 1928, 515–52; 22, 1929, 63–113). Also: Facchinetti, Vittorino, O.F.M., "Attorno ai *Fioretti"* (*FF* 3, 1926, 165–172); Gardner, Edmund G., "The Little Flowers of St. Francis," in *St. Francis of Assisi 1226–1926: Essays in Commemoration* (London, University of London Press, 1926), pp. 97–126; Manzoni, Luigi, "Studi sui Fioretti di San Francesco" (*Miscellanea Francescana* 3, 1888, 116–19, 150–152, 162–68; 4, 1889, 9–15, 78–84, 132–35); Pagnani, Giacinto, O.F.M., "Contributi alla questione dei *'Fioretti di San Francesco'*" (*AFH* 49, 1956, 3–16).

As a general guide to Franciscan problems, there is still nothing to supersede the *Sources for the Life of St. Francis,* John R. H. Moorman, Manchester University Press, 1940. Among the best works in English for a history of the Order, with excellent bibliographies, *cf.*: Rosalind B. Brooke, *Early Franciscan Government: Elias to Bonaventure* (Cambridge University Press, 1959); Decima L. Douie, *The Nature and Effect of the Heresy of the Fraticelli* (Manchester University

Press, 1932); and the work to which this writer would again like to acknowledge his great indebtedness, M. D. Lambert's *Franciscan Poverty* (London, Society for Promoting Christian Knowledge, 1961). Also *cf.*: F. J. Foakes-Jackson and Kirsopp Lake, "The Story of St. Francis of Assisi," in G. G. Coulton, ed., *The Beginnings of Christianity* (London, Macmillan & Co., Ltd., 1922), Part II, pp. 438–463.

Should the reader, after reading the *Fioretti,* feel intrigued by the character of the Saint and wish for a convenient point of departure among his biographies, he can do no better than to begin with the classic of P. Sabatier, *Vie de Saint Francois d'Assise* (Paris, 1894). Very questionable in its portrait of an individualistic Francis ultimately undone by a scheming, nefarious priesthood, Sabatier's *Life*—charming, enthusiastic, brilliantly unreliable—is a basic work. There is, moreover, no better corrective for the saccharine, heavily partisan accounts of the Saint that continue to find publishers and readers. For a very different interpretation of the Saint, *cf.* Father Cuthbert, O.S.F.C., *Life of Saint Francis of Assisi* (Longmans, Green and Co., 1912). In spite of its age and mellow late-nineteenth-century style it remains possibly the best biography we have of the Saint.

If the reader is so unscholarly as to be attracted to historical novels, and cares to admit as much, he should go out of his way to learn enough Italian to read the superb historical novel of R. Bacchelli, *Non ti chiamerò più padre* (Mondadori, 1957), a study of Francis as seen through his father. It is superb.

# Other MENTOR-OMEGA Books

**THE DYNAMICS OF WORLD HISTORY**
by Christopher Dawson

A renowned historian examines the relation between religion and civilization, and shows Christianity as the central, dynamic force in man's historical progression.
(#MQ378—95¢)

**A PREFACE TO METAPHYSICS**   by Jacques Maritain

An introduction to the science of metaphysics in seven brilliant lectures by the distinguished French Neo-Thomist.   (#MP403—60¢)

**AMERICAN CATHOLIC DILEMMA** by Thomas F. O'Dea

A well-known sociologist discusses the contributions of his fellow Catholics to American intellectual life.
(#MP404—60¢)

**THE DEAD SEA SCROLLS AND PRIMITIVE CHRISTIANITY**   by Jean Danielou

A Jesuit Professor at the Catholic Institute of Paris demonstrates the relationship between the facts revealed in the ancient scrolls and the traditional view of Christian faith.   (#MP405—60¢)

**MARIA MONTESSORI: HER LIFE AND WORK**
by E. M. Standing

A friend and colleague of the great educator writes her biography and evaluates her contributions to modern education. With eight pages of photographs.
(#MQ425—95¢)

**PSYCHOANALYSIS AND PERSONALITY**
by Joseph Nuttin

The noted Belgian psychologist discusses the relation between modern depth psychology and Christian philosophy. Newly revised edition.   (#MT426—75¢)

**TWO CENTURIES OF ECUMENISM: THE SEARCH FOR UNITY**   by George H. Tavard

A study of successive efforts at Christian reunion from the Oxford Movement of the last century to the Ecumenical Council of the Church called by the late Pope John XXIII.   (#MT465—75¢)

**THE PAPAL ENCYCLICALS IN THEIR HISTORICAL CONTEXT**   edited by Anne Fremantle

The teachings of the Catholic Church as expressed by the Popes in their official letters.   (#MQ533—95¢)

## LEISURE: THE BASIS OF CULTURE by Josef Pieper

In a series of astonishing essays, the author indicts the 20th century cult of "work" and hectic amusements, which can ultimately destroy both our culture and ourselves. Introduction by T. S. Eliot. (#MP550—60¢)

## CATHOLICISM by Henri de Lubac

One of the world's leading theologians discusses the social traditions and ideals inherent in the teachings of the Church, and their relevancy to modern problems.
(#MT573—75¢)

## DAILY LIFE IN THE TIME OF JESUS
### by Henri Daniel-Rops

A comprehensive study of the land and people, political, economic, scientific, and cultural currents, as they existed in Palestine during the time of Jesus.
(#MQ570—95¢)

## ELEMENTS OF CHRISTIAN PHILOSOPHY
### by Etienne Gilson

The noted French philosopher illuminates the key ideas of the theology of St. Thomas Aquinas.

(#MT489—75¢)

## THE NEW MAN by Thomas Merton

The author of *The Seven Storey Mountain* presents enlightening meditations which point the way the soul must travel to seek and find spiritual reality. (#MP548—60¢)

## THE LOVE OF LEARNING AND THE DESIRE FOR
GOD: A Study of Monastic Culture by Jean Leclercq, O.S.B.

An examination of the manuscripts of the medieval monasteries reveals their role in preserving the culture of the past. By a distinguished scholar and Benedictine monk. (#MT432—75¢)

## OF THE IMITATION OF CHRIST by Thomas à Kempis

The great 15th century classic of devotional literature in a widely acclaimed modern translation of Abbot Justin McCann. (#MT467—75¢)